From Task-Centered Social Work to
Evidence-Based and Integrative Practice

Also available from Lyceum Books, Inc.

Advisory Editor: Thomas M. Meenaghan, *New York University*

Humanistic Social Work: Core Principles in Practice
by Malcolm Payne

Pracademics and Community Change: A True Story of Nonprofit Development and Social Entrepreneurship during Welfare Reform
by Odell Cleveland and Robert Wineburg

Career Reflections of Social Work Educators
by Spencer J. Zeiger

Educating for Social Justice: Transformative Experiential Learning
edited by Julie Birkenmaier, Ashley Cruce, Ellen Burkemper, Jami Curley, R. Jan Wilson, and J. J. Stretch

Regulating Social Work: A Primer on Licensing Practice
by Anthony A. Bibus III and Needha Boutté-Queen

Understanding and Managing the Therapeutic Relationship
by Fred R. McKenzie

Essential Skills for Social Work Practice: Assessment, Intervention, and Evaluation
by Thomas O'Hare

Using Evidence to Inform Practice for Community and Organizational Change
by Maria Roberts-DeGennaro and Sondra J. Fogel

Clinical Assessment for Social Workers: Quantitative and Qualitative Methods, 3rd edition
by Catheleen Jordan and Cynthia Franklin

Contemporary Psychodynamic Theory and Practice
by William Borden

From Task-Centered Social Work to Evidence-Based and Integrative Practice

Reflections on History and Implementation

Edited by

Tina L. Rzepnicki
University of Chicago

Stanley G. McCracken
University of Chicago

Harold E. Briggs
Portland State University

BOOKS, INC.

Chicago, Illinois

© Lyceum Books, Inc., 2012

Published by
LYCEUM BOOKS, INC.
5758 S. Blackstone Ave.
Chicago, Illinois 60637
773 + 643-1903 (Fax)
773 + 643-1902 (Phone)
lyceum@lyceumbooks.com
http://www.lyceumbooks.com

6   5   4   3   2   1   12   13   14   15

ISBN 978-1-933478-99-9

Cover image © Madartists—Dreamstime.com

Library of Congress Cataloging-in-Publication Data

From task-centered social work to evidence-based and integrative practice / [edited by] Tina L. Rzepnicki, Stanley G. McCracken, Harold E. Briggs.
    p.   cm.
ISBN 978-1-933478-99-9 (alk. paper)
1. Evidence-based social work.   2. Social service—Practice.   3. Social service.
I. Rzepnicki, Tina L.   II. McCracken, Stanley Glenn, 1946–   III. Briggs, Harold E. (Harold Eugene), 1955–   IV. Title.
HV10.5.F77   2011
361.3′2—dc22

2011010333

Dedication

We dedicate this book to Laura Epstein (1914–1996), William J. Reid (1928–2003), and a century of scholars at the University of Chicago School of Social Service Administration who gave us the vision of integrating research and practice.

Acknowledgments

We thank the University of Chicago School of Social Service Administration, including Dean Jeanne Marsh; the Centennial Planning Committee, chaired by Dolores Norton, Samuel Deutsch Professor; and the Rhoda G. Sarnat Lecture Fund for supporting the symposium that gave rise to the papers in this volume.

In addition, we are grateful to the peer reviewers who volunteered their time and experience to provide valuable feedback on chapter manuscripts. Their names and organizational affiliations are as follows: Gino Aisenberg, University of Washington; Alida Bouris, University of Chicago; Eileen Brennan, Portland State University; Jonathan Caspi, Montclair State University; Daniel Coleman, Portland State University; Patrick Corrigan, Illinois Institute of Technology; Eileen Munro, London School of Economics; James Nash, Portland State University; Roberto Orellana, Portland State University; John Schuerman, University of Chicago; Bruce Thyer, Florida State University; and Susan Wells, University of British Columbia–Okanagan.

Contents

Preface

Stanley G. McCracken, Tina L. Rzepnicki, and Harold E. Briggs

On June 5, 2009, a symposium focusing on the contribution made by the faculty and graduates of the University of Chicago's School of Social Service Administration (SSA) to the development of evidence-based practice and to an integrative approach to social work practice marked the end of a yearlong celebration of the school's centennial. The present volume includes the papers presented at the symposium and is augmented by additional papers that share the work of others who have studied and taught at SSA. The book's organization reflects that of the conference, with the first section consisting of papers that are more historical and conceptual and the second section comprising papers demonstrating how these approaches are being applied to solving real-world problems in a variety of practice settings.

SSA has a long tradition of both valuing evidence as a resource for practice decision making and recognizing the need to conduct research on the process and outcome of social work practice. Edith Abbott, one of the founders of SSA, placed research and the development of practice knowledge at the center of social work practice and the education of practitioners (see Jeanne C. Marsh's chapter for a detailed review). This tradition continued with the empirical practice movement and practitioner-researcher model, in which scholars such as William Reid, Laura Epstein, Elsie Pinkston, and Edward Mullen at SSA trained social workers to locate and use research to design interventions and to employ research methods such as single-subject designs to evaluate the outcome of these interventions in their practice (Reid, 1994).

Evidence-based practice (EBP) evolved from evidence-based medicine, developed in the 1990s by David Sackett and colleagues at McMaster University. Evidence-based medicine is an approach in which the best research evidence is integrated with patients' values and circumstances and with clinical expertise (Sackett, Rosenberg, Muir Gray, Haynes, & Richardson, 1996). The EBP movement in social work can also be seen as a logical outgrowth of the empirical practice movement. It includes contextual factors in addition to the original elements proposed in evidence-based medicine (Regehr, Stern, & Shlonsky, 2007; McCracken & Rzepnicki, 2010).

In addition to highlighting the importance of evidence for service providers, the empirical practice movement and EBP provided a path to practice integration. Psychotherapy integration is an approach to practice that recognizes the practical, theoretical, and empirical strengths and limitations of the foundational theoretical models.

Like EBP, psychotherapy integration is discussed sometimes as a process and sometimes as a product. The process of psychotherapy integration is an orientation to the study of psychotherapy that is characterized by an openness to seeing the commonalities among the different methods and an interest in promoting dialogue among practitioners from all orientations. The product, integrated therapies, results from efforts to synthesize theories and interventions from two or more traditional schools of therapy (see Stricker & Gold, 2003, for an overview of psychotherapy integration and Borden, 2010, for a discussion of integration in social work).

In the 1970s, Joel Fischer proposed an approach in which social workers would put together behavioral and other empirically based approaches into an eclectic practice based on research rather than a particular theoretical model (Fischer, 1978). While at SSA, Mullen developed the personal practice model, in which practitioners integrate information from personal experience, practice wisdom, theory, and research (Mullen, 1983). Personal practice models are explicit conceptual schemes that express a practitioner's view of practice and provide summary generalizations and guidelines that give general direction to the practitioner's subsequent practice.

Mullen's personal practice model provided a method for practice integration, and others at SSA pulled together elements from various approaches to form integrated approaches. Reid and Epstein integrated elements from brief treatment, general systems theories, behavioral therapy, and the approaches of a variety of social work casework authors to form task-centered practice. Sharon Berlin used the applied-science method to integrate elements from cognitive behavioral therapy and cognitive science research into a new treatment, the cognitive integrative perspective (Berlin, 2002).

The papers in section one review the history, development, and major concepts of empirical practice, EBP, and the integrated treatments mentioned above. In the first chapter of this section, "Learning

by Intervening: Examining the Intersection of Research and Practice,"
Marsh uses the knowledge utilization process to better understand the
process by which practitioners use evidence to inform practice decisions and to evaluate the outcomes of those decisions. She reviews the
history of interest in the intersection of research and practice in social
work, beginning with the 1915 Flexner Report and Edith Abbott's work.
Marsh places practitioners' utilization of research in the context of their
decision making, recognizing that research evidence is but one of many
types of information used in complex decision-making processes.
Finally, she looks at the process of translating evidence into action in
social work practice, critically examining the elements of EBP—the
nature of evidence for practice, the social psychology of expertise, and
the inclusion of client values and expectations in the decision-making
process. Marsh concludes that framing EBP as a clinical decision-making
process is valuable because we can use what we know of the knowledge
utilization process to avoid pitfalls such as emphasizing empirical
knowledge at the expense of theoretical knowledge and focusing on
therapeutic technique at the expense of other curative aspects of the
helping relationship.

Anne E. Fortune's chapter, "Development of the Task-Centered
Model," reviews the development of task-centered practice in the history of empirical practice in social work. She focuses particularly on the
1950s through the mid-1970s, beginning with the formation of the Social
Work Research Group in 1949 and the group's work of defining and disseminating research and integrating it into the social work curriculum.
She noted that during this same period several large-scale social experiments were conducted in a variety of populations, mostly with poor
results, leading reviewers to conclude that social work practice was
ineffective and possibly harmful. This discouraging beginning led to
efforts to infuse accountability into social work practice, to a reexamination of the principles of casework, and to the development of empirical practice in some of the leading schools of social work.

After providing this historical context, Fortune traces the series of
specific research findings and practice assumptions that led Reid and
Epstein to develop task-centered practice beginning in the late 1960s,
and she provides an overview of some of the research on the process
and outcome of task-centered practice in the United States and world-
wide. The chapter ends with a thoughtful consideration of several of
the major contributions that task-centered practice has made to social
work research and practice.

In "The Applied-Science Approach and the Cognitive-Integrative
Perspective," Berlin discusses how she drew upon the applied-science
approach to revise Aaron Beck's cognitive therapy and to develop a different version, the cognitive integrative perspective. Berlin provides

insight into how her practice experience and critical examination of
the research led her to discover conceptual and practical limitations in
cognitive therapy. She particularly noted the lack of attention in traditional cognitive therapy to the role of sociostructural deprivations and
incursions in emotional distress and to the limitations resulting from
the model of memory that informed earlier versions of cognitive therapy. Berlin reviews the principles and research supporting a conceptual
model of memory called Interacting Cognitive Subsystems, from which
she has incorporated a number of key concepts into her cognitive-
integrative perspective.

The second half of the chapter discusses some of the principles of
the cognitive-integrative perspective, as well as the cognitive science
and other research on which these principles are based. She pays particular attention to the effect of sociostructural mechanisms, such as
concrete changes in circumstances, on behavior and emotions. She
concludes that the cognitive-integrative perspective "gives us ways to
generate new social and personal streams of information and to help
people develop the attentional flexibility to notice these discrepancies,
the cognitive and emotional capacity to conceptualize and feel their
significance, and the skills to act on them—to make the most of them."

William Borden and James J. Clark review the current psychodynamic literature and discuss its relevance for EBP in their chapter,
"Contemporary Psychodynamic Theory, Research, and Practice: Implications for Evidence-Based Intervention." They address the ways in
which psychodynamic theory contributes to a deeper appreciation of
the facilitating processes in psychosocial intervention and strengthens
our conceptions of the helping relationship, interpersonal behavior,
and clinical expertise in EBP.

The first of the three sections of this chapter reviews the historical
development and evolution of psychodynamic theory, summarizes the
defining features of the major schools of psychodynamic thought, and
describes core elements of the relational paradigm, which emphasizes
the centrality of relationship and social life in human experience. The
authors describe orienting perspectives in psychodynamic interventions and briefly review and summarize the research on the effectiveness of treatment approaches based on these perspectives. They then
consider the implications of relational theory and research for the
ongoing development of EBP and provide a thoughtful discussion of
ways in which psychodynamic thought can contribute to a broader
understanding of the curative aspects of the helping relationship.

The chapter also highlights the fact that the empirical basis of psychodynamic thinking and intervention is much better documented
than many practitioners realize. The authors suggest that evidence-
based approaches to psychodynamically informed social work practice

will be enhanced as researchers further investigate specific interventions to address particular disorders using methodologically sound approaches, including randomized controlled trials. At the same time they note that "community-based research that supplements traditional, top-down, science-to-practice dissemination with innovative, practice-to-science information flows" has the potential to "open up new opportunities to develop integrative approaches using efficacious relational approaches drawn from multiple schools of psychotherapy."

Julia H. Littell's chapter, "Evidence-Based or Biased? Why Methods of Research Synthesis Matter," provides a transition from the conceptual and historical material in section one to the discussions of implementation and dissemination of EBP in section two. She begins by explaining how research synthesis is used in EBP and by discussing the different methods that researchers use to prepare the three main types of research reviews: traditional narrative reviews, systematic reviews, and meta-analyses. She describes common sources and types of bias that can affect what is presented in research reviews and explains how to correct for or minimize these biases in the review process.

Littell also contrasts empirically based knowledge about the process and methods of research synthesis with common practice and provides an illustration of how different review methods can produce quite different conclusions. Given the considerable amount of research available in some areas of practice and the scarcity of time that practitioners have to locate, read, and critically think about the quality and usefulness of research, it is important that high-quality research syntheses be available if EBP is to be developed and sustained in real-world practice. Littell's chapter thus provides an important caveat about the quality and conclusions of research reviews.

The existence of a good product doesn't mean that people will use it. The papers in section two address the application of EBP in real-world settings. McCracken, Elisabeth Kinnel, Fred Steffen, Margaret Vimont, and Charlotte Mallon, in "Implementing and Sustaining Evidence-Based Practice: Case Example of Leadership, Organization, Infrastructure, and Consultation," describe the effort to implement and sustain evidence-based practice in a large metropolitan social service agency. The chapter begins with a discussion of the five steps of EBP—question formulation, electronic literature search, critically appraising the quality and usefulness of the evidence, integrating evidence with practitioner expertise and client values and preferences, and evaluating the outcome—and a brief overview of the literature on dissemination and implementation of practice innovations. The authors note that the research consistently supports the need to pay attention to leadership, staffing, and other organizational factors when considering adoption of a novel approach to practice.

The rest of the chapter describes the implementation of EBP at that agency, beginning with initial contact and the decision to implement EBP. The authors note that from the start, the project was initiated and sustained by the agency rather than by an academic institution or an outside funder. The description continues through the engagement of and elicitation of support from the agency's leadership and staff, to the training of the staff and application of EBP to program development, and finally to the establishment of EBP as a standard practice within the agency. The authors end with a discussion of lessons learned from the project.

Jennifer F. Bellamy, Sarah E. Bledsoe, Lin Fang, Jennifer Manuel, and Edward J. Mullen, in "Addressing the Barriers to EBP Implementation in Social Work: Reflections from the BEST Project," also discuss implementation of EBP in their review of the BEST (Bringing Evidence for Social Work Training) Project in three community agencies in New York. They used data from the project to discuss barriers to EBP that they identified in a literature review conducted during the early phase of the project. Organizing their discussion around three themes— approaching EBP as a team or organizational process, taking a long-term approach to university-agency partnerships, and supporting an EBP culture of social work practice—they discuss strategies they used to address four groups of barriers (suspicion and distrust, lack of knowledge, limited resources, and lack of fit between research evidence and practice contexts), plus additional challenges and limitations they encountered.

Bellamy et al. found that the strategies they employed in the project were most successful at decreasing barriers related to suspicion and mistrust of research and researchers, at increasing knowledge of the EBP process and skills for searching and evaluating evidence, and at providing some of the resources that are needed for the early steps of the EBP process. They also found that the agency teams needed ongoing support in order to feel like they were engaged in the process from start to finish. For example, they felt the need for support in judging the quality of more complicated research. Finally, the authors found that the training could have better prepared teams to address issues in implementation of new practice methods that were identified in the EBP process. They end the chapter with a discussion of possible strategies for future efforts and of implications for social work education and agency partnership.

Harold E. Briggs and Stephen Edward McMillin shift the focus from EBP used in direct practice to evidence-based management in "Implementing Evidence-Based Management and Evidence-Based Practice in Community Agencies: Lessons from a Case Study." These authors distinguish between a bottom-up approach that mirrors the five steps of

EBP and a top-down approach to evidence-based management that usually involves implementing a specific model of decision analysis for the agency or organization. They identify ten practice principles that agency managers might consider if they wish to adopt EBP and evidence-based management. These principles are then illustrated in a case study of an academic/community partnership between a university and a family-driven, community-based, African American, urban nonprofit agency.

The authors note several points of interest from the case study. They posit that organizational change must be approached in a humanistic, artistic, and culturally specific manner, and that while evidence-based management may seem system- and process-focused, relationship management skills are an essential quality for leaders and for evidence-based management. They noted that planned organizational change should be made gradually, allowing those involved time to adapt, grow, and move forward. The action plan should have a feasible time schedule for implementation of changes in the different components of the program in order to allow for overall program and service integration. For all those involved in the case study—management, staff, clients, and clients' families—the opportunity to learn new ways of communicating, behaving, and working in partnership with others contributed to enhanced productivity and accountability. Briggs and McMillin recommend that in future studies facilitating change and accountability in community organizations, investigators differentiate the types of training needed by staff, such as technical training in client programming involving the EBP process, or training in cultural competency, team building, and leadership skills.

The focus of the first three chapters in section two is relatively narrow—a single agency or small cluster of agencies—in contrast the next two chapters, which address the use of evidence-based methods on a larger, statewide, scale. In "Learning from Data: The Beginning of Error Reduction in Illinois Child Welfare," Tina L. Rzepnicki, Penny R. Johnson, Denise Q. Kane, Diane Moncher, Lisa Coconato, and Barbara Shulman describe an Illinois initiative intended "to identify common patterns of case decision error and to develop a systemic response to improve the state's ability to protect children in families where there have been allegations of abuse or neglect."

The authors begin by describing a framework for understanding human error in an organizational context and then applying their framework to child protection examples uncovered during investigations conducted by the Illinois Department of Children and Family Services' Office of the Inspector General. From these examples, the authors identified several problems in data collection by the child protection investigators, including failure to seek information from multiple sources or to access available information, failure to recognize cumulative risk, and failure to develop a realistic safety plan and monitor cases accordingly. Their efforts to identify common patterns of error revealed a number of practice weaknesses resulting from a lack of critical thinking, a stressful work environment that included staffing shortages and informal incentives for supervisory shortcuts, and an organizational culture that did not use mistakes as learning opportunities.

Rzepnicki et al. then describe how they used these findings to develop actions to reduce error in the child protection system. Their use of a systems perspective and root cause analysis in the Office of the Inspector General allowed them to develop strategies to reduce errors, especially errors that could result in tragic outcomes. The authors note, however, that reducing errors alone is not sufficient for success; it is equally important to anticipate pathways to new errors before injuries occur and to take steps to prevent them.

Ronald H. Rooney and Michael DeJong, in "From Focusing on Deficits to Appreciative Inquiry: Uncovering Promising Practices in Work with Teen Parents," describe a project in which data were used to inform the practice of assisting adolescent parents who are wards of the state. This university/agency collaboration, involving staff from the Illinois Office of the Inspector General and from the Teen Parent Services Network, evolved over five years to produce modifications in goals, objectives, and interventions.The project included a shift from a focus on deficits to a focus on strengths that was influenced by appreciative inquiry—a process in which an outside consultant, rather than solving problems or providing solutions, initiates a process designed to include members of an organization in identifying what is working and in exploring solutions to organizational concerns.

The first phase of the collaboration began with three months of training in working with involuntary clients, in task-centered practice, and in a task-centered approach to supervision of case managers. During this phase an evaluation plan was developed to assess the impact of training on practice, including a test of training content knowledge and an assessment of case records; both of these were completed pre- and post-training. Results from the post-training knowledge test suggested that the training led to an increase in knowledge about task-centered practice and working with involuntary clients. However, evidence of the training's effects on documentation of practice were not immediately discerned from an assessment of case records.

These findings led to the second phase, in which the first author became more immersed in the culture and practice environment of the Teen Parent Services Network. This phase involved case consultation, case record review, and the emergence of appreciative inquiry for exploring in detail situations in which genuine collaboration appeared to occur, followed by the use of this exploration to develop training videos that featured agency staff modeling desired practice modes. The third phase involved further development of the videos and of preliminary training based on the videos; and the fourth phase encompassed final development and implementation of the video training package. The authors end the chapter with a discussion of lessons learned during the collaboration.

Taken together, the chapters in this book describe an approach to EBP that has a number of distinguishing characteristics. First, the approach values evidence as a resource for clinical decision making, and this evidence may come from practice as well as from published research. Sometimes the best available evidence is from one's own practice, as long as it is systematically gathered in a manner that ensures its validity. Not all evidence is equal; nor is all evidence of high quality. At the same time, high-quality evidence is not the exclusive domain of academics; there is a need for practice-based evidence. This is particularly true when practitioners are considering interventions with specific cultural groups and in specific communities, such as rural African-American older adults, urban Hispanic youth, or LGBT immigrants.

Second, this approach recognizes that from the time of initial development of a practice innovation, attention must be paid to issues of dissemination and adoption; otherwise there is a risk of developing innovations that are not feasible and are difficult to adopt and sustain in practice. This may mean that social work scholars and researchers need to encourage and support bottom-up approaches that originate in the field and that involve academics as collaborators and facilitators; involve practitioners, clients and their family members, and community representatives as active partners in developing practice innovations; and acknowledge the practice expertise of the staff who will be adopting the innovation, recognizing that innovations are more likely to be received as additions to rather than replacements of current practice. Researchers need to spend time acting as knowledge brokers, collaborating with and providing consultation to agencies that are translating research into practice.

Third, this approach recognizes the importance of addressing organizational factors in efforts to disseminate and implement practice innovations. This means that clinical researchers and practitioners need to think of organizational factors not as barriers, but as normal aspects of program development, much the way that cultural, developmental, and interpersonal factors are considered normal aspects of treatment planning. Organizations must be involved in and prepared for the process of change. For example, social work services are often delivered by teams, and implementing a practice innovation will result in a shift in roles and responsibilities on a team that must be recognized and facilitated if the innovation is to be adopted rather than rejected. Finally, this approach recognizes the importance of relationship and of relational approaches in EBP. Relationships among team members, staff, clients and their families, administrators, consultants and other change agents, community residents, and the academy provide a context for change. Although formal study of the role of relationship in change is in its infancy (even more so in the implementation literature than in the psychotherapy literature), chapters in both sections of this volume highlight the importance of relationship in the change process.

Even less studied, though extremely important, is the role of cultural diversity in dissemination. Culture is always on the table, whether we are considering the applicability of research to a particular practice setting; nurturing relationships among the key actors in the agency, community, and academy; or deciding whether to implement a practice approach as developed or to adapt it for a different group from the one in which it was developed and studied. One of the most frequent cultural issues in dissemination and implementation is the difference between the change agent (often an academic) and the target audience for change. While these characteristics may not be specific to contributions made by those who have studied and taught at SSA, they have characterized the EBP approach since its beginning.

References

Berlin, S. B. (2002). *Social work clinical practice: A cognitive-integrative perspective.* New York, NY: Oxford University Press.

Borden, W. (2010). Taking multiplicity seriously: Pluralism, pragmatism, and integrative perspectives in clinical social work. In W. Borden (Ed.), *Reshaping theory in contemporary social work: Toward a critical pluralism in clinical practice* (pp. 3–27). New York, NY: Columbia University Press.

Fischer, J. (1978). *Effective casework practice: An eclectic approach.* New York, NY: McGraw-Hill.

McCracken, S., & Rzepnicki, T. (2010). The role of theory in conducting evidence-based clinical practice. In W. Borden (Ed.), *Reshaping theory in contemporary social work: Toward a critical pluralism in clinical practice* (210–233). New York, NY: Columbia University Press.

Mullen, E. J. (1983). Personal practice models in clinical social work. In A. Rosenblatt & D. Waldfogel (Eds.), *Handbook of clinical social work.* San Francisco, CA: Jossey-Bass.

Regehr, C., Stern, S., & Shlonsky, A. (2007). Operationalizing evidence-based practice: The development of an institute for evidence-based social work. *Research on Social Work Practice, 17,* 408–416.

Reid, W. J. (1994). The empirical practice movement. *Social Service Review, 68,* 165–184.

Sackett, D. L., Rosenberg, W. M. C., Muir Gray, J. A., Haynes, R. B., & Richardson, W. S. (1996). Evidence-based medicine: What it is and what it isn't. *British Medical Journal, 312,* 71–72.

Stricker, G., & Gold, J. (2003). Integrative approaches to psychotherapy. In A. Gurman & S. Messer (Eds.), *Essential Psychotherapies* (pp. 317–350). New York, NY: Guilford.

PART I

Evidence-Based Practice: Evolution of a Concept

CHAPTER ONE

Learning by Intervening: Examining the Intersection of Research and Practice

Jeanne C. Marsh

Evidence-based practice. Empirically based practice. Data-driven decision making. Action research. Translational research. Reflexive practice. Knowledge utilization. The currency of these terms, and of other terminology referring to the interaction of research and practice in social work, reflects a growing demand for practitioners to learn from their ongoing work by using research evidence to inform their practice. It also indicates researchers' growing interest in meeting information needs of practitioners by developing evidence that is relevant to practice.

Despite increasing interest in the intersection of research and practice, we know that the research evidence that practitioners need to make decisions may not exist or may not be readily accessible. We also know that our understanding of the knowledge utilization process is underdeveloped. It is the purpose of this chapter to explore the knowledge utilization process to better understand the way practitioners use research evidence to inform practice decisions and evaluate outcomes. The chapter begins with a history of interest in the intersection of research and practice in social work, then places practitioners' utilization of research in the context of their decision making, and finally considers the process whereby evidence is translated into action in social work practice.

Historical Background

Concern with the intersection of research and practice has deep roots in social work, as revealed by the words of Edith Abbott, a founder of the University of Chicago School of Social Service Administration. She wrote in 1931, "If social research is to go on, it can only develop scientifically with the help of well-trained social workers. . . . All the investigating techniques in the world will produce nothing but a multiplication of dullness unless those who are doing the work have a keen understanding of the problems to be solved. Otherwise, the investigator is a headless machine" (E. Abbott, 1931, p. 2). The Flexner Report of 1915, which considered the development of social work as a profession, identified a codified body of knowledge relevant to practice as a critical element in the development of any profession. At the University of Chicago, Edith Abbott placed research and knowledge development at the center of the social work professionalization enterprise. And, as the above quote reveals, she was quite specific that practitioners should be at the center of research development and utilization.

Theories of professions provide a framework for understanding how a codified body of knowledge contributes to the definition of a profession. All professions—social work, law, medicine—are defined by the tasks they complete as well as the evidentiary base they rely on to complete those tasks (A. Abbott, 1988). Given that the tasks of social work are to promote individual well-being and social justice, that those of law are to promote legal justice, and that those of medicine are to promote health and prevent illness, these professions rely on distinct but overlapping knowledge bases to effectively complete these tasks.

Institutional or systems theories of professions propose that professions emerge and develop in relation to other professions in an organizational field (Abbott, 1988). From this perspective, interprofessional relations are determined by the knowledge and skills associated with and controlled by each profession, and research evidence is a fundamental component in the codification of this knowledge and these skills. For example, much of the early research on assertive case management with the chronically mentally ill was conducted at the University of Wisconsin School of Social Work, and the basic principles remain a part of the abstract and specific knowledge base of social work. Researchers in social work and other helping professions continue to conduct research on case management, but the fundamental principles of delivering services in the community to chronically mentally ill clients remain central to the social work service-delivery lexicon. Overall, professions use research evidence to make ongoing claims over the content and control of their work and the work of the other professions.

Despite these deep historical and theoretical roots emphasizing the synergy between practice and research, it is important to acknowledge from the beginning that research evidence represents only one type of information related to the complex decision-making process in which practitioners are involved. This analysis makes clear that specific evidence resulting from research consists of only one consideration among a vast array of considerations that ultimately determine the decisions practitioners make. Too often discussions of evidence-based practice (EBP) fail to articulate that multiple decisions must be made in practice—some of which are appropriately not evidence-based. Further, many discussions fail to define what is meant by evidence and then assume a simple linear process whereby ill-defined evidence maps directly onto ill-defined practice decisions. Thus we begin this discussion of the intersection of research and practice by defining both research evidence and practice decisions.

Defining *Research Evidence* and *Practice Decisions*

Research evidence is defined here as empirical findings deriving from systematic research and analysis, including experimental and quasi-experimental studies, qualitative and quantitative analyses, meta-analyses, and cost-effectiveness studies. Evidence can be generated by researchers, practitioners, or those functioning as researcher-practitioners. *Practitioners* are defined here as individuals working in organizations to provide health and social services or to manage and evaluate the delivery of those services.

Practice decisions are defined here as specific decisions, major and minor, that a practitioner makes in collaboration with a client in the course of providing services. Berlin and Marsh (1993) have identified three major categories of decisions; decisions related to problem assessment, to the course of action, and to the monitoring of progress and evaluation of outcomes. They also examine the knowledge utilization process that informs each of these decision categories—where *knowledge* is defined broadly to include theories, schemas, logic, heuristics, practitioner intuition, and expert opinion, as well as research evidence.

This definition of *practice decisions* derives from a model of social problem solving that undergirds the development of much of American social work research and practice. It recognizes that within each of these broad decision categories are buried an inestimable number of microjudgments that are influenced by universal characteristics of human information processing and problem solving, sources of knowledge, and knowledge-generating tendencies, as well as the organizational and political context of practice.

The field of cognitive psychology has been a rich source of theory and evidence on human information processing, perception, problem solving, and decision making. This research is relevant to helping us understand what goes on in the mind of the social work decision maker during the problem-solving process. The task for the social worker, as for any human information processor, is to select cues, to make sense of them, to go beyond them to resolve ambiguities, and ultimately to draw inferences and make decisions. The research on human information processing is useful for understanding how data are collected, organized, and used to draw inferences and make practice decisions.

Research on human problem solving and decision making—specifically in the clinical context—is the basis for understanding the development of expertise in social work (Berlin & Marsh, 1993; Gambrill, 2005; Sanna, Small, & Cook, 2004). Social workers develop professional expertise by systematically reflecting on how they receive information, give it meaning, transform that meaning into judgment, and check for possible sources of bias. Through this process of reflection on practice decision making, social workers are able to learn from intervening and make more adequate decisions (Berlin & Marsh, 1993).

Under ideal circumstances, social work practitioners make decisions with a stance of open inquiry in order to discover, with the client, new sources of knowledge and new facets of meaning relevant to the decision (Berlin, 2002). Such discoveries are based on multiple sources of information and a variety of thinking processes. Rather than following the normal human instinct to fit incoming information into usual patterns of thought, practitioners engaged in EBP consciously reflect on how they are thinking and consider additional ways of understanding the phenomena in question (Berlin & Marsh, 1993; Berlin, 2002).

Research Evidence and Knowledge Utilization

Fundamental to consideration of EBP and the intersection of research and practice is the expectation that research will be used in practice decision making, and yet we have only a preliminary understanding of the knowledge utilization process (Marsh, 2002, 2003, 2004). Discussions of the use of research in practice can focus on both instrumental and conceptual uses of research. In the first instance, research evidence is identified and used for a specific purpose, to solve a problem. In the second instance, it is used to influence thinking about a problem. Empirical research may be most relevant to solving a specific problem, while theory may be the most likely source for understanding the problem. Despite the fact that EBP focuses largely on the instrumental use of research, early evidence about knowledge utilization (Caplan, Morrison, & Stambaugh, 1975; Weiss & Bucuvalas, 1979) indicates that conceptual use of knowledge may be more common.

In general, social workers—confronted with the imperative to act with and for their clients—might be expected to favor the instrumental use of knowledge. However, a recent survey suggests that this may not be the case and provides insights as to how social workers think about and use knowledge (Cha, Kuo, & Marsh, 2006). A group of social work practitioners were asked to reflect on the utility of various types of knowledge. Specifically, they were asked to rank the following types of information from the most to the least useful: information that is about a social problem or clinical diagnosis, about the effectiveness of social work practice, about a population group, about social work ethics, about the social work profession, about a theoretical perspective, about research methodology, or about epistemological issues in social work research; or information that is useful for advocacy or teaching. The four categories of information that respondents indicated were the most useful could be viewed as a mix of conceptual and instrumental knowledge. Social workers responding to this survey gave the highest ratings to knowledge about the character of particular social problems, about particular population groups, about the effectiveness of particular practice strategies, about social work ethics. Thus, practitioner respondents expressed appreciation for both conceptual and theoretical knowledge, particularly as it is relevant to the everyday in practice.

Findings from this study are consistent with findings from earlier studies of knowledge utilization by social workers. Rosen, Proctor, Morrow-Howell, and Staudt (1995) found that social workers provide primarily conceptual rationales for specific practice decisions. Rosen, Proctor, and Staudt (1999) conducted a literature review that demonstrated that 85 percent of published literature in social work is conceptual and 15 percent is instrumental or empirical. However, there is an important distinction between Cha et al. (2006) and the 1995 and 1999 analyses by Rosen and colleagues. The Rosen studies interpret the relative paucity of instrumental knowledge as a sign of social workers' problematic overreliance on conceptual knowledge, and they advocate for greater generation and utilization of instrumental, empirical evidence. The Cha study, in comparison, documents the types of knowledge that social workers report to be useful, indicating that both conceptual and instrumental knowledge are significantly valued by social work practitioners. The authors further acknowledge that many decisions are made in the course of practice and that different types of knowledge are relevant to different types of decisions.

The Intersection of Research and Practice in EBP

Given the framing of EBP as a clinical decision-making process, it becomes necessary to examine exactly how evidence is translated into action. EBP is grounded in the basic assumption that social work practice is a problem-solving process in which the practitioner and client work together to address three questions: What are the nature and circumstances of the problem? What is the appropriate course of action to resolve the problem? What is the effect of action—that is, what change has occurred that is relevant to adjusting or shifting the course of action and understanding the outcome? Thus, social work practice focuses on a problem or problems defined or co-constructed by the social worker and the client. The ultimate purpose of such collaborations is to enable clients to achieve their goals. Further, the social worker and client engage in a process of ongoing monitoring and evaluation to determine whether client goals have indeed been met. In the profession of social work, practitioners are ethically obligated to focus on clients' goals and to provide clients with the best available services according to the best available evidence (Berlin & Marsh, 1993; Gibbs, 2003).

Consistent with this perspective of social work practice, three fundamental elements define the process of using research findings to aid clinical decision-making: best available evidence, the practitioner's knowledge and judgment, and client values and expectations.

As Gibbs (2003) notes, these elements are grounded in the Code of Ethics of the U.S. National Association of Social Workers (NASW, 1999) in the sections focusing on concern for client preferences, professional expertise, and use of research evidence.

BEST AVAILABLE EVIDENCE

Much of the discussion of EBP has focused on the first element: best available evidence. Further, significant attention has been focused on research evidence about specific interventions and about sets of techniques and procedures that have been tested to evaluate the practice question, What is the appropriate course of action to resolve the problem?—that is, What works? Nonetheless, in EBP, evidence derives from a number of sources: client reports and practitioner observations as well as scientifically generated knowledge or research that is relevant to the questions, What is the nature of the problem? and What is the appropriate solution?

Gibbs provides explicit practical guidelines for the conduct of EBP that focus almost exclusively on available scientifically generated evidence: how to identify it, how to collect it, and how to assess its quality.

He provides this conceptual definition for EBP: "Placing the client's benefit first, evidence-based practitioners adopt a process of lifelong learning that involves posing specific questions of direct practical importance to clients, searching objectively and efficiently for the current best evidence relative to each question, and taking appropriate action guided by evidence" (Gibbs, 2003, p. 6).

The first phrase in Gibbs's definition focuses on client welfare, signaling that improving practice and advancing client welfare are the ultimate aims of social work and of an EBP approach to social work specifically. However, the phrase "searching objectively and efficiently for the current best evidence" is also a central component of the definition and places in the foreground the EBP process of collecting evidence and assessing its quality.

The guidelines that Gibbs provides for finding and assessing the best available evidence focus entirely on electronic searches of databases and rely on prevailing quality standards in social sciences. For example, the highest points for effectiveness studies go to research where subjects are randomly assigned to experimental or control groups (the gold standard of research design), where subjects are blind to whether they are in the treatment or control group, and where the psychometric properties of outcome measures have been assessed. To make this search and assessment process as clear and systematic as possible, Gibbs has developed a set of rating forms and checklists. These forms are designed to enable the practitioners to evaluate and use both quantitative and qualitative studies. They include a worksheet to appraise treatment effectiveness studies that gives the highest ratings to randomized controlled trials; Gibbs advocates the use of such trials to promote consistent evaluation of evidence quality. The expectation is that by following these procedures and using these forms, social work practitioners will be able to identify a set of research findings, "the current best evidence," that will help them make decisions about which course of action to take or which intervention to employ.

The work of Gibbs and others has made a significant contribution by defining clearly and consistently what is meant by best available evidence and by providing a stepwise process for identifying and using such evidence in practice. However, there are some limitations to Gibbs's approach. First, the kinds of electronic searches Gibbs recommends are time-consuming and technology-intensive. His recommendations about searches for and screening and synthesis of research are important in principle; whether it is practical for social workers to engage in this activity is another question.

Second, and perhaps more significantly, some clinical researchers claim that Gibbs's approach and EBP in general are very focused on intervention techniques and that this has the unintended effect of over-emphasizing the least curative factors in the therapeutic endeavor. Specifically, psychotherapy outcome researchers Lambert and Barley (2001) have reviewed over one hundred studies providing statistical analyses of the predictors of outcome and averaging the size of the contribution of each predictor to final outcome. They find that, compared to other factors, psychotherapeutic technique—the typical focus of EBP—explains only about 15 percent of variance in outcome. In other words, they suggest, much of the difference in outcome is determined by client and therapist factors rather than the "best available evidence." The growing interest in common factors—conditions and processes related to positive client outcomes that operate in all interventions—is a response to an overemphasis on evidence-based products as opposed to processes (Cameron & Keenan, 2010; Moos, 2007; Grencavage & Norcross, 1990; Norcross, 2001; Drisko, 2004). There is growing interest in this work that seeks to identify—theoretically or empirically—specific factors in addition to intervention strategies that can be tested to determine their relation to positive service outcomes.

SOCIAL PSYCHOLOGY OF EXPERTISE: KNOWING WHAT KNOWLEDGE IS RELEVANT WHEN

A second consideration in understanding the process of EBP is related to the cognitive psychology of information processing—the knowledge, experience, and judgmental strategies that practitioners bring to the practice situation. This is the preserve of practitioner expertise that all professionally prepared social workers bring to practice from academic learning and professional experience.

In *Informing Practice Decisions*, Sharon Berlin and I focus on the knowledge types and judgmental processes that social workers use to make practice decisions (Berlin and Marsh, 1993). In particular, we describe the types of judgments practitioners make and the human information structures and processes they use to make them. We recognize that in their problem-solving processes practitioners make numerous judgments, both large and small. The research literature on perception, problem-solving, and judgment shows that these judgments are influenced by universal structures and mechanisms of human information processing: the explicit fund of theoretical and substantive knowledge (including research evidence), the implicit practice wisdom developed through experience, and the practitioner's individual inference strategies (Hogarth, 1985; Kahneman, Slovic, & Tversky, 1982; Nesbitt & Ross, 1980).

Because the human perceptual field is confronted with such enormous quantities of information (psychologists estimate that only one-seventieth of what is available in the visual field can actually be perceived), it is well understood that the human mind—including the mind of the social work practitioner—has developed a number of judgmental heuristics, or shortcuts. Social science research on decision making indicates that most decisions are based on a limited number of cues and a small number of thinking strategies. Even though social workers may gather a great deal of information about a client's problems, strengths, and situation, they will necessarily be selective in what they ultimately consider. A rational thinking process is inevitably dominated by prior knowledge and information-processing shortcuts. By reflecting on and understanding their own processes of judgment and decision making, social workers are able to use available scientific and other evidence more critically and creatively. Indeed, instead of following an unconsidered but automatic first inclination to fit incoming information into routine patterns of thought and action, practitioners can expand professional discretion by reflecting on how they are thinking and consider additional information or additional ways of understanding the problem.

Although these ideas related to practitioner reflection and critical thinking are not well-developed in the EBP literature, it is increasingly recognized that practitioner expertise is essential to implementing EBP in real-world clinical practice. McCracken and Marsh (2008) define practitioner expertise as a set of cognitive tools that aid in the interpretation and application of evidence and in the overall conduct of social work practice. These tools for thinking develop over a period of extended practice, so an individual with experience in a given area is likely to respond to a situation with greater insight and experiential background than a novice.

CLIENT VALUES AND EXPECTATIONS

A third consideration in understanding the process of evidence-based decision making is the client's values and expectations for the service encounter. Social work ethics emphasize the client's right to self-determination and the practitioner's obligation to collaborate with the client in the definition of the problems to be addressed as well as in the determination of strategies to address them. This respect for and deference to client values is fundamental to social work professional ethics in the United States (NASW, 1999). McCracken and Marsh (2008) point to the sophisticated clinical and interpersonal skills required to ensure that client values and expectations are incorporated into the decision-making process. Although the principle of honoring client values and expectations is clear, consideration of how to determine the role that the client would like to play in decision making, assess the client's preferences, and provide the client with the information needed for decision making is largely undeveloped in the social work practice literature; it is an area where much more work is needed.

Conclusion

Concern with the intersection of research and practice has been integral to the development of social work as a profession from the beginning. EBP is one expression of this concern, one that builds on and contributes to other empirically based approaches such as task-centered and cognitive integrative approaches. What is gained by framing EBP as a clinical decision-making process? First, it is valuable to use the information we have about knowledge utilization. Sympathy with empirically based approaches has at times led us to overemphasize the utility of instrumental (empirical) knowledge at the expense of conceptual (theoretical) knowledge. In fact, empirical findings tell us that social workers and other helping professionals rely on both instrumental and conceptual knowledge to enhance the effectiveness of day-to-day practice. Second, efforts to advance the development of empirical approaches may have contributed to an overemphasis on the least curative aspect of the helping process, the therapeutic technique. The preponderance of literature on EBP has focused on identifying, collecting, and using information about therapeutic techniques—about what works. While this is critically important, research tells us that a broad set of client and service-provider factors also contribute to the effect of services.

EBP is a process of using research findings to aid clinical decision making that has three elements: best available evidence, practitioner knowledge and judgment, and client values and expectations. A broad definition of EBP places the intersection of research and practice at the intersection of these three circles of the diagram. There is valuable work to be done in all three areas, but this chapter is a call for more work in the areas of practitioner knowledge and judgment and client values and expectations. Over the hundred-year history of the social work profession, much has been learned about synergies between practice and research-by-intervening. It is only by intervening—through thoughtful and thorough examination of all three elements in the EBP process—that we will continue to learn in the next hundred years.

Learning by Intervening 13

References

Abbott, A. (1988). *The system of professions: An essay on the division of expert labor.* Chicago, IL: University of Chicago Press.

Abbott, E. (1931). Research in the program of social worker and agency. Unpublished manuscript. Abbott MSS, box 5, folder 14, Joseph Regenstein Library, University of Chicago.

Berlin, S. (2002). *Clinical social work practice: A cognitive-integrative perspective.* Oxford, UK: Oxford University Press.

Berlin, S. B., & Marsh, J. C. (1993). *Informing practice decisions.* New York, NY: Macmillan.

Cameron, M., & Keenan, E. K. (2010). The common factors model: Implications for transtheoretical clinical social work practice. *Social Work, 55*(1), 63–73.

Caplan, N., Morrison, A., & Stambaugh, R. J. (1975). *The use of social science knowledge in policy decisions at the national level: A report to respondents.* Ann Arbor, MI: University of Michigan Institute for Social Research.

Cha, T., Kuo, E., & Marsh, J. (2006). Useful knowledge for social work practice. *Social Work and Society, 4*(1).

Drisko, J. W. (2004). Common factors in psychotherapy outcome: Meta-analytic findings and their implications for practice and research. *Families in Society, 85,* 81–90.

Gambrill, E. (2005). *Critical thinking in clinical practice: Improving the quality of judgments and decisions* (2nd ed.). New York, NY: John Wiley and Sons.

Gibbs, L. (2003). *Evidence-based practice for the helping professions: A practical guide with integrated multimedia.* Pacific Grove, CA: Brooks/ Cole.

Grencavage, L. M., & Norcross, J. C. (1990). Where are the commonalities among the therapeutic common factors? *Professional Psychology: Research and Practice, 21,* 372–378,

Hogarth, R. (1985). *Judgment and choice.* New York, NY: John Wiley and Sons.

Kahneman, D., Slovic P., & Tversky, A. (1982) *Judgment under uncertainty: Heuristics and biases* (2nd ed.). Cambridge, UK: Cambridge University Press.

Lambert, M. J., & Barley, D. E. (2001). Research summary on the therapeutic relationship and psychotherapy outcome. *Psychotherapy, 38,* 357–361.

Marsh, J. C. (2002). Using knowledge about knowledge utilization. *Social Work, 2,* 101–104.

Marsh, J. C. (2003). Chewing on cardboard and other pleasures of knowledge utilization. *Social Work, 48* (3), 293–294.

Marsh, J. C. (2004). Social work readers describe "useful knowledge." *Social Work, 9,* 533–534.

McCracken, S., & Marsh, J. (2008). Practitioner expertise in evidence-based practice decision making. *Research on Social Work Practice, 18,* 301–310.

Moos, R. H. (2007). Theory-based processes that promote the remission of substance use disorders. *Clinical Psychology Review, 27*(5), 537–551

NASW. (1999). National Association of Social Workers Code of Ethics. Washington, DC: NASW Press.

Nesbitt, R., & Ross, L. 1980. *Human inference: Strategies and shortcomings of social judgment.* Englewood Cliffs, NJ: Prentice Hall.

Norcross, J. C. (2001). Purposes, processes, and products of the task force on empirically supported therapy relationships. *Psychotherapy, 38*, 345–352.

Rosen, A., Proctor, E. E., Morrow-Howell, N., & Staudt, M. (1995). Rationales for practice decisions: Variations in knowledge use by decision task and social work service. *Research on Social Work Practice, 5*(4), 501–523.

Rosen, A., Proctor, E. E., & Staudt, M. (1999). Social work research and the quest for effective practice. *Social Work Research, 23*, 4–14. *Research on Social Work Practice, October 1995; vol. 5, 4: pp. 501–523.*

Sanna, L. J., Small, E. M., & Cook, L. M. (2004). Social problem solving and mental simulation: Heuristics and biases on the route to effective decision making. In E. C. Chang, T. J. D'Zurilla, & L. J. Sanna (Eds.), *Social problem solving: Theory, research and training.* Washington, DC: American Psychological Association.

Weiss, C. H., & Bucuvalas, M. J. (1979). *Social science research and decision-making.* New York, NY: Columbia University Press.

CHAPTER TWO

Development of the Task-Centered Model

Anne E. Fortune

The development of William Reid and Laura Epstein's task-centered model is embedded in the empirical clinical practice movement in the United States, which intended to place social work practice on a scientific basis. This chapter focuses first on the larger empirical practice history and then on the development of task-centered practice within that context.

Empirical Clinical Practice in the United States

Twentieth-century efforts to make social work scientific include legitimating research as a source of data for intervention knowledge, providing evidence on the outcomes of social work practice, building

---

Note: The first section of this chapter is an elaboration of my book chapter "Empirical practice in social work," in Fortune, McCallion, & Briar-Lawson (2010.). The second section is an elaboration of my presentation, "Development of the Task-Centered Model," at the University of Chicago School of Social Service Administration's centennial symposium, From the Task-Centered Approach to Evidence-Based and Integrative Practice, Chicago, IL, June 5, 2009. It also draws on summaries of the task-centered model by Rooney (2010); Fortune, McCallion, and Briar-Lawson (2010); and Videka and Blackburn (2010). My thanks to Eleanor Tolson, Katherine Briar-Lawson, Ronald Rooney, and Tina Rzepnicki for their contributions to this manuscript.

empirical practice models like the task-centered model, and acceptance of evidence-based interventions and decision making.

ESTABLISHING THE RELEVANCE OF A SCIENTIFIC APPROACH

Beginning with Mary Richmond (1917), social work writers attempted to structure intervention with systematic, rational decision making based on empirical knowledge (Kirk & Reid 2002; Reid, 1994). Shortly after World War II, as specialist social work groups began talking about joining forces, researchers organized to define their roles and contributions to social work (Graham, Al-Krenawi, & Bradshaw, 2000).

The Social Work Research Group (SWRG) was founded in 1949. In 1955 it was one of seven professional groups that formed the National Association of Social Work (NASW). From 1963 to 1974 SWRG was a council within NASW, then in a reorganization of NASW, research lost its independent status and recognition. SWRG's substantial accomplishments over its 25 years included defining social work research; integrating research into the role and curricula of schools; disseminating research results through conferences, a newsletter, and the first database of social work research, *Social Work Abstracts;* and improving capacity through workshops and publication of the first social work research textbook: Norman A. Polansky's 1960 *Social Work Research* (Graham et al., 2000; Kirk & Reid, 2002). By the early 1970s, social workers recognized the value of a scientific approach but did not integrate it with social work practice.

RESEARCH ON SOCIAL CASEWORK

During the same period—the 1950s to the 1970s—social work researchers conducted numerous ambitious, large-scale social experiments. These studies for the first time assumed that there were measurable outcomes of practice and that it was desirable to study those outcomes. Subjects included intensive individual psychodynamic services for predelinquent boys (the Cambridge-Somerville study) (Powers & Witmer, 1951); services for mentally impaired older persons in need of protective services (the Benjamin Rose study in Cleveland) (Blenkner, Bloom & Nielsen, 1971); psychodynamic services for families receiving public assistance (the Chemung County, New York, study) (Wallace, 1967); and family-centered casework for multiproblem families (Geismar & Krisberg, 1967). Together, the studies examined work with a cross-section of social work clientele: predelinquent and delinquent boys; girls on probation; bright, disadvantaged minority youth; high school girls; new AFDC recipients; longer-term multiproblem families; and older individuals. The interventions were predominantly psychodynamic approaches, individual and group services, and help with environmental resources.

The outcomes of these social experiments were not encouraging. Several reviews suggested that social work intervention was ineffective or even detrimental (Mullen & Dumpson, 1972; Fischer, 1973). For example, predelinquent youth were as likely to follow criminal careers if they received services (Powers & Witmer, 1951), while older individuals who received intensive social work services died more often than those who did not (Blenkner et al., 1971). These unwanted results spurred two efforts: an age of accountability during which practitioner-researchers attempted to infuse practice with evaluation and measurable outcomes, and a reexamination of the principles of casework, including rethinking psychodynamic approaches and looking to new strategies such as task-centered, cognitive-behavioral, and systems approaches (Kirk & Reid, 2002).

BEGINNINGS OF EMPIRICAL PRACTICE

One approach to the challenge posed by poor outcomes of casework intervention was to further integrate a scientific approach into practice. Intervention models could be built using research, and intervention could include research procedures. The broadest definition of scientific practice was from Reid and Audrey Smith, who wrote that scientifically based or empirical practice includes five elements: empirical language in which key terms can be tied to measurable indicators; use of well-explicated practice models that link interventions and change; priority placed on research-based knowledge as a means of assessment and selecting interventions; use of scientific reasoning, rather than intuition or faith, to make decisions; and use of research methods as an integral part of practice (Reid & Smith, 1981). These assumptions about practice were a response to the interest in effective practice but also a direct challenge to the prevailing psychodynamic and functional interventions.

The new ideas about empirical practice were developed initially at the Columbia University School of Social Work doctoral program in the late 1950s and early 1960s. The context of scientific skepticism and dissatisfaction with psychodynamic casework stimulated a cohort of doctoral students who would become leading proponents of scientific practice (Kirk & Reid, 2002; Reid, 1994). After graduation, they clustered at five schools: University of California, Los Angeles, University of Washington, University of Michigan, University of Wisconsin–Madison, and University of Chicago. At each, they established systematic research programs to improve social work interventions.

Columbia graduate Scott Briar championed the "clinician scientist" and practitioner contribution to intervention knowledge through single-system designs (Blythe, Tripodi, & Briar, 1995). Edward J. Mullen worked on practitioners' individualized models of evidence-based practice, a precursor to the current evidence-based practice (EBP) (Mullen, 1978). Several clusters of faculty and their graduate students refined behavioral group and individual interventions in cumulative research programs. These included Edwin J. Thomas and Sheldon Rose (Michigan graduates), Elsie Pinkston (a University of Kansas psychology graduate), and Columbia graduates Richard Stuart, Tony Tripodi, Irwin Epstein, and Arthur Schwartz (Thomas, 1974; Rose, 1980; Pinkston, Levitt, Green, Linsk, & Rzepnicki, 1982; Stuart, 1977; Schwartz & Goldiamond, 1975; Tripodi & Epstein, 1980; Ivanoff, Blythe, & Tripodi, 1994). Reid and Laura Epstein (a Chicago graduate) developed a new practice approach—the task-centered model—which is based not on behavioral methods but on the results of research on psychodynamic practice (Reid & Epstein, 1972).

These faculty and their students shared a commitment to developing practice through empirical means. All were prolific writers who attempted to integrate their research results and theoretical foundations into new formulations of social work practice that challenged the prevailing psychodynamic interpretations. Their research models focused on intervention; they evaluated change, rather than conducting explanatory research to establish the cause of a problem. They influenced each other and in turn influenced scores of students to continue the development of empirical practice and research on interventions.

While the proponents of empirical practice focused on developmental research, social work intervention theories blossomed as scholars developed models that integrated new ideas from various sources. These nonempirical models included several versions of the generalist model (Compton & Galaway, 1975; Pincus & Minahan, 1973); the life model (Germain & Gitterman, 1980); and general systems (Goldstein, 1973), family systems (Hartman & Laird, 1983), and ecosystems theory (Meyer, 1976). Although these nonempirical models dominated in education and practice (for example, U.S. accreditation standards required generalist practice), gradually the empirical and nonempirical models influenced each other. For example, behavioral (learning) theory and cognitive theory were integrated in cognitive-behavioral theory, task-centered practice incorporated systems theories, and generalist practice included notions of client determination and contracts.

EVIDENCE-BASED INTERVENTIONS

Outside of social work, intervention research was linked primarily to specific problems, rather than models with multiple applications. Interventions were eclectic or nontheoretical. For example, what is now called the National Institutes of Health is organized by area: aging, mental health, drug abuse, and so on. When the federal government agreed to bolster the research infrastructure for social work (on the basis of recommendations in the 1988 NIMH Task Force on Social Work Research; see National Institute of Mental Health, 1991), funding for intervention research was based on problems, not on the theoretical or empirical models developed within social work. Each of the eight research centers that were established focused on a specific area of mental health, as did the research methodology workshops for faculty (Austin, 1999). In 2009, the directory of federally funded grants maintained by the Institute for Advancement of Social Work Research (IASWR, 2009) displayed the specific, focused, and problem-oriented nature of federally funded social work research: grantees focused, for example, on adherence to a low-fat diet, motivational enhancement for drug addicts, treatment of depression among older alcoholics, reduction of HIV risk among drug users, and so on.

Most of the research on social work practice since 1988 has been problem-specific. Because the eclectic interventions in recent research are usually based on best-known practice, the favored interventions are those already supported by evidence—including structured interventions, cognitive-behavioral methods, group interventions, and primary prevention (Reid & Fortune, 2003). As a consequence, there are multiple evidence-supported interventions for narrowly defined problems, while many of the popular social work interventions have not been tested.

A related development in empirical practice was the study of how social workers make decisions about interventions. Many of the Columbia University pioneers had been influenced by James Bieri, who studied clinical decision making (Reid, 1994). Mullen's (1978) personal practice model was a form of decision making using research evidence. Aaron Rosen and Enola K. Proctor (1978) studied clinician decision making from several perspectives. Eventually they developed and tested a structured decision-making system called systematic planned practice and specified the necessary components of practice guidelines (Rosen, 1993; Proctor & Rosen, 2003).

In the mid 1980s, Leonard Gibbs began advocating better reasoning in clinical practice and preparing curricular materials to teach critical thinking (1985, 2003). Gibbs joined Eileen Gambrill (a graduate of Edwin J. Thomas's Michigan program and an ardent behaviorist) to promote critical thinking in the United States (Gambrill, 1990, 1993). Their model was heavily influenced by David Sackett's evidence-based medicine (Sackett, Richardson, & Haynes, 1997), adopted in 1991 by the United Kingdom Health Service, which includes social workers. The Gambrill-Gibbs model involves a seven-step process: 1) being motivated to use EBP; 2) defining an answerable practice question; 3) finding the best available evidence to answer the question; 4) assessing the evidence; 5) integrating the evidence with practice experience, client values, and other relevant factors; 6) implementing and evaluating the intervention; and 7) teaching others (Gibbs, 2003; Gibbs & Gambrill, 1999).

The concurrent developments in problem-based research and critical, rational decision making in the 1980s and 1990s allowed the two to be melded into the EBP decision-making process. Evidence-supported interventions from problem-based research could be retrieved, evaluated, and implemented using the EBP decision-making process. The difficulty, of course, is that the supply of well-validated, evidence-supported interventions is much slimmer in social work than medicine, and the criteria for validation are controversial. For clients with multiple, varied problems, the array of evidence-based guidelines is overwhelming and may not be appropriate for comorbidity. To make the evidence-supported interventions more accessible to practitioners, several organizations assess research in a particular area and summarize the findings. Notable are the Cochrane Collaboration in medicine, founded in 1993, and the Campbell Collaboration for education, criminal justice, and social welfare, founded in 2000. In the United States, rich sources of evidence-supported interventions are available at the National Association of Social Work, the National Institutes of Health, the U.S. Department of Health and Human Services, and many other organizations.

In 2008, the Council on Social Work Education (CSWE) mandated that evidence-based interventions be included in the curricula of U.S. schools of social work (CSWE, 2008). CSWE's accreditation standards did not define *evidence-based intervention*, and there is considerable ambiguity about its meaning. However, Danya International developed a social work EBP curriculum funded by the National Institutes of Health. Collaborators included six social work organizations, including CSWE, and many scholars of EBP, including Mullen and Proctor (Danya International, 2008). The Danya curriculum—called REACH-SW—views EBP as a process to retrieve information and evaluate research evidence. If it is widely adopted, EBP as a decision-making model will be the standard for empirical practice in U.S. social work education. Given the limitations on available valid interventions and on practitioner time to retrieve them, it is likely that EBP decision making will be reintegrated with broader empirical models that provide a framework and practice skills for making sense of EBP.

The Task-Centered Model

Task-centered casework was developed at the University of Chicago School of Social Service Administration by faculty members Reid and

Laura Epstein and their students. Reid was a graduate of the Columbia University doctoral program that influenced so many social work researchers. Epstein was an experienced psychodynamic practitioner, a master's graduate of Chicago, a field educator, and a social work practice teacher. They began developing the task-centered model in 1968 and continued the development through research until their deaths.

THE CATALYST FOR A NEW MODEL

The catalyst for the task-centered model was a study of casework with families who had problems in family relations. In 1965, after six years as a practitioner and five years as an academic, Reid became director of the Center for Social Casework Research at the Community Service Society of New York (CSS). There, he teamed with Ann W. Shyne (a founder of SWRG) to conduct a federally funded four-year field experiment comparing the effectiveness of several types of casework (Reid & Shyne, 1969). The study included 120 intact lower-middle-class families who had applied for services at CSS. Three comparisons of conventional and innovative forms of treatment were planned.

The primary interest was in testing two forms of psychodynamic intervention: ego-modifying casework and ego-supportive casework (Reid & Shyne, 1969). Ego-modifying casework requires advanced skill from the caseworker and is intended to develop insight to change the relationship between the client's ego, id, and superego. Ego-supportive casework is intended to support the client's extant ego functioning. The distinction was central to CSS's developing practice theory and research. The two forms of casework were distinguished by the type of verbal interventions:

> Both supportive and modifying methods were to be directed toward improvement in the client's social functioning and his ability to cope with problems. The supportive method was to attain this end through use of reassurance, advice, and logical discussion of problems in the client's current life situation, without a deliberate aim of increasing his self-understanding or of effecting other internal change. The modifying method, on the other hand, was to utilize techniques that encouraged self-examination by the client so that he might be helped to achieve better social functioning through increased understanding of himself and the dynamics and origin of his behavior. (Reid & Shyne, 1969, 20)

The second comparison of interest involved a relatively new development in casework: interviews with multiple clients simultaneously.

Family members were assigned to be interviewed individually (mothers, for the most part) or jointly (husband and wife).

The third comparison was between continuous, open-ended service—the standard procedure—and planned, short-term treatment. In open-ended service, "neither the recipient nor the practitioner is given any predetermined limits as to amount of input or duration" (Reid & Shyne, 1969, 5). Generally, practitioners expected open-ended treatment to be lengthy—and in this study, a third of the open-ended clients had thirty or more interviews. In planned, short-term service, clients were informed that service would be no longer than eight in-person interviews within three months of intake.

The families were randomly assigned to one of eight groups that each received a different combination of psychosocial interventions (a 2 x 2 x 2 factorial experiment). For example, families in one group received ego-supportive casework with individual interviews in a planned, short-term format. Families in another group received ego-supportive casework with individual interviews in continuous, open-ended service. A third group received ego-modifying casework in individual interviews in a planned, short-term format, and so on. Thus, the design permitted examining each comparison while the other two comparisons were controlled.

The results of the experiment were complex, with some interesting nuances. For example, husbands participated more in planned, short-term treatment. Overall, however, the results were startling (and probably disappointing) to the researchers. For the first comparison—ego-modifying versus ego-supportive casework—analysis of audio tapings revealed no differences in practitioners' use of techniques, regardless of which intervention was prescribed (Mullen, 1968; Reid & Shyne, 1969). Regardless of prescription, practitioners used mostly ego-supportive verbal interventions and almost no core modifying techniques that might develop insight or intrapsychic understanding. Thus an important theoretical distinction was not borne out in practice. (The study illustrates the importance of fidelity checks on intervention!)

In the second comparison—individual versus joint interviews—implementation was also difficult. While there were more joint interviews when joint interviews were prescribed, most were in short-term service. In open-ended service, practitioners usually lapsed to their accustomed individual interviews with mothers. There were no differences in outcome between families with joint interviews and those without, even when joint interviews were successfully implemented.

The final comparison was properly implemented. Families assigned to open-ended service received nearly four times as many interviews; the median number was more than twice as many interviews as in planned, short-term service; and one family received one hundred interviews. With all the additional service, however, families in open-ended service did not have better outcomes than the short-term service recipients. In fact, families in planned, short-term service did better in overall problem situation and on nine of thirty-two outcomes. The outcome measures included caseworker assessments, husband and wife reports, and reports from independent research judges. Most differences were at moderate levels of change, with small numbers of both groups rated as considerably changed, but more open-ended cases rated as unchanged or worse.

These surprising and unwanted results were similar to those from other contemporary studies of social work intervention. Differential interventions based on theoretically inspired distinctions could not be implemented. It was difficult (though not impossible) to get practitioners to change their individually oriented interviewing habits, but it did not make a difference when they did. Most startling was the equivalence or superiority of planned, short-term service. Reid and Shyne devoted much of their analysis to what might be the reason for the difference. Clearly planned, short-term service was not simply a matter of having fewer interviews of the same kind as in open-ended service. Instead, planned, short-term service seemed to evoke different dynamics, motivation, and levels of work from both practitioners and clients.

THE NEW TASK-CENTERED CASEWORK APPROACH

Reid and Shyne's 1969 study served as a catalyst for developing a new treatment model based on what evidence suggested about effective treatment. Having returned to the University of Chicago in 1968, Reid recruited faculty colleague Laura Epstein, and together they developed and began teaching a new planned, short-term model based on psychosocial theory and research.

Reid and Epstein's new model, initially called task-centered casework, incorporated some elements from the brief treatment in the Reid and Shyne study. These elements included a planned, short duration with time limits set at the beginning, a focus on client problems rather than a change in personality, and limited therapeutic goals directly related to the focal problems (Reid & Epstein, 1972). It differed from the earlier casework in that diagnosis was around problems and how to alleviate them (not on personality traits or ego functioning); specific, limited goals were set; and more attention was given to the client's concept of problems and how to deal with them. Additional features, not related to the Reid and Shyne results, were a problem typology, explicit worker-client agreement or contracting, and the specification that change would occur through action, or tasks, rather than solely through verbal support and insight. In-session interventions focused on developing and evaluating tasks that might resolve the clients' problems and that the clients could undertake in their own environments.

Reid and Epstein drew extensively on the work of contemporary casework theorists in developing the task-centered model. The idea of a psychosocial problem (a target problem, or problem-in-living) as the focus of diagnosis and change was drawn from the work of Helen Harris Perlman (Perlman 1957), as were procedures for exploring problems. From Florence Hollis (1964, 1967a, 1967b), Reid and Epstein drew the practitioner's verbal interventions during sessions (the same types of interventions that defined ego-modifying and ego-supportive casework in the Reid and Shyne study). From Ruth Smalley's (1967) functional casework they drew the deliberate use of time, structure, and focus in casework, as well as client self-direction in using help. And from Howard Parad's (1963) and Lydia Rapoport's (1970) formulations of crisis theory, they drew the idea that problems-in-living could be resolved quickly.

The new task-centered model was an eclectic mix of theories and research results. It emphasized client preferences and client action in the environment, limited changes in problems in daily living, planned time limits, a well-defined structure for sessions, and an empirical orientation. The model was controversial, especially because it accorded less importance to the client-practitioner relationship as medium of change. Other key criticisms were that it involved inadequate assessment or diagnosis, which precluded gathering sufficient information for effective intervention; that the duration was too short for important or durable change; that interventions were too superficial to produce lasting change (which requires personality change); that clients were not able to know the best goals for themselves; and that it was impossible to measure goals and outcome.

These criticisms were rooted in the psychodynamic paradigm that Reid and Epstein challenged. Indeed, one of their direct challenges to prevailing theory—and this became a direct contribution to empirical practice—was that one need not get at underlying causes in order to change a problem. In both practice and intervention research, it was acceptable to focus on initiating and sustaining change without understanding or caring about the cause. Despite the criticisms, most practitioners could find some aspect of the task-centered model that was similar to what they were already doing, and this familiarity tempered some of the perceptions of how radical the model was.

An added benefit of the task-centered approach for inexperienced practitioners was that the steps in conducting sessions were laid out according to the phase of treatment. The initial phase focused on problem exploration, contracting around goals and time limits, and development of initial tasks. The middle (and longest) phase focused on results of tasks, progress toward goals, and development of additional tasks through problem-solving steps that were later labeled task planning and implementation (TPIS). The terminal stage (one or two sessions) involved a review of the current status of problems and of problem-solving strategies, and establishment of plans for maintaining gains or tackling incompletely resolved problems. Figure 1 outlines the phases as they were elaborated in 1992 (Reid, 1992). The initial model was not complete, but it did include the basic phases and the task planning processes.

Reid and Epstein began empirical testing and development of their new model immediately. Their first book included reports of three small studies of thirty-two cases in medical social services and psychiatric outpatient services (Reid & Epstein, 1972). The results suggested that the model was useful, but they also led to a number of modifications in the model: more attention was given to the practitioner's role and to how to develop tasks, estimate time limits realistically, handle new problems, and so on. For these trials, Reid and Epstein also devised measures of intermediate outcome (task accomplishment) and ultimate outcome (problem resolution) that continue to be used to assess client progress and the research-practice tools that Reid saw as part of empirical practice.

After publication of the first book on task-centered practice, Reid, the researcher, published more research while Epstein, the practitioner, concentrated on placing task-centered practice squarely in the context of social work and social work education. Epstein's *Helping people* (1980), for example, gave a brilliant portrait of social work, public and private social services, and the growth of the public social welfare system, as well as the task-centered model. It was a popular introductory social work and counseling text that she revised three times, with the final, 4th edition, coauthored with Lester B. Brown and titled *Brief treatment and a new look at the task-centered approach* (2001). She also wrote another book, *Talking and listening*, which positioned the task-centered model in the microskills counseling approach (Epstein, 1985).

The Design and Development
Process for New Interventions

The design and development (D&D) process for developing new interventions, as described by Jack Rothman and Edwin J. Thomas (Thomas, 1984; Rothman, 1980), consists of six steps: problem analysis and project planning, information gathering and synthesis, design, early development and pilot testing, evaluation and advanced development, and

FIGURE 1   Outline of Task-Centered Procedures by Phases

I. Initial Phase (Sessions 1–2)
  1. Discussion of reasons for referral, especially with nonvoluntary client(s)
  2. Exploration and assessment of client-acknowledged target problems and their contexts
  3. Formation of the service contract, including problems and goals to be addressed, explanation of treatment methods, agreement on durational limits
  4. Development and implementation of initial external tasks (see II-5 and 6, below)

II. Middle Phase
  (Each session follows the format below.)
  1. Problem and task review
  2. Identification and resolution of (actual) obstacles
  3. Problem focusing
  4. Session tasks (if two or more clients in session)
  5. Planning external tasks
      a. Generating task possibilities
      b. Establishing motivation
      c. Planning implementation of task(s)
      d. Identifying and resolving (anticipated) obstacles
      e. Guided practice, rehearsal
      f. Task agreement
      g. Summarizing task plan
  6. Implementation of task(s) (between sessions)

III. Terminal Phase (final session)
  1. Review of target problems and overall problem situation
  2. Identification of successful problem-solving strategies used by client(s)
  3. Discussion of what can be done about remaining problems, making use of strategies identified in II, above

Reprinted from W. J. Reid (1992). *Task strategies: An empirical approach to clinical social work.* New York: Columbia University Press, table 1.2, p. 6.

dissemination (Thomas & Rothman, 1994). (For a contemporary elaboration, see Fraser, Richman, Galinsky, & Day, 2009.) Reid and Epstein began their developmental research before D&D was well articulated, but in later publications they were explicit that D&D was the process they used (Reid, 1987a, 1994).

After the early development and pilot testing reported in *Task-centered casework*, Reid and Epstein began a series of randomized experiments to evaluate the model. The first experiment looked at the effectiveness of planning tasks (Reid, 1975), the second at the task-centered process as a whole (Reid, 1978). These evaluations, like much of the later development of the model, engaged student-practitioners in Reid and Epstein's practice classes at the University of Chicago (and later at the University at Albany, State University of New York).

As the model was disseminated, the research spread to doctoral students, community practitioners, and educators at other sites. For example, three large, carefully evaluated experiments were conducted in Britain: on social services, on probation, and on self-poisoners (Goldberg, Gibbons, & Sinclair, 1985). Even after the task-centered model was well accepted, its proponents returned to the initial steps of D&D when approaching a new use of the model (see, for example, Caspi, 2008).

VERBAL INTERVENTIONS, TASK PLANNING AND IMPLEMENTATION, AND TASK STRATEGIES

One component of the developmental research on the task-centered model focused on the mechanisms for change: verbal interventions, task planning, and strategies for using tasks with specific problems.

Given Reid's experience working with Hollis and Shyne, researchers had questions about practitioners' verbal intervention techniques: Were they similar to those in other types of casework? Were they related to outcome? Several studies suggested that task-centered practitioners made less use of exploration, but that exploration continued throughout the course of task-centered casework and was not restricted to the problem-formulation phase (Fortune, 1979a; Reid, 1978; Goldberg et al., 1985). Task-centered practitioners structured treatment more and gave advice more than subjects of previous studies of psychosocial casework (Reid, 1978), and they talked more (Fortune, 1979a). Among adult clients, but not child clients, greater use of advice and explanation about the client's behavior was associated with better outcomes. In short, it appeared that practitioners in the task-centered model were more active, kept the clients focused on the matters at hand, and were more willing to offer advice (Fortune, 1979a).

On the basis of this and other research (Fortune, 1981; Davis, 1975; Ewalt & Kutz, 1976), Reid concluded that advice giving—a no-no in psychosocial casework—had a catalytic function. Clients did not always carry out the practitioner's advice, but the advice stimulated their own successful ideas about how to accomplish tasks or resolve problems (Reid & Shapiro, 1969).

Reid soon added a second way to categorize verbal interventions, one based on the task-centered model's problem-solving structure

(Reid, 1978). Again, studies suggested that problem specification contin-ued throughout treatment, as the practitioner and client explored new aspects of problems in order to develop tasks (Fortune, 1979b; Goldberg et al., 1985; Reid, 1978). About a fifth of intervention-phase interviews were devoted to task planning generally (Reid, 1978; Fortune, 1979b). Predominant task-planning activities were generating alternatives to problem resolution, analyzing obstacles to task accomplishment, estab-lishing incentives and rationales for doing tasks, and review of previous tasks. The more time spent on target problems and tasks, the greater the resolution of client problems (Blizinsky & Reid, 1980).

Once it was established that task accomplishment (an intermediate outcome) was associated with problem resolution and improved overall situation (the ultimate outcome) (Goldberg et al., 1985; Reid, 1978), model developers concentrated on improving the task-planning proc-ess. The initial task-implementation sequence was expanded to include TPIS, with more attention to how the tasks would be done rather than just what the tasks were (Reid, 1978). Family systems theory was incor-porated into assessment and task planning with families, especially in relation to communication and interaction patterns (Reid, 1985). Some tasks were dual-level meta-interventions designed to resolve a problem while also strengthening parental or sibling bonds. The family problem-solving sequence involved paired tasks, one completed in the session (for example, a discussion of conflict resolution between parent and child) and one completed at home after the session (Reid, 1987a). Evalu-ation suggested that shared tasks, done together, were more effective than individual tasks or reciprocal tasks (you clean your room, I'll make your favorite dinner). These family practice developments led to recon-ceptualization of tasks as interventions both within and outside of ses-sions (Reid, 1985, 1987a, 1987b, 1992).

In the late 1980s and early 1990s, Reid's D&D turned from the prac-titioners' and clients' in-session activities to the broader context of which strategies (that is, clusters or sequences of tasks) were more effective with particular problems. In an early work, *The task-centered system*, Reid (1978) included several types of task strategies, including incremental strategies—"a series of tasks of progressive difficulty . . . to help the client gradually achieve his performance goal" (pp. 147–148); interference in escalating sequences of action or interaction; and Haley's (1976) paradoxical tasks and two-sided tasks. He also borrowed eclectically from programs in behavioral and other literature.

Beginning with *Task strategies: An empirical approach to clinical social work*, Reid presented strategies that were specific to particular problems and showed "in detail how an approach can be varied according to the problem for which the client is being seen" (Reid, 1992, p. 13). These strategies included sequences of tasks to deal with target problems related to family problems, coping with stress, increasing social involvement, problem drinking, chronic mental illness, health problems, inadequate resources, and self-monitoring of depression. He also offered task strategies for resolving obstacles such as poor motivation, distorted beliefs, and lack of skill to complete a task. *The task planner* (Reid, 2000) is a compendium of specific target problems—such as alcoholism, elder abuse, withdrawal in children, and gambling—and recommended task strategies for each. Each entry includes a description, a menu of client and practitioner tasks, suggested roles for the practitioner, elaborations or helpful hints, and suggestions for further reading. Many of the entries were developed by Reid's students and community practitioners. The book and its accompanying searchable CD are essentially a database of evidence-based and best practices for client actions that could resolve specific problems within a relatively short time.

When Reid and Epstein first described task-centered casework, they called it a general model that assumed that "certain fundamental principles can be successfully applied to a broad range of situations. . . . A practitioner need not master a large assortment of approaches to cope with the variety of cases . . . but rather can rely on variations of a single approach" (1972, p. 8). Their early D&D focused on the fundamental principles (client determination, action, TPIS, and so on), while later D&D with task strategies became more and more problem-specific and specialized. This development paralleled the problem-oriented focus of federally funded research and the EBP model in the late 1980s. The task-centered model became a curious amalgam of general and problem-specific intervention models. The principles, basic structure, and basic interventions (TPIS) were general, but the task strategies could be specific and were eclectic.

OTHER RESULTS OF D&D WITH THE TASK-CENTERED MODEL

The description of verbal, task planning and implementation, and task strategies interventions illustrates the D&D process for developing an intervention model over twenty-five years. At the same time, other developmental research refined other phases of the model and broadened the scope of the problems and populations with which the task-centered model was used. Problem specification became more sophisticated in response to overeager students, multiproblem families and involuntary clients (Rooney, 1992, 2009; Tolson, Reid, & Garvin, 1994; Trotter, 2006). Problems were placed in a larger context, and changing the context became a legitimate goal (Reid, 1996). Analyzing and overcoming obstacles to task accomplishment became a much more prominent part of the model (Reid, 1992). Unlike other problem-solving approaches, the task-centered model included a technology "for assessing what goes wrong when well-planned goals go awry" (Rooney, 2010). The ending phase was elaborated to include interventions focused not on change but on generalizing and maintaining clients' gains, such as reinforcement of accomplishments, planning to avoid future obstacles, and reviewing problem-solving skills (Brown, 1980; Fortune 1985; Tolson et al., 1994).

Most of the task-centered research was on intervention with individuals, children, adolescents, adults, elderly people, and families (especially those with child-related problems). Interventions were expanded to treatment groups whose members share similar problems and used task-centered structure and buddies or partners so clients could help each other develop and implement tasks (Fortune, 1985; Garvin, 1974; Rooney, 1977). Variations included case management with school children, their teachers, and their parents (Colvin, Lee, Magnano, & Smith, 2008a, 2008b; Vigianni, Reid, & Bailey-Dempsey, 2002); teams with teachers of disturbed students (Magnano, 2009); and case management with frail elderly people (Naleppa & Reid, 2003). In addition, proponents applied a task-centered framework to agency administration (Parihar, 1984), to community practice (Ramakrishnan, Balgopal, & Pettys, 1994), and to supervision of students (Caspi & Reid, 2002). Others integrated task-centered practice into generalist practice—multilevel, multisystems intervention—or melded it with basic social work skills (Epstein, 1980, 1985, 1988; Hepworth, Rooney, Rooney, Strom-Gottfried, & Larsen, 2010; Tolson et al., 1994).

Task-centered practice is the basis of social services in three countries—England, the Netherlands, and Norway (Marsh, 2010; Trotter, 2010; Eriksen, 2010)—and is used on its own or as a component of social work intervention in eleven other countries in Europe, Australia, and Asia. By 2010, there were over 200 publications on the task-centered approach in at least nine languages, including original textbooks in Great Britain, the Netherlands, and Norway (Doel & Marsh, 1992; Eriksen, 1999; Eriksen & Norstrand, 1995; Marsh & Doel, 2005; Jagt & Jagt, 1990; Jagt, 2001, 2008). Although few social work practitioners today identify themselves specifically or exclusively as task-centered practitioners, most make substantial use of components introduced by Reid and Epstein (Kelly, 2008).

The Contribution to Social Work Practice and Research

The task-centered model was created at a critical juncture in social work practice, when concern about the effectiveness of interventions coincided with a willingness to consider new ideas. The task-centered model was a product of that moment, and it also hastened the shift to new practice paradigms.

First, the task-centered model helped break the hold of psychodynamic casework on the practice community, opening the way for other means of conceptualizing psychosocial problems and their resolution. In the 1960s, psychodynamic approaches were dominant and went largely unquestioned except in the case of behavior modification, which was then new and controversial in social work. The task-centered model offered an alternative or intermediate approach that was more acceptable to psychodynamic practitioners than operant-respondent behavior modification. Reid and Epstein (1972) incorporated many ideas from psychosocial casework, which made task-centered practice palatable to many practitioners. They also had a means of validating their ideas through research. The ideas that the practice community eventually accepted included planned, short-term treatment; goal setting and contracting; action orientation (doing something about the problems, not just talking about causes); problem solving; and involving family members and other stakeholders in treatment. All of these concepts are now integral parts of "good social work" (Kelly, 2008).

A second contribution of the model was the integration of research and practice (Videka & Blackburn, 2010). The task-centered model included all five of Reid and Smith's (1981) elements of empirical practice: empirical language, well-explicated links between interventions and change, research-based knowledge for assessment and intervention, scientific reasoning, and research methods as an integral part of practice. In the task-centered model, assessment was based on data from the client; interventions were developed by client and practitioner on the basis of that data, external research evidence (for example, from task planners) and the client's desires; and task accomplishment and goal achievement were measured systematically. Practice and research methods were so well integrated that many neophytes were not aware of a distinction between them.

The task-centered model shared some of the research methods characteristic of Briar's behavioral clinician–scientist model (Blythe & Briar, 1985; Ivanoff, Blythe, & Briar, 1987), such as measurable problems and data-based assessment. However, the task-centered model was not wedded to the single-system research approach that was a core of the clinician-scientist model. Thus Reid and Epstein were able to draw on multiple research paradigms in their D&D, which may have enhanced their credibility and certainly allowed them to evaluate multiple dimensions of the model.

In addition to demonstrating that a practice model could incorporate research methods without becoming rigid or onerous for the practitioner, the model also demonstrated the benefits of D&D. The task-centered model was not the only practice model developed through the use of Thomas and Rothman's (1994) development procedures, but it was a prominent example that was unusual for the long-term persistence of the development work. Many of today's problem-specific intervention models are no longer evaluated after the initial round of D&D, so they are vulnerable to being inappropriate for new clients or settings.

A third contribution to social work practice was the conceptualization of intervention processes (TPIS) as interchangeable pieces that could be subject to research. Interventions were conceptualized as something different from simply time in interviews, as they were in the 1950s and 1960s research, and as something different from Hollis's (1967a, 1967b) verbal interventions. The reconceptualization of *intervention* opened the possibility of mechanisms of change that were not solely psychodynamic. At the same time, behaviorists were elaborating single-system research designs that attempted to isolate key therapeutic elements through the study of intervention interactions, differential intensities of treatment, additive effects of bundled interventions, and "stripping" (removing) pieces of bundled interventions (Hersen & Barlow, 1976).

However, research on TPIS went farther: it assumed that the intervention mechanisms might work similarly for different clients. That is, although the substantive content of a task strategy depended on the client, the process of planning and elaborating tasks was similar among clients. This was the first assumption evaluated by Reid and Epstein, who found that clients who engaged in more task planning were more successful (Reid, 1975, 1978; Blizinsky & Reid, 1980). By conceptualizing interventions as interchangeable and researchable, Reid and Epstein contributed to the current formulations of intervention research.

A fourth contribution of the task-centered model was to field education in social work education. The task-centered courses and practica were a robust forerunner of what are now called "evidence-based practica." For social work students at Chicago, field practica were linked directly to practice courses. While students learned intervention approaches, they implemented them in field agencies linked to the class section. In Reid and Epstein's classes, the students served as practitioners in the developmental research, implementing the task-centered model according to protocols designed to test various aspects of the model. They also participated as clinician-scientists, evaluating their cases according to the research methods incorporated in the task-centered model (that is, measuring task accomplishment and goal achievement). In addition, they were research assistants, interviewing other students' clients for outcome studies and analyzing small sets of data.

Beginning in the 1990s, students (and clients and community practitioners) developed task planners in specific areas of their own interest.

Thus research was a normative part of students' clinical experience. This model of education in EBP is broader than the current model, in which the practitioner is viewed as an information retriever and critical thinker. It should be evaluated to see if it has more durable effects on practitioners' incorporation of EBP than other models.

A side contribution of this field research environment was a re-conceptualization of process recordings as a conceptual learning tool. Traditional process recordings were verbatim transcripts of client-practitioner interactions, with commentary added by the student and field instructor. Process recordings were intended to help students conceptualize the process of what they were doing (Wilson, 1980). However, they focused on neither the conceptual framework of intervention, nor the skills needed to accomplish change. Epstein (1980) developed lists of skills that students needed to employ at each step of the task-centered process—for example, end-phase skills such as assessing change, discussing feelings about termination, and reviewing problem-solving skills. The skills were later elaborated by Eleanor Tolson (Tolson 1985; Tolson et al., 1994). Instead of writing verbatim re-creations of sessions, students of the task-centered model recorded case material on a form organized by components of the model (contract, goals, task review, task planning, and so on). These recording guides helped students conceptualize their practice within the task-centered framework.

At the same time, field instructors could identify and evaluate students' skills quickly. The combination of conceptual recording guide and skills definition and assessment enabled students to learn skills more quickly and to become creative in their use of skills (Tolson, 1985). The specific skills also permitted comparison of various ways to evaluate students (Reid, Bailey-Dempsey, & Viggiani, 1996). Although task-centered recording guides were not unique, they were one of social work's first consistent attempts to define and measure competencies for practice. They helped the social work education community accept that process recordings could include a wide variety of analytical tools for conceptual and skill learning (Graybeal & Ruff, 1995).

Summary

By the 1960s, social work scholars had accepted the credibility of research to evaluate and inform social interventions and were stymied by evidence of poor outcomes with then-dominant psychosocial casework. The dilemma catalyzed movements to develop new models of social intervention. One group of new approaches—behavioral, cognitive-behavioral, and task-centered practice—had empirical bases and were developed using research methods. The behavioral and later cognitive-behavioral approaches imported theory, practice, and research methodology from psychology and adapted them to social problems. The task-centered model was a homegrown social work model. Reid and Epstein drew from psychodynamic theory and from social work's own research findings and then used D&D research to improve and validate the model over more than 30 years.

In 2008, Michael Kelly concluded, "many of the central principles of TCP are now considered simply good social work practice. . . . Its major contribution to the field of social work practice [may be] a sturdy yet flexible practice technology that contains enough rigor to be consistently effective but also enough space to be adapted creatively to an incredible number of social work practice contexts" (2008, p. 199). In addition to creating a new model, Reid and Epstein and their colleagues helped open all of social work to nonpsychodynamic approaches, they integrated research and practice in multiple ways, they reconceptualized intervention (not just outcomes) as researchable, and they integrated field education and empirical practice.

References

Austin, D. M. (1999). A report on progress in the development of research resources in social work. *Research on Social Work Practice, 9*(6), 673–707.

Blenkner, M., Bloom, M., & Nielson, M. (1971). A research and demonstration project of protective services. *Social Casework, 52*, 483–499.

Blizinsky, M. J., & Reid, W. J. (1980). Problem focus and change in a brief treatment model. *Social Work, 25*, 89–98.

Blythe, B. J., & Briar, S. (1985). Developing empirically based models of practice. *Social Work, 30*, 483–488.

Blythe, B. J., Tripodi, T., & Briar, S. (1995). *Direct practice research in human service agencies*. New York, NY: Columbia University Press.

Brown, L. B. (1980). Client problem solving learning in task-centered social treatment. (Unpublished doctoral dissertation). University of Chicago, Chicago, IL.

Caspi, J. (2008). Building a sibling aggression treatment model: Design and development research in action. *Research on Social Work Practice, 16*(6), 575–585.

Caspi, J., & Reid, W. J. (2002). *Educational supervision in social work*. New York, NY: Columbia University Press.

Colvin, J., Lee, M., Magnano, J., & Smith, V. (2008a). The Partners in Prevention Program: Further development of the task-centered case management model. *Research on Social Work Practice, 18*(6), 586–595.

Colvin, J., Lee, M., Magnano, J., & Smith, V. (2008b). The Partners in Prevention Program: The evaluation and evolution of the task-centered case management model. *Research on Social Work Practice, 18*(6), 607–615.

Compton, B. R., & Galaway, B. (1975). *Social work processes*. Homewood, IL: Dorsey.

CSWE (Council on Social Work Education). (2008). Educational policy and accreditation standards. Alexandria, VA: Council on Social Work Education.

Danya International. (2008). Research and empirical applications for curriculum enhancement in social work (REACH-SW): Advanced doctoral students or new instructors edition [CD-ROM].

Davis, I. P. (1975). Advice-giving in parent counseling. *Social Casework, 56,* 346–347.

Doel, M., & Marsh, P. (1992). *Task-centred social work*. Hampshire, UK: Ashgate.

Epstein, L. (1980). *Helping people: The task centered approach*. St. Louis, MO: C. V. Mosby.

Epstein, L. (1985). *Talking and listening: A guide to the helping interview*. St. Louis, MO: C. V. Mosby.

Epstein, L. (1988). *Helping people: The task centered approach* (2nd ed.). Columbus, OH: Merrill.

Epstein, L., & Brown, L. B. (2001). *Brief treatment and a new look at the task-centered approach* (4th ed.). Old Tappan, NJ: Pearson.

Eriksen, R. E. (1999). *Hvordan lære seg oppgaveorientert tilnærming (OOT)? Del I: OOTs teorigrunnlag. Del II: Praktiske tilnærminger*. (How to learn the task-centered approach (TC)? Part one: TC's theoretical basis. Part two: Practical approaches.) Oslo, Norway: Diakonhjemmet høgskole.

Eriksen, R. E. (2010). Task-centered practice in Norway. In A. E. Fortune, P. McCallion, and K. Briar-Lawson (Eds.), *Social work practice research for the 21st century* (pp. 221–226). New York, NY: Columbia University Press.

Eriksen, R. E., & Nordstrand, M. (1995). *Innføring i oppgaveorientert tilnærming (OOT)*. (An introduction to the task-centered approach (TC). Oslo, Norway: Diakonhjemmet høgskole, Høgskolen i Sør Trøndelag og Sosial—og helsedepartementet.

Ewalt, P. L., & Kutz, J. (1976). An examination of advice-giving as a therapeutic intervention. *Smith College Studies in Social Work, 47,* 3–19.

Fischer, J. (1973). Is casework effective? A review. *Social Work, 18*(1), 5–20.

Fortune, A. E. (1979a). Communication processes in task-centered treatment. *Social Work, 24,* 390–396.

Fortune, A. E. (1979b). Problem-solving processes in task-centered treatment with adults and children. *Journal of Social Service Research, 2*(4), 357–371.

Fortune, A. E. (1981). Communication processes in social work practice. *Social Service Review, 55,* 93–128.

Fortune, A. E. (Ed.). (1985). *Task-centered practice with families and groups*. New York, NY: Springer.

Fortune, A. E., McCallion, P., & Briar-Lawson, K. (Eds.), (2010). *Social work practice research for the 21st century*. New York, NY: Columbia University Press.

Fraser, M. W., Richman, J. M., Galinsky, M. J., & Day, S. H. (2009). *Intervention research: developing social programs*. New York, NY: Oxford University Press.

Gambrill, E. (1990). *Critical thinking in clinical practice: Sources of error and how to avoid them*. San Francisco, CA: Jossey-Bass.

Gambrill, E. (1993). What critical thinking offers to clinicians and clients. *Behavior Therapist, 16,* 141–147.

Garvin, C. D. (1974). Task-centered group work. *Social Service Review, 48,* 494–507.

Geismar, L., & Krisberg, J. (1967). *The forgotten neighborhood*. Metuchen, NJ: Scarecrow.

Germain, C. B., & Gitterman, A. (1980). *The life model of social work practice*. New York, NY: Columbia University Press.

Gibbs, L. E. (1985). Teaching critical thinking at the university level: A review of some empirical evidence. *Informal Logic, 7*(2/3), 137–149.

Gibbs, L. E. (2003). *Evidence-based practice for the helping professions: A practical guide with integrated multimedia*. Pacific Grove, CA: Brooks Cole.

Gibbs, L. E., & Gambrill, E. (1999). *Critical thinking for social workers: Exercises for the helping professions* (2nd ed.). Thousand Oaks, CA: Pine Forge.

Goldberg, E. M., Gibbons, J., & Sinclair, I. (1985). *Problems, tasks and outcomes: The evaluation of task-centered casework in three settings*. Winchester, MA: Allen & Unwin.

Goldstein, H. (1973). *Social work practice: A unitary approach* (1st ed.). Columbia, SC: University of South Carolina Press.

Graham, J. R., Al-Krenawi, A., & Bradshaw, C. (2000). The Social Work Research Group/NASW Research Section/Council on Social Work Research, 1949–1965: An emerging research identity in the American profession. *Research on Social Work Practice, 10*(5), 622–643.

Graybeal, C. T., & Ruff, E. (1995). Process recording: It's more than you think. *Journal of Social Work Education, 31*(2), 169–181.

Haley, Jay. (1976). *Problem-solving therapy*. San Francisco, CA: Jossey-Bass.

Hartman, A., & Laird, J. (1983). *Family-centered social work practice*. New York, NY: Free Press.

Hepworth, D. H., Rooney, R. H., Rooney, G. D., Strom-Gottfried, K., & Larsen, J. A. (2010). *Direct Social Work Practice: Theory and Skills* (8 ed.). Pacific Grove, CA: Brooks Cole.

Hersen, M., & Barlow, D. H. (1976). Single-case experimental designs: Strategies for studying behavior change. Oxford, UK: Pergamon.

Hollis, F. (1964). *Casework: A psychosocial therapy*. New York, NY: Random House.

Hollis, F. (1967a). The coding and applications of a typology of casework treatment. *Social Casework, 48*, 489–497.

Hollis, F. (1967b). Explorations in the development of a typology of casework treatment. *Social Casework, 48*, 355–341.

Institute for the Advancement of Social Work Research (IASWR). (2009). Directory of social work research grants awarded by the National Institutes of Health 1993–2009. Retrieved June 29, 2009, from http://www.charityadvantage .com/iaswr/NIHSWRDatabaseRevJUNE2009.pdf.

Ivanoff, A. M., Blythe, B. J., & Briar, S. (1987). The empirical clinical practice debate. *Social Casework 68*(5), 290–298.

Ivanoff, A. M., Blythe, B. J., & Tripodi, T. (1994). *Involuntary clients in social work practice: A research-based approach*. Hawthorne, NY: Aldine de Gruyter.

Jagt, L. (2001). *Moet dat nou? Hulpverlening aan onvrijwillige cliënten*. Houten/Zaventem, Netherlands: Bohn Stafleu Van Loghum.

Jagt, L. (2008). *Van Richmond naar Reid: bronnen en ontwikkeling van taakgerichte* Houten/Zaventem, Netherlands: Bohn Stafleu Van Loghum.

Jagt, L., & Jagt, N. (1990). *Taakgerichte hulpverlening in het maatschappelijk werk.* Houten/Zaventem, Netherlands: Bohn Stafleu Van Loghum.

Kelly, M. (2008). Task-centered practice. In T. Mizrahi & L. Davis (Eds.), *Encyclopedia of Social Work* (20th ed.) (pp. 197–199). Oxford, UK: Oxford University Press.

Kirk, S. A., & Reid, W. J. (2002). *Science and social work.* New York, NY: Columbia University Press.

Magnano, J. (2009). Partners in success: An evaluation of an intervention for children with severe emotional disturbance. (Unpublished dissertation). University at Albany, State University of New York, Albany, NY.

Marsh, P. (2010). Task-centered practice in Great Britain. In A. E. Fortune, P. McCallion, and K. Briar-Lawson (Eds.), *Social work practice research for the 21st century* (pp. 203–207). New York, NY: Columbia University Press.

Marsh, P., & Doel, M. (2005). *The task-centred book.* Abingdon, UK: Routledge.

Meyer, C. H. (1976). *Social work practice* (2nd ed.). New York, NY: Free Press.

Mullen, E. J. (1968). Casework communication. *Social Casework, 49,* 546–551.

Mullen, E. J. (1978). The construction of personal models for effective practice: A method for utilizing research findings to guide social interventions. *Journal of Social Service Research, 2*(1), 45–63.

Mullen, E. J., & Dumpson, J. R. (Eds.), (1972). *Evaluation of social intervention.* San Francisco, CA: Jossey-Bass.

Naleppa, M., & Reid, W. J. (2003). *Gerontological social work: A task-centered approach.* New York, NY: Columbia University Press.

National Institute of Mental Health. (1991). *Building Social Work Knowledge for Effective Services and Policies.* Austin, TX: School of Social Work, University of Texas as Austin.

Parad, H. J. (1963). Brief ego-oriented casework with families in crisis. In H. J. Parad & R. R. Miller (Eds.), *Ego-oriented casework: Problems and perspectives* (pp. 145–164). New York, NY: Family Service Association of America.

Parihar, B. (1984). *Task-centered management in human services.* Springfield, IL: Charles C. Thomas.

Perlman, H. H. (1957). *Social casework, a problem-solving process.* Chicago, IL: University of Chicago Press.

Pincus, A., & Minahan, A. (1973). *Social work practice: model and method.* Itasca, IL: F. E. Peacock.

Pinkston, E. M., Levitt, J. L., Green, G. R., Linsk, N., & Rzepnicki, T. L. (1982). *Effective social work practice: Advanced techniques for behavioral intervention with individuals, families, and institutional staff.* San Francisco, CA: Jossey-Bass.

Polansky, N. A. (Ed.). (1960). *Social work research: Methods for the helping professions.* Chicago, IL: University of Chicago Press.

Powers, E., & Witmer, H. (1951). *An experiment in the prevention of delinquency: The Cambridge-Somerville Youth Study.* New York, NY: Columbia University Press.

Proctor, E. K., & Rosen, A. (2003). The structure and function of social work practice guidelines. In A. Rosen & E. K. Proctor (Eds.), *Developing practice guidelines for social work intervention: Issues, methods, and research agenda* (pp. 108–127). New York, NY: Columbia University Press.

Ramakrishnan, K. R., Balgopal, P. R., & Pettys, G. L. (1994). Task-centered work with communities. In E. R. Tolson, W. J. Reid, & C. D. Garvin (Eds.), *Generalist practice: A task-centered approach* (pp. 339–390). New York, NY: Columbia University Press.

Rapoport, L. (1970). Theories of social casework. In R. W. Roberts & R. H. Nee (Eds.), *Theories of social casework* (pp. 265–312). Chicago, IL: University of Chicago Press.

Reid, W. J. (1975). A test of a task-centered approach. *Social Work, 20,* 3–9.

Reid, W. J. (1978). *The task-centered system.* New York, NY: Columbia University Press.

Reid, W. J. (1985). *Family problem solving.* New York, NY: Columbia University Press.

Reid, W. J. (1987a). Evaluating an intervention in developmental research. *Journal of Social Service Research, 11,* 17–39.

Reid, W. J. (1987b). The family problem-solving sequence. *Family Therapy, 14*(2), 135–146.

Reid, W. J. (1992). *Task strategies: An empirical approach to clinical social work.* New York, NY: Columbia University Press.

Reid, W. J. (1994). Field testing and data gathering on innovative practice interventions in early development. In J. Rothman & E. J. Thomas (Eds.), *Intervention research* (pp. 245–264). New York, NY: Haworth.

Reid, W. J. (1996). Task-centered social work. In F. J. Turner (Ed.), *Social work treatment* (4th ed.). New York, NY: Free Press.

Reid, W. J. (2000). *The task planner: An intervention resource for human service professionals.* New York, NY: Columbia University Press.

Reid, W. J., Bailey-Dempsey, C., & Viggiani, P. (1996). Evaluation of student fieldwork: An empirical study. *Journal of Social Work Education, 32*(1), 45–52.

Reid, W. J., & Epstein, L. (1972). *Task-centered casework.* New York, NY: Columbia University Press.

Reid, W. J., & Fortune, A. E. (2003). Empirical foundations for practice guidelines in current social work knowledge. In E. K. Proctor & A. Rosen (Eds.), *Developing practice guidelines for social work intervention: Issues, methods, and research agenda* (pp. 59–79). New York, NY: Columbia University Press.

Reid, W. J., & Shapiro, B. L. (1969). Client reactions to advice. *Social Service Review, 43,* 165–173.

Reid, W. J., & Shyne, A. W. (1969). *Brief and extended casework.* New York, NY: Columbia University Press.

Reid, W. J., & Smith, A. D. (1981). *Research in social work.* New York, NY: Columbia University Press.

Richmond, M. (1917). *Social diagnosis.* New York, NY: Russell Sage Foundation.

Rooney, R. H. (1977). Adolescent groups in public schools. In W. J. Reid & L. Epstein (Eds.), *Task-centered practice* (pp. 168–182). New York, NY: Columbia University Press.

Rooney, R. H. (1992). *Strategies for work with involuntary clients.* New York, NY: Columbia University Press.

Rooney, R. H. (Ed.). (2009). *Strategies for work with involuntary clients.* New York, NY: Columbia University Press.

Rooney, R. H. (2010). Task-centered practice in the United States. In A. E. Fortune, P. McCallion, & K. Briar-Lawson (Eds.), *Social work practice research for the 21st century*. New York, NY: Columbia University Press.

Rose, S. D. (1980). *A casebook in group therapy: A behavioral-cognitive approach*. Englewood Cliffs, NJ: Prentice-Hall.

Rosen, A. (1993). Systematic planned practice. *Social Service Review, 67*(1), 84–100.

Rosen, A., & Proctor, E. K. (1978). Specifying the treatment process: The basis for effectiveness research. *Journal of Social Service Research, 2*(1), 25–44.

Rothman, J. (1980). *Social R&D: Research and development in the human services*. Englewood Cliffs, NJ: Prentice-Hall.

Sackett, D. L., Richardson, W. S., & Haynes, R. B. (1997). *Evidence-based medicine: How to practice and teach EBM*. New York, NY: Churchill Livingstone.

Schwartz, A., & Goldiamond, I. (1975). *Social casework: A behavioral approach*. New York, NY: Columbia University Press.

Smalley, R. E. (1967). *Theory for social work practice*. New York, NY: Columbia University Press.

Stuart, R. B. (1977). *Behavioral self-management: Strategies, techniques and outcomes*. Hove, UK: Brunner/Mazel.

Thomas, E. J. (1974). *Behavior modification*. Chicago, IL: Aldine.

Thomas, E. J. (1984). *Designing interventions for the helping professions*. Beverly Hills, CA: Sage.

Thomas, E. J., & Rothman, J. (1994). An integrative perspective on intervention research. In E. J. Thomas & J. Rothman (Eds.), *Intervention research: Design and development for human service* (pp. 3–23). New York, NY: Haworth.

Tolson, E. R. (1985). Teaching and measuring task-centered skills: The skill assessment teaching model. In A. E. Fortune (Ed.), *Task-centered practice with families and groups* (pp. 212–226). New York, NY: Springer.

Tolson, E. R., Reid, W. J., & Garvin, C. D. (1994). *Generalist practice: A task-centered approach*. New York, NY: Columbia University Press.

Tripodi, T., & Epstein, I. (1980). *Research techniques for clinical social workers*. New York, NY: Columbia University Press.

Trotter, C. (2006). *Working with involuntary clients* (2nd ed.). Crows Nest, NSW, Australia: Allen & Unwin.

Trotter, C. (2010). Task-centered practice in Australia. In A. E. Fortune, P. McCallion, and K. Briar-Lawson (Eds.), *Social work practice research for the 21st century* (pp. 227–230). New York, NY: Columbia University Press.

Videka, L., & Blackburn, J. A. (2010). The intellectual legacy of William J. Reid. In A. E. Fortune, P. McCallion, & K. Briar-Lawson (Eds.), *Social work practice research for the 21st century*. New York, NY: Columbia University Press.

Viggiani, P. A., Reid, W. J., & Bailey-Dempsey, C. (2002). Social worker–teacher collaboration in the classroom: Help for elementary students at risk of failure. *Research on Social Work Practice, 12*(5), 604–620.

Wallace, D. (1967). The Chemung County evaluation of casework service to dependent multi-problem families: Another problem outcome. *Social Service Review, 41*, 379–389.

Wilson, S. J. (1980). *Recording: Guidelines for social workers*. New York, NY: Free Press.

CHAPTER THREE

The Applied-Science Approach and the Cognitive-Integrative Perspective

Sharon B. Berlin

One of the cherished legacies that our intellectual forebears at Chicago's School of Social Service Administration passed along to subsequent generations of social work scholars is an appreciation for an encompassing approach to developing knowledge. The school's leaders embraced rigorous scholarship, but they were not inclined to frame pathways to knowledge in terms of either-or, superior-inferior choices. Thanks to people like William Reid and Laura Epstein, and even the school's founding mother, Edith Abbott, it has never been a matter of theoretical versus empirical understanding or pragmatism versus empiricism. Rather, all of these approaches have been considered vital. To paraphrase William Reid, empirically derived data and clear theoretical conceptualization, commitments, and values are interdependent contributors to a dynamic configuration of knowledge that is relevant to practice (Reid, 1990).

In some ways this perspective overlaps the parameters of the applied-science approach to developing knowledge for practice. As Teasdale and Barnard (1993) explain, the applied-science approach to understanding mental and therapeutic processes is an iterative process that takes a real-world problem or question as its starting point and then moves back and forth between theory, rigorous experimentation, and real-world applications and evaluations to generate more detailed empirical information, improved theoretical accounts, and, in the case that is the subject of this chapter, advances in cognitive therapy interventions (p. 4). Although the scientists, theorists, and clinicians who participate in this process are not part of a well-coordinated team that is motivated by a singular purpose, in one way or another their work bears on a central question: How does the mind work to create problematic feelings and thoughts, and once caught up in an anxious, depressed, or otherwise maladaptive frame, how does the mind change?

To tell the story of how applied science has shaped the development and evolution of cognitive therapy, one could go as far back as ancient Greek scholars who grappled with understanding how we learn and remember—or not nearly so far back, to 1948 when a group of scientists came together at the Hixon Symposium at the California Institute of Technology. There, the forebears of the cognitive revolution convened to share growing evidence from their respective fields that challenged prevailing antimentalistic explanations of human functioning. At this meeting, the participants also took beginning steps to forge a loose alliance among their various disciplines, including cognitive psychology, computer science, linguistics, neurology, and anthropology. The idea was that a network of cognitive scientists would work to generate a broad range of interdisciplinary insights about the operations of fundamental mental processes (Gardner, 1987).

This chapter starts with the emergence of Aaron Beck's model of cognitive therapy in the 1970s and provides examples of how I have drawn on and contributed to advancements in applied science to revise Beck's model and develop a different version of it, which I call the cognitive-integrative perspective. Although Beck initially developed cognitive therapy to address depression, he and others have subsequently shown how it can be successfully applied to a wider range of mental health problems (e.g., Reinecke & Clark, 2003). Here I focus on the application of cognitive therapy and the cognitive-integrative perspective to depression, but with the understanding that both of these approaches have wider relevance.

I have contributed to this applied-science process primarily by critically examining, recasting, and extending the work of others. I've synthesized research findings, conceptualizations, and practice guidelines generated by scholars representing multiple disciplines; have located gaps in theory and in approaches to practice; and have relied on my own social work theoretical grounding, empirical work, and practice experience to develop a more encompassing conceptual framework and therapeutic approach. The cognitive-integrative perspective is based on the fundamental notion that depression and other mental health problems stem in large part from interactions between current life stressors and memories of difficult past experiences. It incorporates a broad array of therapeutic methods, draws on plausible models of memory and the mind, and should be especially useful for clients whose mental health problems are intertwined with environmental stressors and barriers.

In undertaking this project, my main method was to read extensively across disciplines (including social work, social psychology, social cognitive psychology, clinical psychology, cultural psychology, and neuroscience), engage in dialog with respected scholars in these fields through symposia and publications, piece together findings and ideas about the links between social and mental processes, consider what the emerging picture might mean for social work clients, and finally organize an account that is plausible and practical and has empirical backing (Berlin, 2002). Along the way, this process of theorizing has been stimulated and supported by evidence from multiple interdisciplinary research streams, as well as information I have collected through teaching and my own practice. This latter feedback has provided me with a direct sense of when my ideas are just so many words and when they seem to have traction in the real world.

My research, which was designed to test cognitive therapy interventions (Berlin, 1980, 1985) and to explore how clients accomplish change within the structure of cognitive therapy (Berlin, Mann, & Grossman, 1991), suggests that a lack of attention to ongoing life stresses makes it difficult for clients to alter their negative mind-sets in order embrace a more adaptive approach to daily circumstances. These findings were the red flag that signaled the need for a cognitive therapy that addresses not only negative thoughts, but also the difficult life circumstances that give rise to them.

Cognitive Therapy

When I first started thinking and writing about cognitive therapy as a doctoral student and then a new assistant professor in the 1970s and 1980s, I relied heavily on the prevailing cognitive therapy approach of the time: Aaron Beck's model of cognitive therapy for depression (Beck, Rush, Shaw, and Emery, 1979). As one of the early founders of cognitive therapy, Beck, who started writing about this therapeutic approach in the early 1970s (1972, 1976), distinguished himself from another cognitive therapy pioneer, Albert Ellis (1962), by making the point that the goal of cognitive therapy was not to help clients achieve rational or realistic thinking, but to help them develop a mind-set that was adaptive—that allowed them the mental flexibility to respond to life situations in a functional way.

Another major factor favoring Beck's model was that early on he subjected it to an empirical test. In a landmark paper reported in the first issue of the journal *Cognitive Therapy and Research*, Beck and his associates reported significantly greater improvement for depressed patients receiving cognitive therapy over those receiving pharmacotherapy in a randomized experiment (Rush, Beck, Kovacs, & Hollon, 1977). This early study was the first of many research efforts conducted by Beck and his group and then by a host of others that served to evaluate and further develop cognitive therapy (e.g., Chambless & Peterman, 2004; DeRubeis, Gelfand, Tang, & Simons, 1999; DeRubeis, et al. 2005; Evans et al., 1992; Hollon, et al., 2005; Leahy, 2004).

The more studies are conducted, the more complicated and contradictory the findings tend to be. A case in point is the landmark National Institute of Mental Health Treatment of Depression Collaborative Research Study (Elkin et al., 1989), which found that antidepressants were more effective in reducing symptoms among patients who were severely depressed, that interpersonal psychotherapy was more effective than cognitive therapy for those patients whose depressions were classified as more moderate, and that patients receiving cognitive therapy maintained therapy gains over the long run to a greater extent than patients receiving antidepressants or interpersonal psychotherapy.

Subsequent studies have found that cognitive therapy can be as effective as medication in treating moderate to severe depression, especially when therapists have a high level of experience and expertise (DeRubeis et al., 2005), and that among patients whose treatment is discontinued, those who had received cognitive therapy are less likely to relapse than those who received medication. Furthermore, recipients of cognitive therapy whose treatment is discontinued are no more likely to relapse than are patients receiving medication whose treatment is not discontinued (Hollon et al., 2005). Although cognitive therapy has not held the advantage in every empirical test, its cumulative record in treating problems of anxiety and depression (Barlow, 2007; Leahy, 2004) is very strong and suggests that it is an approach social work should not ignore.

The central idea underlying traditional cognitive therapy is that depressive affect is prompted by negative cognitions. In Beck's model, "cognitions are understood as stream-of-consciousness or automatic thoughts that tend to be in an individual's awareness" (Beck, Epstein, & Harrison, 1983, p. 2). Therapeutic actions include a series of steps designed to help clients replace their negative automatic thoughts with thoughts that represent a fresh, unencumbered look at what is happening and what is possible.

In typical accounts of cognitive therapy (e.g., Beck et al., 1979; A. T. Beck, 2005; J. Beck, 1995), the protocol usually starts with clients self-monitoring negative thoughts to observe them as they are occurring.

Then, with the help of the practitioner, clients learn to reflect on the necessity and utility of these thoughts and ultimately to replace them with assessments that that are more optimistic and compassionate and that encourage adaptive behaviors. Often there is an additional step that includes looking for underlying themes connecting automatic thoughts and considering whether these themes reflect deep-seated beliefs about how one needs to operate to be safe and acceptable in the world. Once clients have identified these beliefs, they are asked to consider whether they are the best guides for their current life. Early on, Beck applied the concept of cognitive schemas to these thematically organized networks of thoughts, suggesting that well-developed, stable, and relatively fixed patterns of thinking are at the root of depression and other mental health problems.

There is a lot to like about Beck's overall approach. It is brief, comprehensible, and flexible, and it has been helpful to countless clients (Leahy, 2004; Reinecke & Clark, 2003). In addition, it has been valuable in prompting therapy theorists of all stripes to look to findings generated by the cognitive and neurological sciences to develop therapeutic accounts that have some basis in how the mind and brain actually work.

Initially I was drawn to cognitive therapy because it offered clear and logical guidelines for helping people let go of the internal dialogues that undermined their efforts to find peace, connection, security, or accomplishment. But as I became more familiar with the model and continued to work with it, I also found several ways in which it seemed limiting. For one thing, the traditional cognitive therapy model maintains a narrow focus on dysfunctional or distorted thoughts and gives relatively little attention to the kinds of ongoing sociostructural deprivations and incursions that create, maintain, and exacerbate them. Given my social work background, my affinity for task-centered practice (Reid & Epstein, 1972), and the research linking poverty, stress, and social isolation to increased rates of depression (Brown & Harris, 1978; Belle, 1982; Grote, et al., 2004; Hobfoll, 1989, 2003; Mirowsky & Ross, 1989), I was quite certain that not only do difficult environmental conditions play a role in contributing to the development of dysfunctional cognitive schemas early in life and in activating them later on, as Beck suggested, but that current difficult circumstances often play a major role in keeping the depressive feelings going, extending them, and making them worse.

Beyond that, Beck's original model rested heavily on a view of the mind as primarily a repository of thoughts and on the assumption that negative thoughts were the source of depressive emotions, but on the basis of my clinical practice, I knew (and my clients knew) that changing thoughts was not enough. It seemed clear that other factors were also at play. As cognitive therapy has evolved, Beck and other theorists associated with his model have become less inclined to argue that thoughts cause emotions (Alford & Beck, 1997; Klosko & Young, 2004), but the primacy of word-based thoughts is still apparent in many contemporary applications (e.g., J. Beck, 1995).

Negative thinking can contribute to depressive feelings, and changing thoughts can contribute to change. But the difficulty with emphasizing thoughts, as our clients tell us and as we experience in our own lives, is that we often respond viscerally—emotionally—before we have an identifiable thought. And these feelings tend to persist even as we are repeating a variety of "cheer-up," "lighten up," "this will pass," "you're not so bad" alternative thoughts in our minds.

It turns out that I wasn't alone in encountering difficulties with aspects of the traditional cognitive therapy model. As I began to search the literature further because of my initial qualms about the adequacy of cognitive therapy, I found out that from the beginning there have been active debates among scientists and clinicians about the role of negative thoughts in depression. For example, many disputed the claim made in the traditional cognitive therapy model that the affective symptoms of depression are the consequence of relatively enduring and stable patterns of negative cognitions. They cited evidence showing that negative thoughts remitted to a normal level in concert with other depressive symptoms once the depressive episode had ended (Simons, Garfield, & Murphy, 1984; Imber et al., 1990; Teasdale, 1988). Others challenged the Beck model for minimizing environmental factors in the etiology of depression (Brown & Harris, 1978; Coyne & Gotlib, 1983). Still others criticized the model for its inability to distinguish between emotional and cognitive meaning (Teasdale & Barnard, 1993; Teasdale, 1996) and for treating cognitions as conscious words and images while ignoring evidence that most of what goes on in the mind is subsymbolic and not accessible to consciousness (Kihlstrom, 1990, 1999).

Even though Beck's model was being widely used, was subject to clinical trials, and often made a positive differences, scholars were becoming increasingly skeptical of the assertion that word-based thoughts constituted the mechanism of change. An early series of laboratory investigations undertaken by Gordon Bower (e.g., Bower, 1981; Bower & Cohen, 1982) and others (Teasdale & Fogarty, 1979) constituted a significant step in addressing Beck's claim that emotional symptoms of depression are the consequences of negative cognitions. Bower found that we tend to access memories and attend to events that are congruent with our current mood. In other words, if we are in a low mood, "we are more likely to remember events previously associated with that mood" (Teasdale & Barnard, 1993, p. 29). In contrast to the cognitive therapy position, this body of work suggested that emotions play a key role in activating negative thinking. Bower went on to incorporate findings regarding mood congruence into an associative network model of the mind in order to come up with an associative network theory of mood congruence.

Versions of associative network models of learning and memory were widely subscribed to by cognitive scientists in the 1980s and provided the basis for Beck's schema concept, in which depressive thoughts are linked in memory via associative pathways (Fiske & Taylor, 1991). Even though these models were often used to depict mind processes in general, they were originally developed to explain verbal learning and recall. They describe how the memory system encodes or translates external experiences into verbal symbols or thought fragments, which are then stored in networks of related thoughts.

There have been numerous trenchant criticisms of these kinds of semantic models of the mind, arguing that they are too static, unidimensional, and slow to accurately depict mind processes (Berlin, 2002, 2006). Eventually these arguments, along with evidence that moderated Bower's initial mood congruence findings, toppled the associative network model.

These later developments prompted a search among theorists and researchers for a way to portray the mind that could account for multiple kinds of memory units, not just thoughts, and that would adequately conceptualize the multilevel, dynamic, malleable patterns of neurological activity that are generated by the brain. John Teasdale, a clinical psychologist who had been treating depressed patients and conducting research on mood biases in depression, started actively looking for such a framework. He found it in a conceptual model of memory called Interacting Cognitive Subsystem (ICS), which had been developed by Phillip Barnard, a cognitive psychologist. Teasdale has been able to use this memory model to provide a plausible and generative explanation of how at least some kinds of depressive disorders are activated, maintained, and resolved (Teasdale & Barnard, 1993; Teasdale, 1997). In turn, I have incorporated key ICS concepts into the core of the cognitive-integrative perspective and elaborated extensively on them.

Interacting Cognitive Subsystems: An Alternative Perspective on the Mind

ICS is a cognitive model of memory that explains how multiple kinds of information (such as thoughts, emotions, and sensations) that are active in memory contribute to an integrated pattern that gives us an overall feeling or an emotional understanding of what is going on. ICS also provides a useful depiction of how various feedback loops within the memory system can work to keep the feeling going as one reacts with additional thoughts, body feelings, and behaviors (and, in my version, also reacts to new events), locking on to depressive themes. Teasdale (1996, 1997) has primarily used ICS to describe the mental processes that unfold when a depression-prone person meets up with inevitable new occurrences of loss or disappointment, but ICS also has the potential for helping us understand a range of other mental states.

There are a lot of technicalities and complexities in ICS, but at the most basic level it is organized around a few ideas: First, ICS incorporates "several qualitatively different kinds of information," or memory codes. Each code represents a distinct aspect of experience: roughly the components of sensations (including body feelings), thoughts, and at the highest level of information integration, the implicational meaning or holistic sense or experiential feel of all this information (Teasdale & Barnard, 1993, p. 50). As Teasdale and Barnard explain, "The concept of 'Implicational' meaning asserts [that] this totality of meaning can be captured 'whole' (at a holistic level), in a way that is qualitatively different from the collection of propositional meanings and sensory information that may contribute to it" (Teasdale & Barnard, 1993, p. 55).

Second, each code has its own separate memory store and information processing activities that are specialized for dealing with that particular type of memory code. Each set of structures, codes, and processes constitutes a cognitive subsystem.

Third, "information processing depends on information flowing from one subsystem to another," where it is copied and transformed into a form appropriate to the receiving subsystem (Teasdale & Barnard, 1993, p. 50).

Fourth, ICS operates on the basis of two kinds of implicit knowledge: if-then knowledge about the information elements that go together to make up a meaningful pattern, and procedural knowledge about actions that follow a given pattern. For example, because of knowledge developed from past experience and genetic loading, the system knows that: *if* an individual sees or hears or feels cues related to loss or failure, *then* the whole integrated depressive pattern is activated; and *if* an individual experiences an overall feeling of heaviness, numbness, and flatness, *then* the individual acts in a way that conserves energy. Because the component bits of information (codes) have been pulled together so many times in the past, the whole implicational pattern and the response to it is likely to be automatically synthesized and activated (Teasdale & Barnard, 1993). Moreover, once this integrated pattern is activated and the person experiences a more-than-words sense of meaning, ICS explains how internal communications can cycle among the subsystems to generate additional thoughts, such as negative rumi-nations ("I'm not normal and never have been normal, a normal person wouldn't feel this way; a normal person would just brush it off, and not brood about how not normal she is"), and body states (say, of empti-ness and lethargy) that sustain and extend the original depressive feel-ing. This is what Teasdale and Barnard (1993) call a pattern of depressive interlock.

ICS recognizes that ongoing environmental events may also provide new information (for example, from criticism, deprivation, or disap-pointment) to the system, which also contributes to this interlock. This insight, which has not been fully exploited by ICS, provided a critical foothold for the cognitive-integrative perspective.

The science behind ICS consists of a wide range of investigations whose findings can be explained according to the framework. For exam-ple, ICS is able to provide an account of empirical evidence regarding mood congruence and incongruence (Miranda & Persons, 1988; Miranda, Persons, and Byers, 1990: Teasdale & Dent, 1987). It is compati-ble with neuropsychological studies that track the multiple areas of the brain involved in generating feelings and thoughts (Damasio, 1999; LeDoux, 1990, 1993, 1996; Siegel, 2007). It is consistent with findings from research on the characteristics of low mood and depression, including the classic study conducted by Nolen-Hoeksema and her col-leagues showing that people who respond to their depressed feelings by ruminating on their internal states are likely to extend these states (Nolen-Hoeksema, 2003; Nolen-Hoeksema & Morrow, 1991; Lyubormir-sky & Nolen-Hoeksema, 1995), as well as studies on mood priming and construct activation (Segal & Ingram, 1994) and on changes in negative thinking with recovery from depression (Teasdale & Barnard, 1993).

More recently, Teasdale and colleagues (Segal, Williams, & Teasdale, 2002; Williams, Teasdale, Segal, & Kabat-Zinn, 2007) have developed and tested a treatment model called mindfulness-based cognitive ther-apy for depression (MBCT), which is based on ICS formulations. MBCT is a psycho-educational approach that is designed to prevent recur-rence of major depression by providing participants with training in mindfulness meditation and by showing them how to use mindfulness to disengage from the interlocking feedback cycles that seem to main-tain depression. A small handful of studies have shown that MBCT is effective in preventing relapse among study participants who have experienced three or more prior episodes of depression, but not for those who have experienced only two previous episodes (Teasdale et al., 2001; Ma & Teasdale, 2004; Kenny & Williams, 2007). A key finding here is that people in the three-or-more episode group were also likely to "report greater childhood adversity and earlier first depression onset" than people in the two-episode group, whose relapses were more often associated with significant life events (Ma & Teasdale, 2004, p. 31).

Although a number of studies have compared MBCT with treatment as usual (seeking support from the family physician or other sources), to date there are no completed studies comparing MBCT with maintenance medication. Such investigations are under way, however, and the results of these studies will help clarify the specific effectiveness of MBCT (Coelho, Canter, & Ernst, 2007). Meanwhile, the finding that an exclusive focus on internal processes is not sufficient for preventing relapse among a subset of depressed individuals gives impetus to social work clinicians' efforts to bring concrete services into their therapeutic work and provides additional support to a major dimension of the cognitive-integrative perspective.

At first glance, ICS may look overly complicated, and from the clinician's perspective, perhaps more cumbersome than useful. However, when one is trying to understand the mind, a complex rendition is probably a good thing. Of course, there is no requirement that clients learn the ins and outs of this system, and clinicians do not necessarily need to master all of its technicalities in order to make good use of it. The beauty of ICS is that it provides a highly plausible and useful framework for understanding the fundamentals of the meaning-making process, and especially for locating various points where one might introduce change (for example, in various streams of information coming into the system, in internal feedback loops, and in attentional processes).

ICS is based on good, albeit incomplete science, it fits with clinical realities, and it accounts for a range of information elements, not just word-based thoughts. With its parallel distributive-processing architecture, in which massive numbers of memory codes from distributed subsystems are transformed in parallel to contribute to an overall pattern, it maps quite closely onto neuropsychological explanations in which massive numbers of neurons from distributed modules in the brain are simultaneously activated or inhibited to settle into a pattern that means something. It incorporates processes of emotion and motivation, it explains why it is so difficult to change automatic patterns of meaning, and it suggests many paths one can take in order to try to change those patterns.

I have devoted many pages and teaching hours to detailing these paths, but fundamentally change depends on discrepancy and selection—or, following Fiske (1993), on options and attention. The discrepancy requirement means that the person has to encounter different kinds of information—that is, information options. The sensory, bodily, and semantic cues coming into the system have to signal differences: sunlight versus clouds, for example, or expressions of understanding from others versus averted eyes and tight smiles. Beyond that, one has to give this information attention, to select it into the system and give it processing priority.

The Cognitive-Integrative Perspective: Creating Personal Change

In developing the cognitive-integrative perspective, I started with Beck's emphasis on the role of thinking processes in shaping human experience, then I took into account critiques of his work that suggested the need for a more encompassing, dynamic, neurologically compatible view of the mind, and I found an alternative account of meaning-making processes in ICS, which seemed to handle these drawbacks. Going beyond ICS, I also looked to additional theoretical and research literature that addresses the ways in which emotions, motivations, life situations, relationships, and actions contribute to an ongoing sense of reality. I reasoned that if the mind generates experience through a synthesis of information from multiple sources (thoughts, emotions, body states, relationships, situational contexts), then these are the domains where discrepancies—different information, new opportunities—need to be created. The next applied-science question was how to take the intellectually satisfying theories about mind processes and social processes and make them pay off in the lives of clients.

In addressing this question, I extracted therapeutic implications from ICS conceptions and linked them to established approaches that I borrowed from a number of therapy models (behavioral, cognitive, environmental, relational, family systems, and more). I then incorporated these therapeutic ideas and steps into guidelines for generating new streams of information from relationships, life situations, thoughts, actions, and emotion.

DIFFERENT ACTIONS

We know from numerous sources that taking action or doing something new generates a variety of powerful informational signals (e.g., Bandura, 1986; Linehan, 1993a; Reid, 1992; Wachtel & Wachtel, 1986). It communicates commitment to ourselves and others and can generate real-world positive outcomes. It provides an internal sense of the self as a doer, and each new step that we successfully undertake increases our confidence that we can negotiate the next one. Indeed, Neil Jacobson and colleagues found that the behavioral components of cognitive-behavioral therapy (graded task assignments, mastery and pleasure schedules, skills training, and general problem solving) were "more effective ways of changing the way people think than treatments that explicitly attempt to alter thinking" (1996, p. 303).

In working with clients who seem likely to benefit from learning how to take constructive steps on their own behalf, the cognitive-integrative perspective draws on variations of two fundamental action strategies: learning to implement new skills (Bandura, 1986; Linehan, 1993a; Reid, 1990) and learning to tolerate but not act on feelings that can lead to maladaptive responses such as avoidance (Chambless & Gillis, 1993; Linehan, 1993a, b; Salkovskis, 1996; Wachtel, 1997). Of course, a key issue in all action strategies is that in order to gain action proficiency, one has to engage in the action repeatedly, which requires persistence. Persistence, in turn, requires carefully calibrated steps, emotionally compelling goals, at least small successes along the way, and the ability to attend to these improvements and let them mean something. All of this depends on at least a moderately responsive environment and on careful coaching and encouraging support along the way (Bandura, 1986; Klinger, 1996; Linehan, 1993a, 1993b). There is no such thing as a simple behavioral intervention.

DIFFERENT THOUGHTS

As a stand-alone strategy, changing thoughts may not be sufficient to alter ingrained memory patterns. Still, the fact that thoughts are a part of the overall configuration of implicational meaning suggests that they are worthy targets of change. The cognitive-integrative perspective builds on guidelines offered by traditional cognitive therapy for helping clients to become aware of their thought processes and to consider whether those thought processes are a useful assessment of what is happening currently or are more a product of mind-habits that were originally generated by past experiences.

The cognitive-integrative perspective adds additional depth and detail to the therapeutic steps offered by Beck and his colleagues by incorporating insights from other sources about how one might take a mental step back from habitual thought patterns in order to make way for new information. These sources include Jean Piaget (1930), who introduced the concept of decentering; Robert Kegan (1982), who built on Piaget's work with his notion of emergence from embeddedness; Teasdale (1997), who talks about rolling another mind into place; and Marsha Linehan (1993b) and Zindel Segal and colleagues (2002), who introduced mindfulness practice as a way to help clients stay focused on the present moment.

Various forms of cognitive therapy have been criticized because they require some capacity for metacognition. In practice, social workers encounter countless clients who have had very little opportunity to develop the skill of metacognition, in part because as they were growing up no one was very interested in what they were thinking. But opportunities for positive difference can be offered in these situations as well. As Peter Fonagy (1997) suggests, when clients see that their circumstances have improved, the contrast between how they believed things had to be and how they are now opens up a recognition that sometimes one's beliefs don't always tell the whole story, and thus that those believes might be worth examining. Clients' capacity to reflect on their own thoughts can be further fostered and enhanced throughout the therapeutic interchange as the therapist models reflection, prompts and labels client reflection, and shows genuine interest in clients' thoughts (Berlin, 2002; Fonagy, 1997).

DIFFERENT EMOTIONS

In the last decade, a great deal of work has been accomplished in tracking the multiple parts of the brain involved in generating emotions (Damasio, 1999, 2003; Fredrickson, 2001; Greenberg, 2002, Klinger, 1996; LeDoux 1996; Siegel, 1999, 2007). This work has prompted more precise approaches for helping clients regulate their difficult emotions and build on their more positive, generative ones (Greenberg, 2002). I have incorporated this work into the cognitive-integrative perspective to provide guidelines for helping clients to access discrepant emotional experiences.

Emotion theorists tell us that emotions are multicomponent processes that unfold in two phases, which are sometimes termed the low-road phase and the high-road phase (Greenberg, 2002). In a situation of threat, for example, threat cues are first picked up on the low road—specifically by the thalamus—and then relayed to the amygdala, which reads the danger patterns and "broadcasts an emergency distress signal to other parts of the brain and the body" to activate expressive and physiological responses (Greenberg, 2002, p. 157). In the second, or high-road phase, this same information is conveyed more slowly to the neocortex. When the latter part of the process occurs, we are able to feel the impact of incoming information on our bodies and draw on memory associations to conceptualize the situation (Greenberg, 2002; LeDoux, 1990, 1993, 1996; Whalen et al., 1998).

It is clear, however, that the neocortex, or "the thinking brain, . . . cannot really intervene in time to prevent the initial emotional response" (Greenberg, 2002, p. 157). On the other hand, just as soon as our high-road awareness of cognitive and body reactions clicks on, it is possible to engage in conscious emotion-regulation strategies to modify or modulate what happens next on the low road. Making use of our prefrontal cortex can make the difference in whether we extend our emotions and just "let 'er rip" or use our awareness of our reaction as a signal for taking a breath, releasing body tension, accepting and riding out the wave of feelings, and perhaps then coming at the situation again from a broader perspective (Berlin, 2010).

In this process, emotional regulation is not a matter of using our higher brain to try to block whatever emotion we are feeling, which often has the paradoxical effect of intensifying and extending the emotion (Wachtel, 1993). Instead, the idea is to acknowledge the feeling; to create a working distance from it by observing, naming, and explaining it; and to calm the activation by accepting and allowing it and engaging in self-soothing activities, such as deep breathing, relaxation, and showing compassion to the self (Berlin, 2002; Greenberg, 2002). Following Spinoza, who wrote, "an emotion cannot be restrained nor removed unless by an opposed and stronger emotion" (1677/1967, p. 195), Leslie Greenberg (2002) and Linehan (1993a, 1993b) also suggest that the best way to change a maladaptive emotional state is to replace it or transform it through a kind of synthesis with an alternative emotion—perhaps finding feelings of anger to replace or transform fear, or allowing fear to give way to loneliness. Given Barbara Fredrickson's (2001) analysis of the attention-broadening and resource-building capacity of positive emotions, we can also encourage clients to generate, search for, and make the most of incipient positive feelings. Finally, in order to change emotions, we might also choose to give serious attention to changing the situation that gives rise to them in the first place.

DIFFERENT SOCIAL RELATIONSHIPS AND SITUATIONS

Drawing on logic, practice experience, social work literature, and empirical and theoretical accounts from other sources, the cognitive-integrative perspective asserts that we are not likely to revise and adjust our memory patterns if our ongoing relationships and life circumstances continue to supply us with the kind of information that fits well enough with the old memory patterns to add to them and keep them active (Berlin, 2010).

One might expect that in the forty years since Beck wrote his groundbreaking work, psychological scientists would have begun to at least explore the ways which life circumstances work to shape and constantly reshape clients' state of mind, but empirical work on this question comes primarily from other sources (Berlin, 2010). In giving his perspective on this turn of events Albert Bandura contends that the discipline of psychology is proceeding down two divergent routes: one seeking to clarify basic mechanisms governing human functioning through a microanalysis of the inner workings of the mind and the other centering on a macroanalysis of the influences of social factors in human development, adaptation, and change. He notes that we lack a theory that can bridge these two approaches and says that we need a comprehensive theory that can "merge the analytic dualism by integrating personal and social foci of causation within a unified causal structure" to show how "sociostructural influences operate through psychological mechanisms to produce behavioral effects" (2001, pp. 5–6).

I can't claim that in the cognitive-integrative perspective I have isolated this mechanism, but I do know from decades of social work research and scholarship that concrete changes in circumstances create big discrepancies. If a client repeatedly encounters informational cues signaling that her relationships and life circumstances are different and positive, there is the potential that she will (or can be helped to) attend to them, recognize their significance, take action based on them, and build new memories about them. This seems to be a significant and obvious step toward overcoming the analytic dualism that Bandura underscores in his critique.

In my search for scholarly work bearing on this issue, I located a number of empirical and conceptual sources that provided a strong rationale for the cognitive-integrative perspective's position on the importance of environmental information in creating personal change, including a number of social work sources (e.g., Finn & Jacobson, 2003; Grote, et al., 2004; Ife, 2001; Kemp, 2010; Meyer, 1983; Reid & Epstein, 1972; Ungar, 2002); the classic works of Brown and Harris (1978) and Hobfoll (1989; 2003); analyses of person-environment interaction (Caspi, 1993; 2005; Magnusson, 1990; Mischel, 2004); research on the role of the environment in child development (e.g., Masten & Coatsworth, 1998); community studies on the effects of social stress on mental health (Belle, 1982; Mirowsky and Ross, 1989); and studies of the role of culture in psychological processes (e.g., Kitayama, 2002). I was able to extract therapeutic implications from these and other works to create guidelines for practitioners as they attempt to make new streams of relational and environmental information available to clients. These include guidelines for enhancing the relational support flowing from the therapeutic relationship (e.g., Finn, 2010; Jordan, 2003; Miller, 2002; Wachtel, 2008), for supporting family resilience (e.g., Walsh, 2003; Aponte, 1994; Jacobson & Christensen, 2000), for providing concrete help (e.g., Finn & Jacobson, 2003; Henly & Lyons, 2000; Grote et al., 2004; Kemp, Whittaker, & Tracy, 2002; Reid & Epstein, 1972), and for engaging in community-based efforts to improve life conditions (e.g., Henggeler, Schoenwald, Borduin, Rolland, & Cunningham, 1998; McKay, Nudelman, McCadam, & Gonzales, 1996).

GOALS AND MOTIVATIONS

If new information is available that runs counter to clients' expectations, assessments, and overall feelings, the next question is, What can we do to increase the probability that clients will pay attention to it—that the mind will select it into the system and give it processing priority?

According to Teasdale and Barnard (1993), decisions about which competing streams of information to select are regulated by goals. In many instances, these are survival-related goals or motivations that have been developed to protect against threats to one's vulnerability—to minimize personal contact in order to avoid humiliation, to achieve perfection in order to overcome personal flaws, and to always be in control in order to avoid anxious free fall. When one encounters informational cues that bear on these kinds of goals, the system automatically recognizes the cues and gives them priority. If these goals cannot be achieved and yet are hard to relinquish, the stage is set for a "depressive interlock," in which attention focuses on a narrow band of self-perpetuating experience (Pyszczynski, Hamilton, Herring, & Greenberg, 1989). On the other hand, if there are competing goals that are the product of self-regulation efforts, they are also introduced into and stored in the memory system. If cues related to the new goals are available, one can consciously direct attention to those cues, mull them over for a bit, take an action step toward them, and feel the difference (Baumeister, Heatherton, & Tice, 1994). In general this is the kind of process that the cognitive-integrative perspective prompts clients to engage with.

By way of illustration:

Violet is feeling depressed and defeated because her car broke down in the middle of the street, because it is a horribly cold day, because she had an argument with a colleague, and because she feels so far behind at work that she doesn't know how she will ever catch up. She can put words on what she is feeling, but the overall feeling of defeat and despair goes beyond words. It is made up of sensory information—visual and auditory cues that come from standing underneath a steel-gray sky, hearing the wind, and feeling the ice pellets against her skin; a feeling of heaviness in her chest, a clenched jaw, and an almost physical paralysis. In combination, these elements are more than enough to activate the readily available memory pattern of defeat.

How long will Violet stay stuck in this feeling? It depends on what else is going on and whether other information elements get processed.

Time passes and she's back in the car. She got it fixed, she has the heater on, and she is heading home. Even as the old sense of defeat is still simmering, new information is now available: the car is warm, the crisis is over, she is in a safe space. She could keep on fretting and fuming about her bad luck, how things never work out, how her day is ruined—or she could remind herself of her goal to roll with the punches, then direct her attention to the new cues: She could notice the warmth from the heater, notice that her body is more relaxed, and remind herself that she got the car fixed, that she faced a problem and solved it. As she notices these differences, feels them, gives them mind-space, it is likely that they will create an experiential shift—from hopeless defeat to something like recovery from defeat tinged with satisfaction. This is a whole different feeling, one that doesn't deny the defeat, but is a few steps distant from it.

In this example, motivation to open up to changing circumstances and possibilities directs attention to a broader set of cues and thus is an important ingredient in forging an experiential shift. Goals and motivations are key both in keeping Violet stuck and in holding out the possibility of release. On the one hand, her memory system keeps activating the old goals, the imperatives she adopted at some point in the past to stave off loneliness, failure, humiliation, or weakness so whenever she brushed up against one of these feelings, she was automatically given defensive responses that kept her struggling along the same old narrow, dead-end pathways. On the other hand, a new goal, say of feasible accomplishment—or even better, of self-acceptance—can remind her that she can give up the struggle, can step off the old path and have a different experience.

Eric Klinger (1996) helps us understand that the strength and persistence of our defensive goals comes in large part from their link to our fundamental motivation to survive. Even though our lives are directed by biologically based survival motives, these basic motives also carry a heavy overlay of the values of our culture and the hopes and fears that come from our individual experiences. Drawing on evidence from laboratory studies and neuroanatomical descriptions, Klinger talks further about the memory system's hair-trigger response to goals that bear on survival. In his account, cues related to significant goals immediately activate a low-road "proto-emotional" alarm in the limbic system of the brain. This rapid, nonconscious general alarm tunes the system in to whatever is happening and then activates other expressive, cognitive, and motor processes.

Accordingly, the cognitive-integrative perspective holds that in order for new discrepant information to be noticed and processed, old defensive goals need to be disengaged, and new, more forward-looking ones need to be radically strengthened so they can keep us alert to opportunities for opening up, lightening up, and making things better. In thinking about how to do this, I've drawn from numerous sources in the social work and social psychological literature that shed light on the kinds of goals and goal-achievement strategies are most likely to lead to positive outcomes (e.g., Fredrickson, 2001; Gollwitzer & Moskowitz, 1996; Mischel, Cantor, & Feldman, 1996; Carver, 1996; Baumeister, 1996; Reid & Epstein, 1972; Reid, 1992). In particular, I've borrowed from Markus and Nurius's (1986) classic work on possible selves to lay out a set of steps for helping clients develop positive goals—or in Markus and Nurius's terms, positive possible self-memories. As they explain, in order for representations of hoped-for selves to gain traction, they have to be feasible, accessible (frequently used), and filled with specific, vivid, and emotionally compelling detail. By anticipating desired outcomes, planning steps to take to accomplish them, conducting mental simulations of how the actions will unfold, and practicing them in real life, one lays down and strengthens memory representations of the details of an emerging self and creates a stronger emotional alarm that signals opportunities for further development.

Conclusion

Aaron Beck made a brilliant move when he recognized that depressed people hang on to the residues of difficult past experiences by engaging with memory patterns that keep generating assessments and expectations that are more in line with past events than current possibilities. As applied science has progressed, we have also come to understand that the power of people's thoughts is based not just on words, but also on the motivations, emotions, current life circumstances, and capacity for skilled action that ground those words and give them an experiential feel.

The cognitive-integrative perspective gives us ways to help people generate new social and personal streams of information and develop the attentional flexibility to notice new options, the cognitive and emotional capacity to conceptualize them and feel their significance, and the skills to act on them—to make the most of them. In the short run, controlled empirical tests are needed to determine whether these additions to the cognitive therapy model make a difference. This will be a critical step. Meanwhile, some accounts suggest that taking knowledge that already exists, pulling it together, trying it out, filling in the gaps, and making new knowledge out of it has a place in the applied-science approach.

References

Alford, B. A., & Beck, A. T. (1997). *The integrative power of cognitive therapy.* New York, NY: Guilford.

Aponte, H. (1994). *Bread and spirit: Therapy with the new poor.* New York, NY: W. W. Norton.

Bandura, A. (1986). *Social foundations of thought and action: A social cognitive theory.* Englewood Cliffs, NJ: Prentice-Hall.

Bandura, A. (2001). Social cognitive theory: An agentic perspective. *Annual Review of Psychology, 52,* 1–26.

Barlow, D. H. (Ed.). (2007). *Clinical handbook of psychological disorders* (4th ed.). New York, NY: Guilford.

Baumeister, R. F. (1996). Self-regulation and ego threat: Motivated cognition, self-deception, and destructive goal setting. In P. M. Gollwitzer & J. A. Bargh (Eds.), *The psychology of action: Linking cognition and motivation to behavior* (pp. 27–47). New York, NY: Guilford.

Baumeister, R. F., Heatherton, T. F., & Tice, D. M. (1994). *Losing control: How and why people fail at self-regulation.* New York, NY: Academic Press.

Beck, A. T. (1972). *Depression: Causes and treatment.* Philadelphia, PA: University of Pennsylvania Press.

Beck, A. T. (1976). *Cognitive Therapy and the emotional disorders.* Madison, CT: International Universities Press.

Beck, A. T. (2005). The current state of cognitive therapy: A 40-year retrospective. *Archives of General Psychiatry, 62,* 953–959.

Beck, A. T., Epstein, N., & Harrison, R. (1983). Cognitions, attitudes, and personality dimensions in depression. *British Journal of Cognitive Psychotherapy, 1,* 1–16.

Beck, A. T., Rush, A. J., Shaw, B. F., & Emery, G. (1979). *Cognitive therapy for depression.* New York, NY: Guilford.

Beck, J. (1995). *Cognitive therapy: The basics and beyond.* New York, NY: Guilford.

Belle, D. (Ed.). (1982). *Lives in stress: Women and depression.* Beverly Hills, CA: Sage.

Berlin, S. (2010). Why cognitive therapy needs social work. In W. Borden (Ed). *Reshaping theory in contemporary social work: Toward a critical pluralism in clinical practice* (pp. 30–50). New York, NY: Columbia University Press.

Berlin, S. B. (1980). Cognitive-behavioral intervention for problems of self-criticism among women. *Social Work Research and Abstracts, 16,* 19–28.

Berlin, S. B. (1985). The effect of relapse prevention on the durability of self-criticism problem change. *Social Work Research and Abstracts, 21,* 21–33.

Berlin, S. B. (2002). *Social work clinical practice: A cognitive-integrative perspective.* New York, NY: Oxford University Press.

Berlin, S. B. (2006). Review of R. L. Leahy (Ed.), Contemporary cognitive therapy. *Social Service Review, 80,* 194–196.

Berlin, S. B., Mann, K. B., and Grossman, S. F. (1991). Task-analysis of cognitive therapy for depression. *Social Work Research and Abstracts, 27,* 3–11.

Bower, G. H. (1981). Mood and memory. *American Psychologist, 36,*129–148.

Bower, G. H., & Cohen, P. R. (1982). Emotional influences in memory and thinking: Data and theory. In M. S. Clark and S. T. Fiske (Eds.), *Affect and cognition* (pp. 291–332). Hillsdale, NJ: Lawrence Erlbaum Associates.

Brown, G. W., & Harris, T. (1978). *Social origins of depression.* London, UK: Tavistock.

Carver, C. S. (1996). Some ways in which goals differ and some implications of those differences. In P. M. Gollwitzer & J. A. Bargh (Eds.), *The psychology of action: Linking cognition and motivation to behavior* (pp. 645–672). New York, NY: Guilford.

Caspi, A. (1993). Why maladaptive behaviors persist: Sources of continuity and change across the life course. In D. C. Funder, R. D. Parke, C. Tomlinson-Keasey, and K. Widaman (Eds.), *Handbook of personality: Theory and research* (pp. 343–376). Washington, DC: American Psychological Association.

Caspi, A. (2005). Personality development: Stability and change. *Annual Review of Psychology, 56,* 453–484.

Chambless, D. L., & Gillis, M. M. (1993). Cognitive therapy of anxiety disorders. *Journal of Consulting and Clinical Psychology, 61,* 248–260.

Chambless, D. L., & Peterman, M. (2004). Evidence on cognitive-behavior therapy for generalized anxiety disorder and panic disorder. In R. L. Leahy (Ed.), *Contemporary cognitive therapy: Theory, research, and practice* (pp. 86–115). New York, NY: Guilford.

Coelho, H. F., Canter, P. H., Ernst, E. (2007). Mindfulness-based cognitive therapy: Evaluating current evidence and informing future research. *Journal of Consulting and Clinical Psychology, 75,* 1000–1005.

Coyne, J. C., & Gotlib, L. H. (1983). The role of cognition in depression: A critical appraisal. *Psychological Bulletin, 94,* 472–505.

Damasio, A. (1999). *The feeling of what happens: Body and emotion in the making of consciousness.* New York, NY: Harcourt Brace.

Damasio, A. (2003). *Looking for Spinoza: Joy, sorrow, and the feeling brain.* New York, NY: Harcourt.

DeRubeis, R. J., Gelfand, L. A., Tang, T. Z., & Simons, A. D. (1999). Medications versus cognitive behavioral therapy for severely depressed outpatients: Meta-analysis of four randomized comparisons. *American Journal of Psychiatry, 156,* 1007–1013.

DeRubeis, R. J., Hollon, S. D., Amsterdam, J. D., Shelton, R. C., Young, P. R., Salomon, R. M., O'Reardon, J. P., Lovett, M. L., Gladis, M. M., Brown, L. L., Gallop, R. (2005). Cognitive therapy versus medications in the treatment of moderate to severe depression. *Archives of General Psychiatry, 62,* 409–416.

Elkin, I., Shea, T., Watkins, J. T., Imber, S. D., Sotsky, S. M., Collins, J. F., Glass, D. R., Pilkonis, P. A., Leber, W. R., Docherty, J. P., Fiester, S. J., Parloff M. B.

(1989). National Institute of Mental Health Treatment of Depression Collaborative Research Program: General effectiveness of treatments. *Archives of General Psychiatry, 46*, 971–982.

Ellis, A. (1962). *Reason and emotion in psychotherapy.* Englewood Cliffs, NJ: Prentice Hall.

Evans, M. D., Hollon, S. D., DeRubeis, R. J., Piasecki, J. M., Grove, W. M., Garvey, M. J., & Tuason, V. B. (1992). Differential relapse following cognitive therapy and pharmacotherapy for depression. *Archives of General Psychiatry, 49*, 802–808.

Finn, J. L. (2010). Love and justice: A silenced language of integrated practice? In W. Borden (Ed.), *Reshaping theory in contemporary social work: Toward a critical pluralism in clinical practice* (pp. 179–209). New York, NY: Columbia University Press.

Finn, J. L., & Jacobson, M. (2003). *Just practice: A social justice approach to social work.* Peosta, IA: Eddie Bowers.

Fiske, S. T. (1993). Social cognition and social perception. *Annual Review of Psychology, 44*, 155–194.

Fiske, S. T., & Taylor, S. (1991). *Social cognition* (2nd edition). New York, NY: McGraw-Hill.

Fonagy, P. (1997). Multiple voices versus metacognition: An attachment theory perspective. *Journal of Psychotherapy Integration, 7*, 181–194.

Fredrickson, B. L. (2001). The role of positive emotions in positive psychology: The broaden-and-build theory of positive emotions. *American Psychologist, 56*, 218–226.

Gardner, H. (1987). *The mind's new science* (2nd ed.). New York, NY: Basic Books.

Gollwitzer, P. M., & Moskowitz G. B. (1996). Goal effects on action and cognition. In A. W. Kruglanski (Ed.), *Social psychology: Handbook of basic principles* (pp. 361–399). New York, NY: Guilford.

Greenberg, L. S. (2002). Integrating an emotion-focused approach to treatment into psychotherapy integration. *Journal of Psychotherapy Integration, 12*, 154–189

Grote, N., Bledsoe, S. E., Swartz, H. A. & Frank, E. (2004). Culturally relevant psychotherapy for perinatal depression in low-income OB/GYN patients. *Clinical Social Work Journal, 32*, 327–347.

Henggeler, S. W., Schoenwald, S. K., Borduin, C. M., Rolland, M. D., & Cunningham, P. B. (1998). *Multisystemic treatment of antisocial behavior in children and adolescents.* New York, NY: Guilford .

Henly, J. R., & Lyons, S. (2000). The negotiation of child care and employment demands among low-income parents. *Journal of Social Issues, 56*, pp. 683–706.

Hobfoll, S. E. (1989). Conservation of resources: A new attempt at conceptualizing stress. *American Psychologist, 44*, 513–524.

Hobfoll, S. E. (2003). Resource loss, resource gain, and emotional outcomes among inner city women. *Journal of Personality and Social Psychology, 84*, 632–643.

Hollon, S. D., DeRubeis, R. J., Shelton, R. C., Amsterdam, J. D., Salomon, R. M., O'Reardon, J. P., Lovett, M. L., Young, P. R., Human, K. L., Freeman, B. A., and Gallop, R. (2005). Prevention of relapse following cognitive therapy versus medications in moderate to severe depression. *Archives of General Psychiatry, 62*, 417–422.

Ife, J. (2001). *Human rights and social work: Towards rights-based practice*. New York, NY: Cambridge University Press.

Imber, S. D., Pilkonis, P. A., Sotsky, S. M., Elkin, I., Watkins, J. T., Collins, J. F., Shea, T. M., Leber, W. R., & Glass, D. R. (1990). Mode specific effects among three treatments for depression. *Journal of Consulting and Clinical Psychology, 58,* 352–359.

Jacobson, N. S., & Christensen, A. (2000). *Integrative couple therapy: Promoting acceptance and change*. New York, NY: W. W. Norton.

Jacobson, N. S., Dobson, K. S., Truax, P. A., Addis, M. E., Koerner, K., Gollan, J. K., Gortner, E., & Prince S. E. (1996). A component analysis of cognitive-behavioral treatment for depression. *Journal of Consulting and Clinical Psychology, 64,* 295–304.

Jordan, J. V. (2003). Valuing vulnerability: New definitions of courage. Working Paper No. 102. Wellesley, MA: Stone Center.

Kegan, R. (1982). *The evolving self*. Cambridge, MA: Harvard University Press.

Kemp, S. P. (2010). Place matters: Toward a rejuvenated theory of environment for direct social work practice. In W. Borden (Ed.), *Reshaping theory in contemporary social work: Toward a critical pluralism in clinical practice* (pp. 114–145). New York, NY: Columbia University Press.

Kemp, S. P., Whittaker, J. K., & Tracy, E. M. (2002). Contextual social work practice. In M. O'Melia and K. K. Miley (Eds.), *Pathways to Power: Readings in contextual social work practice* (pp. 15–35). Boston, MA: Allyn and Bacon.

Kenny, M. A., & Williams, J. M. G. (2007). Treatment-resistant depressed patients show a good response to mindfulness-based cognitive therapy. *Behaviour Research and Therapy, 45,* 617–625.

Kihlstrom, J. F. (1990). The psychological unconscious. In L. A. Pervin (Ed.), *Handbook of personality: Theory and research* (pp. 445–464). New York, NY: Guilford.

Kihlstrom, J. F. (1999). The psychological unconscious. In L. A. Pervin and O. P. John (Eds.), *Handbook of personality: Theory and research* (2nd ed.) (pp. 424–442). New York, NY: Guilford.

Kitayama, S. (2002). Cultural and basic psychological processes: Toward a system view of culture. *Psychological Bulletin, 128,* 89–96.

Klinger, E. (1996). Emotional influences on cognitive processing with implications for theories of both. In P. M. Gollwitzer & J. A. Bargh (Eds.). *The psychology of action: Linking cognition and motivation to behavior* (pp. 168–192). New York, NY: Guilford.

Klosko, J., & Young, J. (2004). Cognitive therapy of borderline personality disorder. In Leahy, R. L. (Ed.), *Contemporary cognitive therapy: Theory, research, and practice*. New York, NY: Guilford.

Leahy, R. L. (Ed.). (2004). *Contemporary cognitive therapy: Theory, research, and practice*. New York, NY: Guilford.

LeDoux, J. E. (1990). Information flow from sensation to emotion plasticity in the neural computation of stimulus value. In M. Gabriel & J. Moore (Eds.), *Learning and computational neuroscience: Foundations of adaptive networks* (pp. 3–52). Cambridge, MA: MIT Press.

LeDoux, J. E. (1993). Emotional networks in the brain. In M. Lewis & J. M. Haviland (Eds.), *Handbook of emotions* (pp. 109–118). New York, NY: Guilford.

LeDoux, J. E. (1996). The emotional brain: The mysterious underpinnings of emotional life. New York, NY: Simon & Schuster.

Linehan, M. M. (1993a). *Skills training manual for treating borderline personality disorders*. New York, NY: Guilford.

Linehan, M. M. (1993b). *Cognitive-behavioral treatment of borderline personality disorder*. New York, NY: Guilford.

Lyubormirsky, S., & Nolen-Hoeksema, S. (1995). Effects of self-focused rumination on negative thinking and interpersonal problem solving. *Journal of Personality and Social Psychology, 69*, 176–190.

Ma, S. H., & Teasdale, J. D. (2004). Mindfulness-based cognitive therapy for depression: Replication and exploration of differential relapse prevention effects. *Journal of Consulting and Clinical Psychology, 72*, 31–40.

Magnusson, D. (1990). Personality development from an interactional perspective. In L. A. Pervin (Ed.), *Handbook of personality: Theory and research* (pp. 193–222). New York, NY: Guilford.

Markus, H. R., & Nurius, P. S. (1986). Possible selves. *American Psychologist, 42*, 954–961.

Masten, A. S., & Coatsworth, J. D. (1998). The development of competence in favorable and unfavorable environments: Lessons from research on successful children. *American Psychologist, 53*, 205–220.

McKay, M. M., Nudelman, R., McCadam, K., & Gonzales, J. J. (1996). Addressing the barriers to mental health services for inner city children and their caretakers. *Community Mental Health Journal, 32*, 353–361.

Meyer, C. H. (1983). *Clinical social work in the ecosystems perspective.* New York, NY: Columbia University Press.

Miller, J. B. (2002). How change happens: Controlling images, mutuality, and power. Work in Progress, No. 96. Wellesley, MA: Stone Center.

Miranda, J., & Persons, J. B. (1988). Dysfunctional attitudes are mood state dependent. *Journal of Abnormal Psychology, 97*, 76–79.

Miranda, J., Persons, J. B., & Byers, C. (1990). Endorsement of dysfunctional beliefs depends on current mood state. *Journal of Abnormal Psychology, 99*, 237–241.

Mirowsky, J., & Ross, C. E. (1989). *Social causes of psychological distress.* New York, NY: Aldine de Gruyter.

Mischel, W. (2004). Toward an integrative science of the person. *Annual Review of Psychology, 55*, 1–22.

Mischel, W., Cantor, N., & Feldman, S. (1996). Principles of self-regulation: The nature of willpower and self-control. In E. T. Higgins & A.W. Kruglanski (Eds.), *Social psychology: Handbook of basic principles* (pp. 329–360). New York, NY: Guilford.

Nolen-Hoeksema, S. (2003). *Women who think too much: How to break free of overthinking and reclaim your life.* New York, NY: Macmillan.

Nolen-Hoeksema, S., & Morrow, J. (1991). A prospective study of depression and posttraumatic stress symptoms after a natural disaster: The 1989 Loma Pieta earthquake. *Journal of Personality and Social Psychology 61*, 115–121.

Piaget, J. (1930). *The child's conception of physical causality.* London, UK: Routledge & Kegan Paul.

Pyszczynski, T., Hamilton, J., Herring, F., & Greenberg, J. (1989). Self-regulatory perseveration and the depressive self-focusing style: A self-awareness theory of reactive depression. *Psychological Bulletin, 102*, 122–138

Reid, W. J. (1990). Change-process research: A new paradigm? In L. Videka-Sherman & W. J. Reid (Eds.), *Advances in clinical social work research, 11*(1), 17–37.

Reid, W. J. (1992). *Task strategies: An empirical approach to clinical social work.* New York, NY: Columbia University Press.

Reid, W. J., & Epstein, L. (1972). *Task-centered casework.* New York, NY: Columbia University Press.

Reinecke, M. A., & Clark, D.A. (Eds.). (2003). *Cognitive therapy across the life span: Evidence and practice.* New York, NY: Cambridge University Press.

Rush, A. J., Beck, A. T., Kovacs, M., & Hollon, S. (1977). Comparative efficacy of cognitive therapy and pharmacotherapy in the treatment of depressed outpatients. *Cognitive Therapy and Research, 1,* 17–38.

Salkovskis, P. M. (1996). The cognitive approach to anxiety: Threat beliefs, safety seeking behavior, and the special case of health anxiety and obsessions. In P. M. Salkovskis (Ed.), *Frontiers of Cognitive Therapy* (pp. 48–74). New York, NY: Guilford.

Segal, Z. V. & Ingram, R. E. (1994). Mood priming and construct activation in a test of cognitive vulnerability to unipolar depression. *Clinical Psychology Review, 14,* 247–274.

Segal, Z. V., Williams, J. M. G., & Teasdale, J. D. (2002). *Mindfulness-based cognitive therapy for depression.* New York, NY: Guilford.

Siegel, D. J. (1999). *The developing mind.* New York, NY: Guilford

Siegel, D. J. (2007). *The mindful brain: Reflection and attunement in the cultivation of well being.* New York, NY: W. W. Norton.

Simons, A. D., Garfield, S. L., & Murphy, G. E. (1984). The process of change in cognitive therapy and pharmacotherapy for depression: Changes in mood and cognition. *Archives of General Psychiatry, 41,* 43–48.

Spinoza, B. (1677/1967). *Ethics* (Part 4). New York, NY: Hafner.

Teasdale, J. D. (1988). Cognitive vulnerability to persistent depression. *Cognition and Emotion, 2,* 247–274.

Teasdale, J. D. (1996). Clinically relevant theory: Integrating clinical insight with cognitive science. In P. M. Salkovskis (Ed.), *Frontiers of cognitive therapy* (pp. 26–47). New York, NY: Guilford

Teasdale, J. D. (1997). The mind in place in mood disorders. In D. M. Clark & C. C. Fairburn (Eds.), *Science and practice of cognitive behavior therapy* (pp. 26–47). Oxford, UK: Oxford University Press.

Teasdale, J. D. & Barnard, P. J. (1993). *Affect, cognition, and change: Re-modeling depressive thought.* London, UK: Laurence Erlbaum & Associates.

Teasdale, J. D., & Dent, J. (1987). Cognitive vulnerability to depression: An investigation of two hypotheses. *British Journal of Clinical Psychology, 26,* 113–126.

Teasdale, J. D., & Fogarty, S. J. (1979). Differential effects of induced mood on retrieval of pleasant and unpleasant events from episodic memory. *Journal of Abnormal Psychology, 88,* 248–257.

Teasdale, J. D., Scott, J., Moore, R. G., Hayhurst, H., Pope, M., & Paykel, E. S. (2001). How does cognitive therapy prevent relapse in residual depression: Evidence from a controlled trial. *Journal of Consulting and Clinical Psychology, 69,* 347–357.

Ungar, M. (2002). A deeper, more social ecological social work practice. *Social Service Review, 76,* 480–497.

Wachtel, E. F., & Wachtel, P. L. (1986). *Family dynamics in individual psychother-apy*. New York, NY: Guilford.

Wachtel, P. L. (1993). *Therapeutic communication*. New York, NY: Guilford.

Wachtel, P. L. (1997). *Psychoanalysis, behavior therapy, and the relational world*. Washington, DC: American Psychological Association.

Wachtel, P. L. (2008). *Relational theory and the practice of psychotherapy*. New York, NY: Guilford.

Walsh, F. (2003). Family resilience: A framework for clinical practice. *Family Process, 42*(1), 1–18.

Whalen, P. J., Rausch, S. L., Etcoff, N. L., McInerrny, S., Lee, M. B., & Jenike, M. A. (1998). Masked presentations of emotional facial expressions modulate amygdala activity without explicit knowledge. *Journal of Neuroscience, 18*, 411–418.

Williams, J. M. G., Teasdale, J. D., Segal, Z.V., & Kabat-Zinn, J. (2007) *The Mindful way through depression: Freeing yourself from chronic unhappiness*. New York, NY: Guilford.

CHAPTER FOUR

Contemporary Psychodynamic Theory, Research, and Practice: Implications for Evidence-Based Intervention

William Borden and James J. Clark

Over the last quarter century critiques and reformulations of psychodynamic thought have brought about major shifts in theoretical perspectives, empirical research, and methods of intervention. The growing emphasis on interdisciplinary study has enlarged the scope of understanding, and emerging formulations have been shaped by findings in the fields of neuroscience, cognitive psychology, developmental psychology, personality psychology, and social psychology. Theory and research have increasingly centered on conceptions of relationship, interpersonal behavior, and social life, and clinicians have introduced integrative models of intervention in efforts to engage a wider range of clients, broaden the scope of practice, strengthen the empirical base of treatment, and improve outcomes. Research findings provide strong support for the efficacy of psychodynamic approaches in the treatment of problems in functioning associated with a range of conditions, including acute stress reactions, posttraumatic stress disorder, depression, personality disorders, and other mental disorders (Fonagy, Roth, & Higgitt, 2005; Gibbons, Crits-Christoph, & Hearon 2008; Shedler, 2010).

In spite of these developments, there is surprisingly little consideration of psychodynamic theory, research, or practice models in the contemporary social work literature. Many educators, researchers, and practitioners continue to reject psychodynamic perspectives because of perceived conflicts with the humanistic identity of the profession and the growing emphasis on evidence-based intervention. Unfortunately, many critics have only limited awareness of the major innovations that have occurred, and their accounts fail to reflect the range of relational approaches, social perspectives, and pragmatic concerns that now shape the broader domain of understanding and practice. Additionally, widespread neglect of important research findings supporting the core propositions of psychodynamic theory and the evidence produced by major psychodynamic psychotherapy research investigations have contributed to this strange situation (Shedler, 2010; Weinberger & Westen, 2001; Westen, 1998).

This chapter focuses on the ways in which psychodynamic theory deepens our understanding of facilitating processes in psychosocial intervention and strengthens conceptions of the helping relationship, interpersonal behavior, and clinical expertise in emerging models of evidence-based practice. In the first section we review the development of theoretical perspectives in the psychodynamic tradition, summarize the defining features of the major schools of thought, and describe the core elements of the relational paradigm. We identify empirical lines of inquiry that corroborate basic assumptions and concepts in psychodynamic understanding. In the second part we describe orienting perspectives in psychosocial intervention, summarize empirical findings on the effectiveness of treatment approaches, and consider the implications of relational theory and research for continued development of evidence-based intervention. As we show, the empirical basis of psychodynamic understanding and intervention is far better documented than many clinicians realize, and contemporary psychodynamic thinking deepens appreciation of essential concerns and facilitating processes in social work practice.

The Development of Psychodynamic Understanding

Clinical scholars have come to distinguish two fundamental perspectives in the development of psychodynamic thought: the drive paradigm, based on Sigmund Freud's classical instinct theory, and the relational paradigm, which emphasizes the central role of relationship and social life in human experience. Although Freud's drive psychology served as the guiding paradigm in classical psychoanalytic thought through the first half of the 20th century, growing numbers of thinkers challenged his theoretical system and enlarged the scope of psychodynamic understanding, emphasizing concepts of relationship and social life. The following overview, drawn from more extended accounts of the history of psychodynamic thought, outlines the contributions of early revisionists and theoretical developments in Great Britain and the United States that have shaped contemporary relational and social perspectives (for further review of theoretical systems and practice models, see Borden, 2000, 2008, 2009a).

THE EMERGENCE OF RELATIONAL AND SOCIAL PERSPECTIVES

While Freud's patriarchal insistence on theoretical orthodoxy dominates many accounts, a more careful study of the historical record reveals that even during its earliest period psychoanalysis was characterized by a robust intellectual diversity usually informed by the empirical observations of working clinicians. Alfred Adler, Otto Rank, and Sándor Ferenczi, originally members of Freud's inner circle, rejected the core tenets of drive psychology and increasingly emphasized conscious motives, relational experience, and social life in their conceptions of personality development, vulnerability, and problems in living. Interventions focused on the crucial functions of the helping relationship, interpersonal interaction, and experiential learning in efforts to facilitate change and growth.

Adler regarded people as social beings, emphasizing notions of interconnectedness and interdependence in his conceptions of relational life, and his integrative models of intervention encompassed family and community perspectives (Adler, 1927/1992). He introduced active strategies in pragmatic approaches to treatment, employing what we would now describe as cognitive, behavioral, educational, and task-centered methods.

Rank centered on concepts of autonomy, dependency, and relationship in fashioning humanistic and existential models of personality, emphasizing notions of self-determination, will, responsibility, and action in his formulations of the helping process (Rank, 1936). His ideas informed the development of the functional school of casework and shaped basic assumptions and principles of intervention in the collective wisdom of social work practice (Borden, 2009a).

Ferenczi focused on the role of relational life and events in the outer world in his conceptions of vulnerability and trauma; like Adler, he emphasized the social, cultural, political, and economic contexts of problems in living. He was increasingly troubled by the constraints of classical psychoanalytic technique and introduced active methods of intervention, including behavioral strategies and relaxation techniques, in efforts to reduce the length of treatment and improve outcomes. He realized the crucial role of the therapeutic alliance in the helping process; emphasized the sustaining functions of the practitioner's attunement, empathy, and responsiveness; and viewed the client-worker relationship as a collaborative, mutually supportive partnership. He introduced the "rule of empathy" as a principle of intervention and came to see emotion as the transformative element of change and growth (Ferenczi, 1933/1980).

This first generation of revisionist thinkers, marginalized in most accounts of the psychodynamic tradition, prefigures the emergence of relational and social perspectives as well as the growing emphasis on integrative approaches in contemporary practice.

The pervasive experience of trauma, loss, and mourning after World War I was a crucial influence in the development of relational perspectives in Great Britain in the 1920s. Ian Suttie challenged the individualism of Freud's classical psychoanalytic thought, emphasizing the role of family dynamics, social life, and culture in his conceptions of personality development, resilience, vulnerability, and problems in living (Suttie, 1935). He theorized that innate needs for love and relationship are the fundamental motivational forces in personality development, and he focused on the role of "social interest" and the generative functions of "fellowship" and community involvement in his conceptions of health, well-being, and fulfillment (Suttie, 1935). In his models of psychosocial intervention, he stressed the curative functions of interactive experience and of the helping relationship.

The following generation of thinkers, including W. R. D. Fairbairn, Donald W. Winnicott, and John Bowlby, continued to expand psychoanalytic theory through the second half of the 20th century. Fairbairn challenged Freud's classical drive paradigm and introduced models of personality development that would serve as the foundation for contemporary object relations psychology. In his theoretical system, the self is structured through internalization and representation of interpersonal experience, and fundamental needs for contact and relationship shape behavior across the course of life (Fairbairn, 1952).

Winnicott described the crucial functions of caretaking figures in the emergence of the self, and he regarded relational provisions and the constancy of care in the holding environment of infancy and early childhood as crucial determinants of maturation, health, and well-being. He increasingly centered on subjective experience in elaborating his developmental formulations, emphasizing notions of inner coherence, authenticity, agency, personal meaning, and creativity. As the leader of the Independent Tradition in Great Britain, Winnicott was committed to a pragmatic ethics in his approach to intervention. He eschewed standard models of treatment and remained steadfast in his efforts to carry out what he called "experiments in adapting to need" (Winnicot, 1971).

Bowlby's formulations of attachment, influenced by Darwinian thought and developmental biology, deepened understanding of the bond between children and caretakers, enlarging conceptions of personality development and relational life. His attachment theory emerged as an orienting perspective in empirical study of the mother-child relationship. Drawing on cognitive psychology, Bowlby theorized that individuals internalize and represent fundamental elements of relational experience, forming working models of self and others that guide processing of information, patterns of interpersonal behavior, and modes of adaptation through life. In the domain of intervention he stressed the sustaining functions of the helping relationship and demonstrated how conceptions of attachment deepen understanding of interpersonal behavior in worker-client interaction over the course of treatment (Bowlby, 1988).

In the United States the interpersonal school, shaped by the contributions of Harry Stack Sullivan, Karen Horney, Eric Fromm, and Clara Thompson, introduced social and cultural perspectives that enlarged conceptions of personality development, relational life, and psychosocial intervention. Beginning in the 1930s, Sullivan drew on American pragmatism and the social thought of Jane Addams, George Herbert Mead, Charles Cooley, Edward Sapir, and William Thomas in fashioning process-oriented models of personality, centering on the dynamics of interpersonal behavior and social life. He viewed the practitioner as a participant-observer in the helping process, and emphasized the role of interpersonal interaction and experiential learning in formulations of change and growth.

Horney expanded conceptions of self through the 1940s and examined the ways in which social and cultural conditions influence personality development, gender identity, patterns of relational life, and problems in functioning. She came to view the defining feature of neurosis—"a special form of human development antithetical to human growth"—as alienation from the core self, originating in pathogenic conditions in the social environment (Horney, 1950, p. 13). In her formulations of dysfunction, fear and anxiety constrict ways of being, relating, and living, limiting realization of potential. She introduced interpersonal conceptions of defense and described vicious circles of thought, emotion, and behavior that perpetuate problems in living

In the late 1970s Heinz Kohut introduced a relational perspective that centered on the development of the self and the phenomenology of subjective experience. In his developmental schema, he characterized the essential connection between the self and others as the "selfobject relationship" and assumed that this bond is essential for the maturation of a cohesive sense of self (Kohut, 1977). He saw the person as a social being embedded in a relational matrix, and his formulations of health and well-being emphasized the sustaining functions of relationship across the course of life.

RELATIONAL SCHOOLS OF THOUGHT

The contributions of the foregoing thinkers have shaped the development of three schools of thought in the wider field of psychodynamic understanding, broadly characterized as object relations psychology, interpersonal psychoanalysis, and self psychology. We briefly review the orienting perspectives, core concepts, and empirical lines of inquiry that have shaped thinking and practice in each tradition.

Object Relations Perspectives

Contemporary object relations perspectives, extending the theoretical formulations of Fairbairn and Bowlby, explore the ways in which motivational, cognitive, and affective processes influence subjective states of self, perceptions of relational life, and ongoing patterns of interpersonal functioning. Theorists assume that basic prototypes of connection, established over the course of early relational life, are preserved in the form of internalized representations of self and others. Although thinkers believe that core representations originate in interpersonal experience, they assume that inner models of relational life are influenced by individual differences in constitution and temperament, early developmental experience, unconscious fantasy processes, and life events; accordingly, they do not regard schemas as true representations of actual experience (see Borden, 2000, 2008). Presumably, the particular representations guiding perception and behavior at any given time are influenced by emerging needs, interpersonal contexts, and life circumstances. Theorists have increasingly drawn on empirical findings in neuroscience and cognitive psychology in their efforts to expand understanding of the dynamics of inner models of self, others, and interactive experience (Westen, 2005).

Formulations of psychopathology in object relations theory center on the nature of inner representations and the ways in which models of self and others influence perceptions of experience, activate defensive processes, precipitate maladaptive behaviors, and perpetuate problems in functioning. Conceptions of intervention emphasize the central role of the helping relationship and sources of experiential learning through client-practitioner interaction in efforts to enlarge inner models of relational life, reorganize maladaptive defensive processes, and strengthen capacities to negotiate interpersonal life (see Borden, 2008 and 2009a, for elaboration of these concepts and for case illustrations).

Object relations perspectives have increasingly informed empirical studies of personality development, psychopathology, and psychosocial intervention over the last decade. Developmental lines of study explore the nature of caretaking experience, patterns of attachment, and emerging capacities to engage in relational life. Empirical findings corroborate the assumption that infants are preadapted to form attachments and engage in complex forms of interaction with caretaking figures (see, e.g., Beebe & Lachmann, 1998; Fonagy & Target, 2007; Schore, 2003a, 2003b; Stern, 1985). Cognitive research on perception, memory, and learning has provided considerable support for object relations formulations of unconscious mental processing and mental representations of self, others, and relational life (Westen, 1998, 2005; Westen & Gabbard, 2002a, 2002b). Longitudinal studies document the critical role of attachment styles and dyadic care-giving systems in the development of personality organization, relational capacities, interpersonal functioning, and patterns of coping and adaptation (see, e.g., Fonagy, 2001; Fonagy & Target, 2007; Sroufe, Egelund, Carlson, & Collins, 2005). Researchers have generated considerable evidence for the stability of interpersonal patterns over time (see Luborsky & Barrett, 2006; Westen, 1998). In the field of social psychology, object relations perspectives have informed the study of social perception, causal attribution, and interpersonal influence (Aronson, 1992; Masling & Bornstein, 1994; Westen, 1998).

In the domain of psychosocial intervention, researchers have explored the ways in which inner models of relational experience and patterns of social cognition perpetuate problems in functioning associated with depression, acute stress reactions, posttraumatic stress disorders, personality disorders, and other forms of developmental psychopathology (see reviews by e.g., Blatt & Homann, 1992; Fonagy & Target, 2007; Luborsky & Barrett, 2006; Masling & Bornstein, 1994; Roth & Fonagy, 2005; Shedler, 2010; Westen, 1998, 2005). Converging lines of study in cognitive neuroscience support conceptions of transference formulated in object relations theory, emphasizing the ways in interpersonal situations activate inner representations of self and others; motivational, cognitive, and affective processes; and corresponding patterns of behavior (Cozolino, 2002; Westen & Gabbard, 2002a, 2002b).

Interpersonal Perspectives

Contemporary interpersonal perspectives, building on the contributions of Sullivan and Horney, focus on interactive behavior in the social fields of relational life. These thinkers introduce process-oriented conceptions of the self, exploring the interactive determinants of personality, defensive operations, and patterns of interpersonal behavior in the context of the social environment. Integrative practitioners view object relations and interpersonal approaches as complementary perspectives, assuming that there is an isomorphic relationship between inner models of self and others, and interactive experience and observable patterns of behavior in interpersonal life.

From the perspective of Sullivan's developmental psychology, the experience of dependency and conditions of care in infancy and childhood inevitably generate vulnerability, fear, and anxiety as individuals negotiate the opportunities and constraints of their social surroundings. Over the course of development, Sullivan theorizes, people elaborate repetitive patterns of behavior in ongoing efforts to reduce fear and anxiety, maximize security and satisfaction, and preserve connections with others. His formulations of problems in living, or "dynamisms of difficulty," emphasize the ways in which defensive processes perpetuate maladaptive patterns of thought, feeling, and action (Sullivan, 1953). The concept of interpersonal complementarity is a basic principle of interpersonal theory: The individual's patterns of behavior tend to evoke particular types of reactions from others, which reinforce negative self-appraisals and expectations of others (Wachtel, 2008).

Conceptions of dysfunction focus on defensive strategies and vicious circles of thought, feeling, and behavior that perpetuate problems in living. Sullivan describes the clinician as a participant-observer in the interpersonal field of the helping process. In working from an interpersonal perspective, the clinician and client explore maladaptive patterns of behavior as they emerge in the helping process, engaging opportunities for experiential learning that foster the development of relational capacities and interpersonal skills.

Clinical researchers have drawn on interpersonal perspectives in conceptualizing interactive processes in empirical studies of treatment processes and outcomes (see, e.g., Benjamin, 1993; Luborsky & Crits-Christoph, 1990; Strupp & Binder, 1984). They have examined the relationship between social information processing and transference phenomena, focusing on motivational, cognitive, and affective elements and activation of interpersonal scripts or schemas that specify particular patterns of interpersonal behavior (Westen, 2005). A growing body of research provides support for the effectiveness of interpersonal approaches in the treatment of problems in functioning associated with a range of conditions, including depression, anxiety disorders, and personality disorders (for reviews of empirical findings see Gibbons, Crits-Christoph & Hearon, 2008; Luborsky & Barrett, 2006; Roth & Fonagy, 2005; Shedler, 2010).

Self Psychology

Contemporary thinkers have expanded Kohut's model of personality development, psychopathology, and psychotherapy, enlarging conceptions of self, vulnerability, and relational life. Notions of motivation continue to focus on the fundamental need to establish a unitary, integrated sense of self and on the sustaining functions of relationship across the course of life. Formulations of personality development emphasize the ways in which the attunement, responsiveness, and empathic provisions of caretakers or "selfobjects" facilitate the emergence of a cohesive sense of self. Theorists assume that caretaking functions of primary figures are internalized as psychic structure over the course of development, and facilitate efforts to regulate emotion and maintain stability in the sense of self. Failures in empathic responsiveness over the course of caretaking undermine the development of the self, leading to structural deficits and defensive patterns of behavior. Disorders of the self are characterized by ongoing difficulties in preserving cohesion in identity and sense of self, in regulating emotion, in maintaining self-esteem and morale, in negotiating interpersonal life, and in pursuing meaningful goals (Borden, 2000; 2009a).

Conceptions of intervention in self psychology focus on the crucial functions of relational provisions in efforts to strengthen the self and interpersonal functioning. The clinician's empathic attunement and responsiveness to emerging needs foster the development of psychic structure, strengthening the integrity of the self and the capacity to make use of relational experience. Self psychological perspectives affirm ongoing needs for connection, interdependence, and affirmation across the life course.

Over the last quarter century, studies of mother-infant interaction have provided empirical support for Kohut's conceptions of development, showing that babies and caretakers mutually influence internal affective states and that lapses in attunement over the course of caretaking have adverse effects on infants (Beebe & Lachmann, 1988; Stern, 1985, 2004). Empirical findings suggest that patterns of affect, cognition, and behavior established in infancy and early childhood shape subsequent interpersonal functioning and adjustment (Westen, 1998). Drawing on Kohut's formulations, Schore (2003a, 2003b) has elaborated a neurobiological model of the development of the self, focusing on the experience-dependent maturation of the right brain. He introduces neurobiological and self psychological conceptions of trauma, posttraumatic stress disorders, and borderline personality organization, and explores the ways in which interactive experience over the course of intervention influences the neurobiology of regulatory structures. In the domain of intervention, a substantial body of research on the core conditions of the helping relationship and on management of strain and rupture in the therapeutic alliance documents the crucial role of the practitioner's empathic attunement and responsiveness in determining the process and outcomes of treatment (for reviews see Horvath, 2006; Roth & Fonagy, 2005; Wampold, 2007).

THE RELATIONAL PARADIGM

The foregoing schools of thought emerged as independent perspectives in psychodynamic understanding over the second half of the 20th century, and there was little interaction among members of differing groups in the development of foundational concepts and methods. In the early 1980s, however, clinical scholars began to carry out comparative studies of theoretical perspectives in attempts to identify the defining features and overlapping elements of differing frameworks. In their seminal work, Jay Greenberg and Stephen Mitchell (1983) described orienting perspectives that shaped the development of object relations psychology, interpersonal theories, and self psychology, and distinguished two competing paradigms in psychodynamic thought: Freud's drive model and the relational model.

In subsequent formulations of the relational paradigm, Mitchell (1993, 1997, 2000) fashioned a conceptual synthesis that linked ideas and methods across the major schools of thought. We briefly outline conceptions of personality development; health and well-being; and vulnerability, psychopathology, and problems in living encompassed in the relational paradigm (for extended accounts see Borden, 2000, 2008, 2009a).

Personality Development

In the shift from Freud's drive psychology to the relational paradigm, as Mitchell (1988) explains, "Mind has been redefined from a set of predetermined structures emerging from inside an individual organism to transactional patterns and internal structures derived from an interactive, interpersonal field" (p. 17). Relational theorists view relations with others—actual and internalized—as core constituents of human experience. The basic unit of attention is not the person but the interactive field of self, others, and relational life. Conceptions of motivation and personality development emphasize fundamental needs for attachment and relationship across the course of life. Interpersonal experience and social life shape the emergence of the person; the self is constituted in a relational matrix.

From the perspective of self psychology, theorists focus on the crucial functions of caretaking figures and relational provisions that facilitate the establishment of a cohesive sense of self. From the perspective of object relations theory, internalization of interpersonal experience mediates the development of self-organization and capacities for relatedness. Prototypes of connection, established in infancy and childhood, are structured in the form of internalized representations of self and others, influencing subjective states, perceptions of persons, and patterns of interpersonal behavior. From the perspective of the inter-personal school, personality or self is shaped by relational life and mediated by ongoing interaction with others in social contexts.

Empirical domains of study in neuroscience, developmental psy-chology, cognitive psychology, social psychology, and experimental psychology corroborate fundamental propositions underlying rela-tional conceptions of personality, including notions of unconscious motivational, cognitive, and affective processes; mental representations of self, others, and interactive experience; conceptions of defense; and the origins of personality and social dispositions in childhood (for sys-tematic reviews of empirical research, see Fonagy & Target, 2007; Luborsky & Barrett, 2006; Shedler, 2010; Westen, 1998, 2005).

Health and Well-Being

Subjective states, inner representations of self and others, and patterns of interpersonal functioning are central domains of concern in concep-tions of health and well-being. Theorists focus on the development of core structures of personality or self and corresponding capacities for relationship that influence patterns of behavior. The fully functioning person is characterized by a cohesive sense of self and identity, affirm-ing but realistic views and expectations of self and others, stable pat-terns of interpersonal functioning, and fulfilling relationships. The individual establishes flexible ways of being and relating that facilitate efforts to form attachments, participate in social life, and assimilate new experiences. Winnicott, Horney, and Kohut emphasize subjective domains of experience in their conceptions of health, well-being, and fulfillment, focusing on notions of aliveness, authenticity, creativity, morale and self-esteem, personal meaning, and purpose. Most theorists include concepts of mastery, coping, and self-actualization in their accounts of health and adaptive functioning (Borden, 2008, 2009a).

Just as thinkers emphasize the central role of relational life in the development of the person, they focus on the sustaining functions of social interaction and community across the course of life. Adler, for example, argues that the development of social interest—what he defines most broadly as a sense of fellowship and identity with the whole of humanity—is a crucial determinant of health, well-being, and the common good. In his accounts of personal and social development, the individual comes to feel a deep sense of connection with human-kind, recognizes the interdependence of relational life, empathizes with others, and realizes that the welfare of any one individual depends on the well-being of the larger community. Constructive relationships and sustaining communities are characterized by mutual respect, attune-ment and empathy, trust, cooperation, and personal equality (Adler, 1927/1992).

Greenberg and Mitchell (1983) review traditions of social and political thought that provide philosophical contexts of understanding for relational conceptions of health, fulfillment, and well-being, focusing on the work of Rousseau, Hegel, and Marx. In their account of relational perspectives, human nature is characterized by "feelings of natural affiliation and mutual concern," and "satisfactions and goals are realizable only within a community" (1983, pp. 401–402).

Vulnerability, Psychopathology, and Problems in Living

The orienting perspectives of the relational schools of thought have shaped differing conceptions of vulnerability, psychopathology, and problems in living. One group of thinkers emphasizes "arrests" or "deficits" in the development of the self that compromise ways of being, relating, and living. Kohut, for example, traces structural deficits in the organization of the self to earlier lapses in care that limit development of capacities to regulate emotion, integrate experience, and engage in relational life. Winnicott centers on the ways in which cumulative trauma undermines the development of the self, and he distinguishes true-self and false-self states of experience in his formulations of authenticity, defensive processes, and maladaptive behavior.

A second group of theorists, influenced by object relations psychology, traces the origins of maladaptive behavior to internalized representations of interpersonal experience that limit patterns of functioning. Bowlby, for example, describes the ways in which rigid working models of self, other, and modes of interactive experience distort perceptions of relational life and precipitate maladaptive patterns of behavior.

A third group of thinkers, influenced by the interpersonal school, focuses on outer domains of experience, emphasizing observable patterns of behavior in the social field that perpetuate maladaptive cycles of thought, feeling, and action. Sullivan rejected diagnostic classifications of mental disorders, viewing them as reductive, and preferred to speak of "dynamisms of difficulty" and "problems in living." Most interpersonal theorists view patterns of behavior as having been learned over the course of relational life—originating in adaptive ways of negotiating experience in light of particular requirements—and emphasize the role of learning in change and growth.

In Mitchell's formulation of the relational paradigm, the social field is the fundamental organizer of personality or self, and thinkers regard disruptions in caretaking experience, traumatic events, and adverse social environments as major determinants of vulnerability. The first generation of theorists focused on the nature of caretaker-child relationships and critical periods of care in infancy and early childhood in formulations of problems in functioning. More recently, however, following critiques of theory and research, investigators have broadened the scope of study to consider the ways in which relationships, life events, and social conditions influence problems in living across the course of life (see Borden, 2008; 2009a).

While these more recent theorists recognize the adverse effects of deprivation and trauma in conceptions of vulnerability and dysfunction, they emphasize the organizing and sustaining functions of maladaptive behavior. Following Mitchell's formulations, they assume that psychopathology is self-perpetuating because it is embedded in global ways of being, relating, and living that persons have established over the course of development. There is "a pervasive tendency to preserve the continuity, connections, and familiarity of one's personal, interactional world" (Mitchell, 1988, p. 33).

In Mitchell's schema, although vicious circles of thought, feeling, and behavior may be limiting, these patterns of functioning serve important purposes. The individual perpetuates maladaptive ways of being and relating in an effort to preserve cohesion and continuity in subjective experience and the sense of self. What is new is threatening because it lies beyond the bounds of experience in which the individual recognizes the self as a cohesive, continuous being. From the perspective of object relations formulations, the individual perpetuates dysfunction also in order to preserve connections with the internal representations and presence of others. "What is new is frightening because it requires what one experiences as the abandonment of old loyalties, through which one feels connected and devoted" (Mitchell, 1988, p. 291). In the domain of interpersonal life, the individual perpetuates maladaptive behavior in an effort to regulate fear and anxiety and to maximize safety and security. Following Sullivan's formulation, "security operations steer (the individual) into familiar channels and away from the anxiety-shrouded unknown" (Mitchell, 1988, p. 291; see Borden, 2000, 2008, and 2009a, for further elaboration of these concepts).

A growing number of psychodynamic thinkers have emphasized social, cultural, political, and economic contexts of vulnerability in their conceptions of need, problems in living, and clinical practice. Social injustice and inequality have emerged as central themes in critiques of psychotherapy, and practitioners continue efforts to make psychodynamically oriented forms of intervention more available to the poor as well as to racially and ethnically marginalized groups. In doing so, they are making pragmatic use of psychodynamic concepts and methods and introducing realistic, flexible modes of intervention (see, e.g., Ornstein & Ganzer, 2005; Wachtel, 2008). Beyond the domain of clinical practice, thinkers have explored the ways in which psychodynamic points of view enlarge understanding of social problems and inform policy development. Robert Coles has engaged psychodynamic perspectives in his seminal accounts of race, class, and poverty (Coles, 1997). Psychodynamic thought has informed Paul Wachtel's writings on racism and social justice, and his critiques of individualism and consumerism in American culture are shaped by the political and social orientation of the interpersonal tradition (Wachtel, 1999, 2008). Neil Altman has drawn on relational perspectives and critical social theory in his accounts of race, class, poverty, and the urban environment (Altman, 2006).

Orienting Perspectives in Psychosocial Intervention

Drawing on the schools of thought encompassed in the relational paradigm, scholars and practitioners have outlined basic assumptions, core concepts, and essential concerns that inform integrative approaches to assessment, case formulation, treatment planning, and intervention (see Borden, 2008, for an overview of practice guidelines). These thinkers recognize the fundamental importance of common factors that are believed to facilitate change and growth and that operate across the foundational schools of thought in contemporary psychotherapy. These include the sustaining functions of the helping relationship, the setting of the intervention, conceptual frameworks that provide plausible explanations of the origins of problems in functioning and that specify interventions that carry the potential to help, and the core activities of the intervention (Frank & Frank, 1991; Wampold, 2007; Borden, 2009b; Clark, 2009). In formulating conceptions of intervention from relational lines of understanding, however, these thinkers emphasize the fundamental role of the practitioner-client relationship in the process of change and the functions of interpersonal interaction and experiential learning in efforts to negotiate problems in living.

From the perspective of self psychology, the practitioner's empathic attunement and responsiveness as a "selfobject" strengthen the integrity of the self and foster the development of capacities to enrich and make use of relational experience. From the perspective of object relations psychology, the practitioner provides reparative experiences over the course of interaction that modify inner models of self and others, reorganize dysfunctional patterns of defense, and foster more adaptive ways of being, relating, and living. From the perspective of the interpersonal school, the practitioner is inevitably engaged in the client's maladaptive patterns of behavior as a participant-observer in the relational field of intervention. Following Sullivan's formulations, these theorists view the clinician as a participant-observer and emphasize the reciprocal nature of therapeutic interaction. Ongoing interaction between client and worker facilitates efforts to identify vicious circles of behavior and to strengthen capacities to process information, regulate emotion, and negotiate interpersonal experience.

Theorists of the interpersonal school consider the ways in which the client and the practitioner shape the process and outcome of intervention, and their conceptions of the helping relationship acknowledge mutual sources of recognition, empathy, and influence. This deepens appreciation of subjective experience and mutuality in the helping process. The focus on the dynamics of the client-practitioner relationship and current patterns of interaction distinguish contemporary relational models of intervention from classical psychoanalytic approaches that emphasize principles of neutrality and exploration of childhood conflict (Borden, 2008, 2009a).

Conceptions of transference and countertransference, as developed in object relations thought and interpersonal psychoanalysis, center on inner models of relational life and the reciprocal nature of interactive experience in the social field. From the perspective of object relations theory, formulations of transference emphasize the ways in which inner models of self and others influence perceptions of experience, constructions of meaning, and patterns of interpersonal behavior. From the perspective of the interpersonal school, conceptions of transference emphasize patterns of expectation and learning established over the course of relational life. Research in the field of cognitive neuroscience provides empirical support for these formulations of transference. To the degree that the helping relationship corresponds to prototypes from the past, it is likely to activate similar patterns of motivation, affect, thought, conflict, defense, and interpersonal behavior (Luborsky & Barrett, 2006; Westen & Gabbard, 2002a, 2002b; Westen, 2005).

The practitioner's countertransference reactions are conceptualized as role-responsive complements or counterparts to the client's behavior, serving as sources of data that deepen understanding of interactive processes that perpetuate problematic patterns of thought, feeling, and action. Enactments of maladaptive behavior in the helping process facilitate efforts to clarify problematic modes of interaction and to establish more effective ways of negotiating interpersonal life.

The helping relationship, accordingly, facilitates change and growth in a variety of ways, providing crucial sources of experience, understanding, and learning. In their formulations of facilitating processes, relational thinkers emphasize the sustaining functions of the therapeutic alliance and the constancy of care in the holding environment of intervention; the role of experiential learning through interpersonal interaction; and interpretive procedures that deepen understanding of self, interpersonal behavior, and life experience. More recently, practitioners have identified reinforcement, modeling, and identification as key processes in client-worker interaction and have emphasized use of tasks outside of sessions to facilitate development of crucial skills in living (Borden, 2009a; Wachtel, 2008).

From a psychodynamic perspective, clinicians assume that the core activities of intervention carry the potential to facilitate change and growth across multiple domains of functioning, helping clients to strengthen capacities to experience emotion and process subjective experience; to deepen awareness of unconscious realms of experience; to reorganize cognitive schemas and meaning structures, including models of self, others, and interactive experience; to engage stimuli that precipitate fear and anxiety; to expand coping capacities and problem-solving skills; and to strengthen relational capacities, interpersonal functioning, and social networks. Empirical studies of psychodynamic interventions suggest that enhanced interpersonal functioning strengthens morale, self-esteem, and subjective well-being and reduces problems associated with all forms of psychopathology (Binder, Strupp, & Henry, 1995; Luborsky & Barrett, 2006; Roth & Fonagy, 2005; Shedler, 2010). From the perspective of cognitive neuroscience, thinkers hypothesize that the core activities of intervention modify the structures of associational networks established over the course of development and foster formation of new, adaptive linkages and patterns of behavior (Cozolino, 2002; Schore, 2003a, 2003b; Westen & Gabbard, 2002a, 2002b; Westen, 2005).

Psychodynamic Theory, Empirical Research, and Evidence-Based Practice

Evidence-based social work practice must draw upon the best available science to guide assessment, treatment design, and intervention. Unfortunately, there has been surprisingly little consideration of psychodynamic theory or research in emerging models of evidence-based social work interventions. One reason might be that influential EBP advocates have worked from strongly held ideas that are assumed to be generally valid but are nonetheless at odds with the realities of clinical practice. Many recent approaches to psychotherapy research, for example, assume that manualized short-term intervention packages can adequately treat "psychopathology that is highly malleable, that most patients can be treated for a single problem or disorder, that psychiatric disorders can be treated independently of personality factors unlikely to change in brief treatment, and that experimental methods provide a gold standard for identifying useful psychotherapeutic packages" (Westen, Novotny, & Thompson-Brenner, 2004, pp. 632–633). On the other hand, the psychodynamic approaches described here work from a set of competing assumptions—for example, that clients typically present with chronic, interacting, comorbid, biopsychosocial disorders that shape and are shaped by personality development throughout the lifespan and in the context of interpersonal relationships. These divergences have led some psychodynamic clinicians to reject current psychotherapy research as fundamentally flawed. However, leading psychodynamic psychotherapy researchers have argued that there are compelling clinical, scientific, and ethical arguments for continuing and enhancing empirical work, cautiously and rigorously (Fonagy, Roth, & Higgitt, 2005; Shedler, 2010). Any careful review of the psychodynamic psychotherapy research literature will reveal strong commitments to building a viable evidence base that can be disseminated into and implemented in practice settings. Additionally, it is likely that psychodynamic psychotherapists will be among the most demanding consumers of evidence-based technologies precisely because they will approach research findings with strong clinical skepticism that rejects treatment studies that have poor ecological validity.

Such skepticism is well-advised: many acclaimed psychotherapy research studies, including randomized, controlled trials highlighting cognitive-behavioral technologies, are plagued by significant client dropout rates; focus primarily on symptom-reduction; exclude therapist, client, and therapeutic alliance factors, and frequently reveal high rates of client relapse by one year post-treatment (Fonagy, Roth, & Higgitt, 2005; Lambert & Ogles, 2003; Westen, Novotny, & Thompson-Brenner, 2004). Additionally, a reanalysis of the data set for the landmark National Institute of Mental Health Treatment of Depression Collaboration Research Program—a randomized controlled trial of cognitive therapy, interpersonal therapy, pharmacological therapy (with imipramine), and a double-blind placebo (Elkin, 1994)—has revealed significant differences across treatment conditions that were not detected in earlier analyses. By categorizing subjects by depressions phenomenologically subtyped as generated through disruptions of valued, interpersonal relationships versus disruptions of the effective, positive sense of self, more recent analysts discovered that treatment outcomes were not influenced by specific treatment approaches, but rather were significantly related to pretreatment client personality factors, pretreatment client interpersonal relationships, and the quality of therapeutic alliances (Blatt, Zuroff, & Hawley, 2009).

It is empirically responsible, therefore, to ask whether psychodynamic approaches, especially those that involve clients for fifty sessions and longer, might provide the sustained engagement required for comorbid, complex disorders typically seen in community settings. Indeed, recent investigations of psychodynamic approaches have generated a substantial body of literature focusing on case formulations, establishment of the practitioner-client relationship and helping alliances, core processes, and outcomes of intervention. Although exhaustive review of empirical findings is beyond the scope of this chapter, critical evaluations of process and outcome studies are provided by Luborsky and Barrett (2006), Messer and Warren (1995), Roth and Fonagy (2005), Shedler (2010), and Siefert, Defife, and Baity (2009).

Additionally, contemporary reviews of the empirical literature show that many outcome studies provide support for the efficacy of psychodynamic models of intervention in the treatment of problems in functioning associated with a range of conditions, including major depressive disorder, borderline personality disorder, panic disorder, posttraumatic stress disorder, and certain types of substance abuse and dependence (Gibbons, Crits-Christoph, & Hearon, 2008; Luborsky & Barrett, 2006; Roth & Fonagy, 2005; Shedler, 2010). Leichsenring (2009) reviewed thirty-one studies and found that psychodynamic psychotherapy was consistently superior to supportive therapies, treatment as usual, and placebo conditions, and as effective as cognitive-behavioral therapies targeted for major depression, pathological grief, anxiety disorders, posttraumatic stress disorder, somatoform disorder, bulimia, anorexia, borderline personality disorder, avoidant personality disorder, Cluster C personality disorders, and opiate dependence disorder.

Leischenring and Rabung (2009) performed a meta-analysis that included twenty-three studies of published and nonpublished investigations of long-term psychodynamic psychotherapy. Conducted from 1960 to 2008, the studies included 1,053 clients and 257 controls. Results suggested that long-term psychodynamic psychotherapy was effective for complex mental disorders, including personality disorders, chronic mental disorders, and multiple mental disorders (Leischenring & Rabung, 2009). While all such meta-analyses must be interpreted with caution due to the limited number of acceptable studies and the lack of follow-up data, this study strongly refutes any claim that psychodynamic approaches should be rejected out of hand as an essential category of evidence-based intervention (Glass, 2009).

Shedler (2010) provides a careful account of empirical evidence that provides strong support for the efficacy of psychodynamic intervention. His review of meta-analyses of treatment outcome studies shows that effect sizes for psychodynamic therapy were as large as those reported for other approaches that are represented as evidence-based and empirically supported. He notes the recurring finding that persons who received psychodynamically oriented treatment maintained therapeutic gains and continued to improve over time. He suggests that nonpsychodynamic therapies may be effective in part because experienced practitioners use methods that are fundamental to psychodynamic forms of intervention.

Practitioners and researchers have begun to outline basic tasks and essential concerns in formulations of interpersonal expertise in the domain of evidence-based intervention. According to guidelines introduced in the American Psychological Association task force report on evidence-based practice, the expert practitioner seeks to establish a therapeutic alliance, strengthen the client's engagement in the helping process, monitor the dynamics of client-practitioner interaction, and address conditions that limit progress. The clinician encodes and decodes verbal and nonverbal responses and responds empathically to the client's explicit and implicit experiences and concerns, creating a supportive atmosphere that fosters exploration, openness, and change (see American Psychological Association Presidential Task Force on Evidence-Based Practice, 2006, p. 277).

Empirical findings document the crucial role of the helping relationship in all forms of intervention, and psychodynamic researchers emphasize the ways in which the therapeutic alliance and patterns of interaction influence the process and outcome of treatment (Horvath, 2006; Norcross, 2002; Roth & Fonagy, 2005; Wampold, 2007). Relational theorists describe a range of defensive strategies and patterns of behavior that potentially compromise engagement in the helping process, challenge the establishment of the therapeutic alliance, and precipitate strain and rupture over the course of intervention, limiting opportunities for change and growth (Borden, 2008, 2009a). Anthony Roth and Peter Fonagy (2005) stress the importance of clinical judgment in the application of strategies and techniques, management of the therapeutic alliance, and monitoring of interpersonal processes in their formulations of evidence-based intervention, reminding us that therapeutic effectiveness requires more than "narrow technical competence" (p. 52). Engagement of theoretical understanding across the relational schools of thought will deepen conceptions of interactive experience and facilitating processes in development of more complex formulations of integrative approaches and evidence-based intervention.

Conclusion

The theoretical systems that shape contemporary psychodynamic thought enlarge conceptions of personality development, health and well-being, and vulnerability, psychopathology, and problems in functioning. Converging lines of study, centering on conceptions of relationship, interpersonal behavior, and experiential learning, deepen appreciation of facilitating processes in psychosocial intervention. Continued development of theoretical understanding and empirical research will strengthen approaches to assessment, case formulation, treatment planning, and intervention in integrative approaches and evidence-based practice (Luborsky & Barrett, 2006). Evidence-based approaches to psychodynamically informed social work practice will be enhanced as researchers focus further investigation on specific interventions in the treatment of specific disorders using multiple randomized controlled studies that address identified methodological weaknesses (Gibbons, Crits-Christoph, & Hearon, 2008). At the same time the important epistemological and methodological reforms advocated by Clark (2009); Fonagy, Roth, and Higgitt (2005); Lambert and Ogles (2003); and Westen (2007) can advance clinician-researcher alliances leading to the ecologically valid, community-based psychotherapy research programs required to substantially develop evidence-based practices. We speculate that community-based research that supplements traditional top-down, science-to-practice dissemination with innovative, practice-to-science information flows will open new opportunities to develop integrative approaches using efficacious relational strategies drawn from multiple schools of psychotherapy (Borden, 2009a, 2009b).

References

Adler, A. (1927/1992). *Understanding human nature*. (C. Brett, Trans,). Oxford, UK: Oneworld.

Altman, N. (2006). *The analyst in the inner city: Race, class and culture through a psychoanalytic lens*. Hillsdale, NJ: Analytic Press.

American Psychological Association Presidential Task Force on Evidence-Based Practice. (2006). Evidence-based practice in psychology. *American Psychologist, 61*(4), 271–285.

Aronson, E. (1992). *The social animal*. New York, NY: W. H. Freeman.

Beebe, B., & Lachmann, F. M. (1998). The contribution of mother-infant mutual influence to the origins of self and object representations. *Psychoanalytic Psychology, 5*, 305–337.

Benjamin, L. (1993). *Diagnosis and treatment of personality disorders: A structural approach*. New York, NY: Guilford.

Binder, J., Strupp, H., & Henry, W. (1995). Psychodynamic therapies in practice: Time-limited psychodynamic psychotherapy. In B. Bonger & L. Beutler (Eds.), *Comprehensive textbook of psychotherapy* (pp. 48–63). New York, NY: Oxford University Press.

Blatt, S., & Homann, E. (1992). Parent-child interactions in the etiology of dependent and self-critical depression. *Clinical Psychology Review, 12*, 47–91.

Blatt, S. J., Zuroff, D.C., & Hawley, L. (2009). Factors contributing to sustained therapeutic gain in outpatient treatments of depression. In R. A. Levy & S. J. Ablon (Eds.), *Handbook of evidence-based psychodynamic therapy* (pp. 279–301). New York, NY: Humana Press.

Borden, W. (2000). The relational paradigm in contemporary psychoanalysis: Toward a psychodynamically informed social work perspective. *Social Service Review, 74*(3), 352–379.

Borden, W. (2008). Contemporary object relations psychology and psychosocial intervention. In A. Roberts (Ed.), *Social workers' desk reference* (pp. 305–310). New York, NY: Oxford University Press.

Borden, W. (2009a). *Contemporary psychodynamic theory and practice: Toward a critical pluralism.* Chicago, IL: Lyceum.

Borden, W. (2009b). Taking multiplicity seriously: Pluralism, pragmatism, and integrative perspectives in social work practice. In W. Borden (Ed.). *Reshaping the domain of theory in contemporary social work.* New York, NY: Columbia University Press.

Bowlby, J. (1988). *A secure base.* New York, NY: Basic Books.

Clark, J. J. (2009). Contemporary psychotherapy research: Implications for substance misuse treatment and research. *Substance Use and Misuse, 44,* 1–19.

Coles, R. (1997). *Doing documentary work.* New York, NY: Oxford University Press.

Cozolino, L. (2002). *The neuroscience of psychotherapy.* New York, NY: Norton.

Elkin, I. (1994). The NIMH Treatment of Depression Collaborative Research Program: Where we began and where we are. In A. E. Beren and S. L. Garfield (Eds.), *Handbook of psychotherapy and behavior change* (4th ed.) (pp 114–139). New York, NY: Wiley.

Fairbairn, W. R. D. (1952). A synopsis of the development of the author's views regarding the structure of the personality. In *Psychoanalytic studies of the personality* (pp. 162–182). London, UK: Tavistock.

Ferenczi, S. (1933/1980). The confusion of tongues between adults and the child: The language of tenderness and passion. In M. Balint (Ed.) & E. Mosbacher et al. (Trans.), *Final contributions to the problems and methods of psychoanalysis* (pp. 156–167). London, UK: Karnac.

Fonagy, P. (2001). *Attachment Theory and Psychoanalysis.* New York, NY: Other Press.

Fonagy, P., Roth, A., & Higgitt, A. (2005). Psychodynamic psychotherapies: Evidence-based practice and clinical wisdom. *Bulletin of the Menninger Clinic, 69*(1), 1–58.

Fonagy, P., & Target, M. (2007). The rooting of the mind in the body: New links between attachment theory and psychoanalytic thought. *Journal of the American Psychoanalytic Association, 55* (2), 411–456.

Frank, J., & Frank, J. (1991). *Persuasion and healing.* Baltimore, MD: Johns Hopkins University Press.

Gibbons, M., Crits-Christoph, P., & Hearon, B. (2008). The empirical status of psychodynamic therapies. *Annual Review of Clinical Psychology, 4,* 93–108.

Glass, R. M. (2009). Psychodynamic psychotherapy and research evidence: Bambi survives Godzilla? *Journal of the American Medical Association, 300*(13), 1587–1589.

Greenberg, J., & Mitchell, S. (1983). *Object relations in psychoanalytic theory.* Cambridge, MA: Harvard University Press.

Horney, K. (1950). *Neurosis and human growth.* New York, NY: Norton.

Horvath, A. (2006). The alliance in context: Accomplishments, challenges, and future directions. *Psychotherapy: Theory, Research, Practice, Training, 43*(3), 258–263.

Kohut, H. (1977). *The restoration of the self.* Madison, CT: International Universities Press.

Lambert, M. J., & Ogles, B. M. (2003). The efficacy and effectiveness of psychotherapy. In M. J. Lambert (Ed.), *Bergin and Garfield's handbook of psychotherapy and behavior change* (5th ed.) (pp. 139–193). New York, NY: John Wiley & Sons.

Leichsenring, F. (2009). Psychodynamic psychotherapy: A review of efficacy and effectiveness studies. In R. A. Levy & S. J. Ablon (Eds.), *Handbook of evidence-based psychodynamic therapy* (pp. 3–27). New York, NY: Humana Press.

Leichsenring, F., & Rabung, S. (2009). Effectiveness of long-term psychodynamic psychotherapy: A meta-analysis. *Journal of the American Medical Association, 300*(13), 1587–1589.

Luborsky, L., & Barrett, M. (2006). The history and empirical status of key psychoanalytic concepts. *Annual Review of Clinical Psychology, 2,* 1–19.

Luborsky, L., & Crits-Christoph, P. (1990). *Understanding transference: The CCRT method.* New York, NY: Basic Books.

Masling, J., & Bornstein, R. (1994). *Empirical perspectives on object relations theory.* Washington, DC: American Psychological Association.

Messer, S., & Warren, S. (1995). *Models of brief psychodynamic psychotherapy.* New York, NY: Guilford.

Mitchell, S. (1988). *Relational concepts in psychoanalysis.* Cambridge, MA: Harvard University Press.

Mitchell, S. (1993). *Hope and dread in psychoanalysis.* New York, NY: Basic Books.

Mitchell, S. (1997). *Influence and autonomy in psychoanalysis.* Hillsdale, NJ: Analytic Press.

Mitchell, S. (2000). *Relationality.* Hillsdale, NJ: Analytic Press.

Norcross, J. (2002). *Psychotherapy relationships that work: Therapist contributions and responsiveness to patients.* New York, NY: Oxford University Press.

Ornstein, E., & Ganzer, C. (2005). Relational social work: A model for the future. *Journal of Contemporary Social Services, 86*(4), 565–572.

Rank, O. (1936). *Will therapy.* (J. Taft, Trans.). New York, NY: Knopf.

Roth, A., & Fonagy, P. (2005). *What works for whom? A critical review of psychotherapy research* (2nd ed.). New York, NY: Guilford.

Schore, A. (2003a). *Affect dysregulation and disorders of the self.* New York, NY: Norton.

Schore, A. (2003b). *Affect regulation and the repair of the self.* New York, NY: Norton.

Shedler, J. (2010). The efficacy of psychodynamic psychotherapy. *American Psychologist, 65*(2), 98–109.

Siefert, C. J., Defife J. A., & Baity, M. R. (2009). Process measures for psychodynamic psychotherapy. In R. A. Levy & S. J. Ablon (Eds.), *Handbook of evidence-based psychodynamic therapy* (pp. 157–178). New York, NY: Humana Press.

Sroufe, A., Egelund, B., Carlson, E. A., & Collins, W. A. (2005). *The development of the person.* New York, NY: Guilford.

Stern, D. (1985). *The Interpersonal World of the Infant.* New York, NY: Basic Books.

Stern, D. (2004). *The Present Moment in Psychotherapy and Everyday Life.* New York, NY: Norton.

Strupp, H., & Binder, J. (1984). *Psychotherapy in a new key.* New York, NY: Basic Books.

Sullivan, H. S. (1953). *The interpersonal theory of psychiatry.* New York, NY: Norton.

Suttie, I. (1935). *The origins of love and hate.* London, UK: Kegan Paul.

Wachtel, P. (1999). *Race in the mind of America: Breaking the vicious circle between blacks and whites.* London, UK: Routledge.

Wachtel, P. (2008). *Relational theory and the practice of psychotherapy.* New York, NY: Guilford.

Wampold, B. (2007). Psychotherapy: The humanistic (and effective) treatment. *American Psychologist, 2*(8), 857–873.

Weinberger, J., & Westen, D. (2001). Science and psychodynamics: From arguments about Freud to data. *Psychological Inquiry, 12*(3), 129–132.

Westen, D. (1998). The scientific legacy of Sigmund Freud: Toward a psychodynamically informed psychological science. *Psychological Bulletin, 124*(3), 333–371.

Westen, D. (2005). Implications of research in cognitive neuroscience for psychodynamic psychotherapy. In G. Gabbard, J. Beck, & J. Holmes (Eds.), *Oxford Textbook of Psychotherapy* (443–449). New York, NY: Oxford.

Westen, D. (2007). Discovering what works in the community: Toward a general partnership of clinicians and researchers. In S. G Hofmann & J. Weinberger (Eds.), *The art and science of psychotherapy* (pp. 3–30). New York, NY: Routledge.

Westen, D., & Gabbard, G. (2002a). Developments in cognitive neuroscience: Conflict, compromise, and connectionism. *Journal of the American Psychoanalytic Association, 50,* 53–90.

Westen, D., & Gabbard, G. (2002b). Developments in cognitive neuroscience: Implications for theories of transference. *Journal of the American Psychoanalytic Association, 50,* 99–134.

Westen, D., Novotny, C. M., & Thompson-Brenner, H. (2004). The empirical status of empirically supported psychotherapies: Assumptions, findings, and reporting in controlled clinical trials. *Psychological Bulletin, 130*(4), 631—663.

Winnicott, D. (1971). *Therapeutic consultations in child psychiatry.* New York, NY: Basic Books.

CHAPTER FIVE

Evidence-Based or Biased? Why Methods of Research Synthesis Matter

Julia H. Littell

Like experience, evidence is cumulative. Empirical evidence evolves as new studies confirm, modify, or contradict results of previous research. Thus, the evidence base for practice is constantly growing and changing in light of new information. How can practitioners keep up with the diverse and rapidly growing sources of evidence?

Credible research reviews can provide valuable syntheses of the best available evidence on many topics that are relevant for practice. Research syntheses can tell us what is known about the nature and extent of certain problems or conditions, the reliability and accuracy of various assessment instruments, the efficacy and effectiveness of interventions, and so forth. "Ideally, practitioners should be able to rely on reviewers to isolate the best evidence for them and to distill it for its essence to guide practice decision making. Unfortunately, conventional reviews have fallen far short of such expectations" (Gibbs, 2003, p. 153). Many published research reviews use selective and haphazard methods for finding, critically appraising, and synthesizing results across studies; these reviews do not produce reliable summaries of evidence for practice (Littell, 2008; Petticrew & Roberts, 2006). Given wide variations in the quality and credibility of research reviews, it is important to know how to judge evidence summaries.

This chapter begins with a discussion of the uses of research synthesis in evidence-based practice. To address concerns about the varied quality of research reviews, I describe the methods reviewers use to locate, critically appraise, and summarize research results, focusing on three predominant types of research reviews (traditional reviews, systematic reviews, and meta-analyses). I discuss common sources of and types of bias that affect research reviews, and show how these biases can be taken into account (or at least minimized) in the review process. Finally, I contrast the science of research synthesis with common practice, and I use an illustration to show that different review methods can lead to very different conclusions.

Research Synthesis and Evidence-Based Practice

The term evidence-based practice has been applied to disparate approaches. One approach, derived from models of evidence-based medicine (Sackett, Rosenberg, Gray, Haynes, & Richardson, 1996; Straus, Richardson, Glasziou, & Haynes, 2005), emphasizes the integration of the best research evidence with clinical expertise and consumer values to produce informed decisions about individual cases. Leonard Gibbs (2003) explicated the process of EBP for the helping professions (Gibbs & Gambrill, 2002), and Philip Davies (2004) extended the process to policy making.

A second approach, one that is most prominent in the United States, involves the identification of clinical interventions that meet certain criteria and standards of evidence (these are sometimes called evidence-based practices, empirically supported treatments, or empirically validated treatments). Following this second approach, governmental and professional organizations have developed criteria for effective and efficacious interventions. Prominent examples are the prestigious Blueprints for Violence Prevention series (Mihalic, Fagan, Irwin, Ballard, & Elliott, 2004); the National Registry of Evidence-Based Programs and Practices (Substance Abuse and Mental Health Services Administration, 2007); the Society for Prevention Research standards for efficacy, effectiveness, and broad dissemination (Flay et al., 2005); and the American Psychological Association Society of Clinical Psychology (Chambless et al., 1998; Chambless & Ollendick, 2001). Concerns about the standards of evidence and methods used to compile influential lists of effective practices have been raised (e.g., by Gandhi, Murphy-Graham, Petrosino, Chrismer, & Weiss, 2006; Gorman 2003; Littell, 2005, 2008) and will be considered below.

Regardless of which approach is taken EBP relies, in part, on the synthesis of research results across studies. Research synthesis is important because the results of multiple studies provide more robust information than results of any single study. Just as we would not rely on one person's views as a valid indicator of public opinion, we should not rely on a single study for definitive answers to important questions for policy or practice. Studies use different samples, research designs, measures, and analytic approaches, and these sampling and methodological characteristics can affect results (Wilson & Lipsey, 2001). Like a survey of a large population, careful syntheses of results across studies are useful in identifying central trends and variations.

Further, research syntheses can address questions that were not considered in the primary studies under review by assessing whether and how results vary across samples, settings, treatments, study designs, and measures. Research syntheses can capitalize on variations that occur within and across studies to explore what works best for whom and under what conditions.

BUILDING EVIDENCE

In a now-famous article, titled "What can you build with thousands of bricks?" Mark Lipsey (1997) noted that studies tend to pile up, like used bricks. Crafted for a particular purpose and potentially useful in certain contexts, studies tend to be discarded if they are thought to be inapplicable or no longer useful. In 1997, Lipsey argued that relatively little attention had been paid to the types of knowledge that could be derived from entire bodies of empirical research. He noted that evidence from the many completed evaluation studies could be compiled to develop new knowledge about which facets of interventions matter and which do not.

Just as diverse structures (such as homes, temples, prisons, and town halls) can be constructed from bricks, research reviews can be created for many purposes. Reviews can focus on questions about the incidence or prevalence of certain conditions, the accuracy of diagnostic or prognostic tests, relative effects of alternative interventions, treatment costs, and so on. Reviewers can consider averages or variations across studies. They can look for patterns of results within and across studies that may be accounted for by moderator variables, examining whether and how research results vary by study design features, population and sample characteristics, intervention characteristics, and setting (cultural, geographical, political, agency, or temporal contexts).

If form follows function, then good research syntheses will aim to achieve specific objectives and will be designed and constructed to meet those objectives. Different raw materials (study designs) and construction (synthesis) methods are called for in reviews that aim to achieve different objectives.

As in building construction, skilled reviewers use detailed blueprints (called protocols), raw materials (studies) that are fit for the purpose of the review and meet certain criteria and quality standards, and skilled construction methods (appropriate techniques for synthesizing results across studies).

TRADITIONAL APPROACHES TO RESEARCH SYNTHESIS

Traditional narrative research reviews are common in social work and the social sciences. Traditional reviews rely on convenience samples of published studies, narrative descriptions of selected studies, and cognitive algebra or "vote counting" to synthesize results across studies.

In traditional research synthesis, a convenience sample of published studies is usually obtained with keyword searches of one or more bibliographic databases. Some keyword searches are more sensitive (likely to identify relevant studies) than others, and some are more specific (likely to omit irrelevant studies) than others. Keyword searches may miss relevant studies that are contained in the database but are improperly indexed or do not use the words that are included in the keyword search string. Different databases will, of course, produce different results, as will different portals. Moreover, most bibliographic databases do not contain relevant, rigorous studies that are unpublished. In recent years, reviewers have become more careful to document which databases and strategies they used to find studies, but search strategies are rarely documented at the level of detail needed for replication (Patrick et al., 2004).

Traditional reviews rarely explain how studies were selected for inclusion; nor do they tell which studies were omitted and why. Indeed, explicit inclusion and exclusion criteria are usually absent. Instead, reviewers usually provide narrative descriptions of selected studies, with little information about the larger pools of studies from which they were drawn. Thus reviews can be based on biased samples of studies, and readers have no way to know about the nature or extent of this selection bias.

Formal assessments of study quality are absent in most traditional, narrative reviews. Reviewers may mention selected methodological features, but this type of analysis is frequently uneven in narrative reviews. It is often unclear whether reviewers are reliably extracting important details from primary studies (that is, whether two people reading the same research report would have the same observations and conclusions). Indeed, consistent appraisals of previous studies are difficult to achieve, in part because many published reports provide incomplete information on study design, implementation, and result characteristics.

Traditional reviews usually employ some form of cognitive algebra to arrive at summary statements about the weight of the evidence. Statements such as "most studies suggest" involve some form of mental math, but it is rarely clear how the math was performed. Some reviews make this more explicit, using vote counting to indicate how many studies produced results that support or refute a hypothesis. Vote counting usually relies on the results of tests of statistical significance in the primary studies, and these tests are affected by sample size. Small studies may lack the statistical power needed for detection of statistically significant differences, even when clinically meaningful effects are present; on the other hand, very large studies are so sensitive that small (and virtually meaningless) differences will appear to be statistically significant. Thus, a tally of statistically significant results is potentially misleading. Traditional research reviews are vulnerable to many well-documented sources and types of bias that can affect the validity of research reviews.

Sources and Types of Bias

Biases that affect research reviews include systematic errors and omissions that arise in the identification and sampling of relevant studies, in the conduct of the included studies themselves, and in the extraction and interpretation of data from studies. Issues of research design and implementation affect the validity of conclusions that can be drawn from primary studies included in a review. Confirmation and allegiance biases can also affect conclusions drawn from primary studies and research reviews. Publication, dissemination, and reporting biases affect the availability of empirical evidence and have important implications for research reviews as well.

RESEARCH DESIGN AND IMPLEMENTATION ISSUES IN PRIMARY STUDIES

Much has been written about design and implementation issues that can affect the validity of conclusions drawn from empirical research. Validity is not a property of research methods; there are no research designs or techniques than ensure valid results. Rather, validity is a property of the inferences that are based on research results (Shadish, Cook, & Campbell, 2002). In general, bias is any systematic error that distorts those results or their interpretation.

High-quality materials are needed to produce reliable evidence summaries. The best materials for this task depend on what we are building—that is, on the purpose of the research synthesis. In any case, standards of evidence must be set to avoid the garbage in, garbage out problem.

Randomized controlled trials are considered the gold standard in research on intervention effects, yet implementation and analytic problems can compromise the validity of conclusions based on such trials. Poorly implemented or improperly analyzed randomized controlled trials are sometimes called queasy experiments because they produce dubious results. Shadish, Cook, and Campbell (2002) showed that a critical analysis of study design and implementation issues is needed to determine whether there are plausible alternative explanations for study results. Simple hierarchies of evidence based on overall research designs are inadequate for judging the credibility of research results (Wells & Littell, 2009). Nevertheless, randomized controlled trials have been privileged over other study designs.

There are many critiques of the raw materials that go into research reviews. Concerns have been expressed about improper randomization procedures (Schulz & Grimes, 2002), differential attrition, and failure to conduct intent-to-treat analyses in randomized controlled trials (Littell, Popa, & Forsythe, 2005), as well as about the failure in some studies to account for common factors that affect outcomes across treatments (Jensen, Weersing, Hoagwood, & Goldman, 2005). Other problems include over-reliance on tests of statistical significance (versus clinically meaningful effect sizes); use of multiple outcome measures, multiple subgroups, post hoc sample refinement, and multiple tests of significance (fishing for effects); failure to adjust for clustering in cluster randomized controlled trials; and an absence of long-term follow-up (Gandhi et al., 2006; Gorman, 2003).

The development of scientific standards for the conduct and reporting of different types of studies has been an important step in addressing many of these concerns. For example, the CONSORT statement was developed to improve reporting on randomized controlled studies (Moher et al., 2010; Schulz et al., 2010). Initially published in 1996, this statement was widely adopted by medical journals and was revised in 2001 and 2010. Similar reporting standards and guidelines exist for many other types of studies (see www.equator-network.org and APA Publications and Communications Board Working Group on Journal Article Reporting Standards, 2008).

CONFIRMATION AND ALLEGIANCE BIASES

Confirmation bias is the tendency to seek and accept information that corroborates prior expectations and to ignore evidence to the contrary.

This very human tendency is well-documented (Fugelsang, Stein, Green, & Dunbar, 2004; Nickerson, 1998). Allegiance bias occurs when investigators' prior beliefs about the superiority of one approach over another predict research results (Luborsky et al., 1999). Confirmation and allegiance biases may be present in research reviews that use evidence selectively (Littell, 2008) and those that draw conclusions that benefit the reviewers or their sponsors. For example, Jørgensen and colleagues (2006) found that reviews sponsored by pharmaceutical companies were less likely to raise concerns about the methodological limitations of drug trials and more likely to draw favorable conclusions about the companies' products, compared with independent Cochrane reviews of the same products (Jørgensen, Hilden, & Gøtzsche, 2006).

PUBLICATION, DISSEMINATION, AND REPORTING BIASES

Studies with statistically significant, positive results are significantly more likely to be published than equally credible studies that have nonsignificant or negative results (Dickersin, 2005; Hopewell, Loudon, Clarke, Oxman, & Dickersin, 2009; Scherer, Langenberg, & von-Elm, 2007; Song et al., 2009; Torgerson, 2006). The reasons for this are complex. First, investigators may think that nonsignificant results are not informative (one investigator told me, "We didn't find anything"). Second, investigators are less likely to submit null results for publication (Dickersin, 2005; Song et al., 2009) because they think that no one will publish null results. Third, peer reviewers and editors may prefer studies with statistically significant results and those that support their own hypotheses (Mahoney, 1977). However, a recent meta-analysis suggests that publication bias appears to occur early, before the presentation of findings at conferences or submission of manuscripts to journals; thus, investigators appear to be the primary source of publication bias (Song et al., 2009).

Studies with statistically significant and positive results are published more rapidly (Hopewell, Clarke, Stewart, & Tierney, 2001), are cited and reprinted more often (Egger & Smith, 1998), and are more likely to be published in English (Egger, Zellweger-Zahner, et al., 1997) than studies of equal merit with nonsignificant or negative results. Thus, studies with statistically significant, positive results are easier to locate than other studies, especially when searches are conducted in English.

When studies have mixed results, statistically significant and positive results are more likely to be included in conference presentations and published reports than other, equally valid findings (Song et al., 2009). Significant results are mentioned more often and are reported more fully than nonsignificant results (Chan & Altman, 2005; Chan, Krleza-Jeric, Schmid, & Altman, 2004; Chan, Hróbjartsson, Haar, Gøtzsche, & Altman, 2004; Dwan et al., 2008; Williamson et al., 2006).

On the basis of analyses of several cohorts of studies, Song and colleagues (2009) concluded that the dissemination of research findings is likely to be a biased process. Publication, dissemination, and outcome reporting biases appear to be cumulative and lead to inflated estimates of intervention effects. Although publication and dissemination biases are ubiquitous, they are often ignored in the social science literature.

Systematic Reviews

Systematic reviews aim to minimize bias in the review process by developing and following a detailed protocol, using transparent, well-documented, replicable procedures to locate, analyze, and synthesize results of prior studies (Cooper, Hedges, & Valentine, 2009; Higgins & Green, 2008; Littell, Corcoran, & Pillai, 2008; Petticrew & Roberts, 2006). These procedures include the use of:

Explicit inclusion and exclusion criteria for eligible studies
Systematic strategies for locating all potentially relevant studies, regardless of their publication status
Structured data extraction and coding of information from included studies
Formal assessment of study qualities and the risk of bias in included studies
Inter-rater agreement on key decisions about such elements as study eligibility, data extraction, and coding
Meta-analysis (when appropriate) to synthesize quantitative results across studies

In the protocol for a systematic review, reviewers describe the study population, interventions, comparisons, outcomes, and study designs that will and will not be included (Higgins & Green, 2008; Littell, Corcoran, & Pillai, 2008). Ideally, the protocol will be published (or at least made publicly available) in advance of the review, so that readers can tell whether it was closely followed. The Cochrane and Campbell Collaborations routinely publish peer-reviewed protocols for systematic reviews before authors embark on the reviews themselves. Published protocols reduce opportunities for undetected, intentional or unintentional selection bias in decisions about which studies to include.

Because systematic reviews can address different questions, they are not limited to randomized controlled trials; nor are they limited to quantitative studies. Qualitative research can be used to better understand service delivery processes, implementation issues, client characteristics, and contextual conditions that may explain variations in results (see, for example, Harden, Brunton, Fletcher, & Oakley, 2009; Thomas et al., 2004). Methods for the synthesis of qualitative data and mixed or multiple methods are currently under development.

In addition to keyword searches of multiple electronic databases, systematic reviews use a variety of techniques to find relevant gray literature—eligible studies that are unpublished or hard to find. These strategies include hand searching key journals, scanning other reference lists and conference abstracts, and multiple contacts with networks of scholars and other key informants to identify research that is in progress, in press, or unpublished. Potentially useful unpublished papers include program evaluation reports, government-funded studies, and other research reports that have not been submitted for publication.

Working independently, two or more reviewers scan titles and abstracts and decide which studies may meet their inclusion criteria. Full text reports are retrieved when studies are thought to be eligible for the review or eligibility is unclear. On the basis of their readings of the full text, two reviewers make independent decisions about study eligibility; they resolve their disagreements by consulting with a third reviewer or by contacting the study authors for more information. Specific reasons for excluding studies are documented on a case-by-case basis.

Reviewers use a structured format to extract data from included studies. Usually this is done independently by two or more reviewers to make it possible to check the reliability of data extraction. Information is gathered on the study design, implementation, sample characteristics, interventions, outcomes measures, data collection methods, statistical procedures, and results. A formal assessment of the strength of the evidence and the risk of bias is conducted to gauge the credibility of each study's results.

Many schemes have been developed to aid in the assessment of the quality, credibility, and validity of research results. Overall study-design hierarchies are inadequate for this purpose. Deeks and his colleagues (2003) identified almost 200 scales and checklists that were developed for evaluating random controlled trials and nonrandomized studies. They found that only a handful of these tools were appropriate for use in systematic reviews, and virtually all needed to be modified for such reviews. Recently, the Cochrane Collaboration adopted a risk-of-bias framework to assess the credibility of results of research on intervention effects (Higgins & Green, 2008).

Meta-Analysis

When possible, synthesis of data across studies is performed with meta-analysis, a set of statistical procedures used to combine and analyze data across quantitative studies. Meta-analysis can be used to estimate overall averages, assess variations, identify potential sources of variation, and assess or adjust for biases in a set of studies (Lipsey & Wilson, 2001a; Littell, Corcoran, & Pillai, 2008). Study results are usually expressed as effect sizes. An effect size is any metric that describes the strength and direction of a relationship (e.g., odds ratio, correlation coefficient, Cohen's *d*). Overall averages are calculated using inverse variance methods, which weight study results by their precision; this means that larger studies have more influence than smaller studies in overall estimates.

Forest plots are used to show study-level effect size and overall weighted averages. Heterogeneity tests indicate whether variations in ES across studies are likely due to sampling error alone, or whether there are important differences in results across studies. Moderator analyses can be used to see whether certain characteristics of the research designs, study participants, measures, interventions, or comparison conditions are associated with variations in effect size. Various graphical displays and statistical tests can be used to present and investigate results of multiple studies (Anzures-Cabrera & Higgins, 2010; Cooper, Hedges, & Valentine; 2009; Higgins & Green, 2008), and a number of techniques are available to assess and adjust for publication bias and related issues in a set of studies included in a meta-analysis (Rothstein, Sutton, & Bornstein, 2005).

Criticisms of meta-analysis have focused on the apples-and-oranges problem. Since no two studies are alike, questions arise about conditions under which cross-study syntheses are valid. Similar problems occur in survey research: no two people are alike, yet we combine data from many people to understand larger trends and patterns. Lipsey and Wilson (2001b) observed that studies have "personalities"; that is, they consist of interrelated webs of substantive and methodological features, and they take on distinct characteristics.

As in social surveys, whether a meta-analysis should have a homogeneous or heterogeneous sample of studies depends on its central research questions and objectives. Meta-analysts have argued that it is sensible to combine apples and oranges if we are interested in fruits (Rosenthal & DiMatteo, 2001). Some heterogeneity is desirable when reviewers want to examine potential subgroups (apples versus oranges) or moderators of effects. Caution is needed when reviewers are making inferences about potential moderators, however, as intervention, sample, and methodological features are often confounded within studies in a review.

It is important to note that meta-analyses are not always conducted within a systematic review framework. In fact many (if not most) published meta-analyses in social work and psychology are not based on systematic reviews. Many meta-analyses rely on convenience samples of published studies; thus, they are vulnerable to the same dissemination and selection biases that plague traditional research reviews. The omission of valid unpublished studies tends to inflate overall estimates of effect size in meta-analysis (Hopewell, McDonald, Clarke, & Egger, 2007).

Systematic reviews do not always include meta-analysis. For example, the Cochrane Collaboration publishes systematic reviews that come up empty—that is, reviews that find no studies that meet the stated inclusion criteria. Without any data there is, of course, no opportunity for meta-analysis. Empty reviews can, however, provide good justification for investment in new research. When two or more quantitative studies are available, a systematic review can include meta-analysis. Some systematic reviews include multiple meta-analyses and several meta-analytic techniques. For example, most Cochrane and Campbell reviews employ separate meta-analyses (forest plots) for conceptually distinct outcomes.

Recent advancements in meta-analysis are the result of extensive development, application, and testing of new methods. Similarly, scholars have studied the reliability and validity of alternative methods for handling other steps in the review process, such as searching for studies and extracting data from study reports. The use of empirical evidence to improve and guide research reviews has fueled the growing science of research synthesis.

The Science and Practice of Research Synthesis

The science of research synthesis involves the development, testing, and use of reliable and valid methods in research reviews. Scientific approaches to research synthesis are not new. Early examples of systematic reviews and meta-analyses appeared in the fields of education and psychology (Chalmers, Hedges, & Cooper, 2002; Petticrew & Roberts, 2006). Following mounting empirical evidence of bias in the dissemination and synthesis of research results, multidisciplinary groups of scholars have worked to develop and test methods to minimize bias and error in the identification, analysis, and synthesis of research results. The Cochrane Collaboration and the Campbell Collaboration produce rigorous systematic reviews and meta-analyses in the fields of health care and social services respectively. Guidelines, standards, and procedures for these reviews (Higgins & Green, 2008) are based on empirical evidence of biases that affect the identification, critical appraisal, and synthesis of empirical research. Much of this methodological literature is contained in the Cochrane Library, and protocols for systematic reviews are published in the Cochrane and Campbell Libraries before these reviews are conducted. Explicit standards for reporting systematic reviews and meta-analyses have been developed by the PRISMA group (Liberati et al., 2009; Moher et al., 2009).

Elsewhere I have argued that the science and practice of research synthesis have not been closely connected (Littell, 2005, 2008). Many reviewers seem to be unaware of current standards for reviews and the methodological research upon which these standards are based. For example, some U.S. government agencies and professional associations promote research syntheses that deviate substantially from the evidence-based guidelines for reviews developed by the Cochrane Collaboration and the PRISMA group. Systematic reviews produced by the U.S. Evidence-Based Practice Centers (funded by the U.S. Agency for Healthcare Research and Quality) follow transparent rules and procedures, but these rules and procedures are not always informed by the best empirical evidence about the review process. Some Evidence-Based Practice Centers routinely ignore unpublished studies, despite evidence that this practice is likely to produce biased results (Hopewell et al., 2007).

Many research reviews have been conducted to determine whether certain interventions work. As Gandhi and colleagues (2006) noted, some prominent lists of evidence-based practices seem to have low standards, requiring only one or two trials with evidence of positive effects. Most of these lists rely on tests of statistical significance in the primary studies and pay little attention to potential methodological problems in randomized controlled trials.

The following example drawn from my own work illustrates the gap between the science and practice of research synthesis and shows that different review methods can lead to very different conclusions.

SYSTEMATIC REVIEW AND META-ANALYSIS: AN EXAMPLE

My colleagues and I conducted a systematic review and meta-analysis of effects of multisystemic therapy for families of youth with social, emotional, and behavioral problems. Initially developed in juvenile justice and later extended to mental health and other settings, multisystemic therapy is a home- and community-based intervention that is widely used to prevent out-of-home placement and improve youth and family functioning (Henggeler, Schoenwald, Borduin, Rowland, & Cunningham, 1998; Henggeler, Schoenwald, Rowland, & Cunningham, 2002).

Conducted under the auspices of the Cochrane and Campbell Collaborations, our review included randomized controlled trials of licensed multisystemic therapy programs conducted in any country and published before 2003 (we are in the process of updating this review with new data). We screened 266 titles and abstracts, retrieved ninety-five full-text reports, identified thirty-five studies (some with multiple reports, many that were unfinished), and found eight studies that met our inclusion criteria. Details of the search procedures are provided in Littell, Popa, & Forsythe (2005). Six of the eight studies were conducted by multisystemic therapy program developers in the United States, one was conducted at four sites in Norway (with data analysis conducted in collaboration with multisystemic therapy developers), and one study was conducted by an independent team at four sites in Ontario, Canada. Our analysis of multiple reports on these studies showed that there were problems with the implementation and analysis of randomized designs in most studies (for example, failure to conduct intent-to-treat analysis, and the use of unstandardized observation periods).

Separate meta-analyses were performed for twenty-one conceptually distinct outcomes, including measures of incarceration, hospitalization, delinquency, drug use, peer relations, psychiatric symptoms, and family functioning. Multisystemic therapy had no discernable advantages over regular juvenile justice services in the most rigorous trial (the independent study in Ontario, which was the largest trial and the only study that conducted full intent-to-treat analysis). Other studies indicated that multisytemic therapy has some positive effects, but results were inconsistent across studies, and there were no outcomes on which multisystemic therapy had overall positive, significant results.

Results of this systematic review are at odds with widespread claims about the effectiveness of multisystemic therapy. To explore these discrepancies, I conducted an analysis of other published reviews of the research on this treatment modality (Littell, 2008). Analysis of thirty-seven published reviews of research on multisystemic therapy showed that most reviews used narrative summaries of convenience samples of published studies (Littell, 2008). Almost all of these reviews concluded that multisystemic therapy works—that is, researchers concluded that the approach was superior to the other interventions to which it was compared. Some reviewers concluded that multisystemic therapy was consistently effective across populations, problems, and settings. These reviews did not use systematic strategies to find, critically appraise, and synthesize results of relevant studies. To better understand how reviewers had appraised evidence, I conducted a detailed analysis of a single multisystemic therapy trial and analyzed the ways in which the results of that trial were characterized in published reviews (Littell, 2008).

In 1987, Brunk, Henggeler, and Whelan published a report on a study in which forty-three families of abused and neglected children were randomly assigned to parent training groups or multisystemic therapy. Thirty-three families completed treatment and provided data on outcomes immediately after treatment (there were no follow-up data). Outcome data were obtained on thirty scales and subscales. With two-tailed tests and a significance level set at p<.05, by chance we would expect to find statistically significant results favoring one of the groups on 1.5 of the thirty measures. Results of the Brunk study showed differences that favored the multisystemic therapy group on five outcome measures, differences that favored the parent training group on two measures, and no differences on twenty-two measures; results were not reported for one outcome measure.

Brunk and her colleagues (1987) provided subgroup means for pre- and post-tests for all seven outcome measures that were statistically significant, but provided these details for only twelve of the twenty-two nonsignificant results. Full reporting of significant results and incomplete reporting of nonsignificant results is an example of outcome reporting bias.

In the abstract of their article, Brunk and her colleagues (1987) detailed five conclusions from the results of the study: that the parent training group performed better on measures of parental social isolation; that the multisystemic therapy group performed better on measures of parent-child interaction; and that both groups showed reductions in psychiatric symptoms, stress, and problem severity (there were no significant between-group differences in the last three domains). This appears to be a balanced summary of the study's results.

Content analysis of published reviews of the Brunk study suggested that reviewers provided unbalanced summaries of it (Littell, 2008). Most reviewers used a single phrase to describe the results of the Brunk investigation, highlighting results that favored the multisystemic therapy group. These reviews failed to convey the relative advantages and disadvantages of each intervention, and the equivalent results of the two treatments in some domains. Confirmation bias is a plausible explanation for a selective focus on outcomes that favored one treatment over another.

Prior to 2010, the Brunk study was the only controlled trial of multisystemic therapy in cases of child abuse and neglect. Yet some reviewers and experts cited this study—of thirty-three families with mixed post-treatment results and no follow-up data—as evidence that multi-system therapy is effective in cases of child abuse and neglect (e.g., Burns, Schoenwald, Burchard, Faw, & Santos, 2000; Kazdin & Weisz, 1998). This conclusion is misleading.

THE HAZARDS OF HAPHAZARD REVIEWS

It is clear that research reviews that use shoddy materials and inferior construction techniques cannot provide a firm foundation for practice and policy. Petticrew and Roberts (2006) termed traditional review methods "haphazard" because traditional reviews do not follow detailed protocols; traditional methods for finding, critically appraising, and synthesizing data from multiple studies are not transparent; and these methods are vulnerable to well-known sources of bias.

Traditional reviews tend to rely on biased samples of studies and do not provide consistent or thorough assessment of the methodological qualities of included studies. Without methods to deal with publication and dissemination biases, haphazard reviews are likely to miss rigorous unpublished studies that had negative or nonsignificant results, as well as nonsignificant results obtained in published studies. Thus haphazard reviews are likely to present inflated effect sizes that favor prominent programs. Narrative descriptions of studies are insufficient as they do not reliably capture important qualities of primary studies and do not provide careful assessment of the risk of bias in component studies.

Our natural methods of filtering, analyzing, and synthesizing complex information are not always reliable. The human brain is adept at pattern recognition, but it can identify patterns that are irrelevant. Cognitive algebra and vote counting are clearly insufficient for complex mathematical tasks, such as the weighting of data to account for variations in sample size and precision. Further, it is often difficult for people (including researchers) to change firmly held beliefs, even when faced with data that contradict these views. Haphazard review methods lack the structure, safeguards, and sophistication needed to produce unbiased conclusions.

Fortunately, better alternatives are available. Systematic reviews and meta-analyses can use the science of research synthesis to produce credible summaries of empirical research.

Conclusions

Research synthesis is an important tool for evidence-based practice, but there are wide variations in the quality of research reviews. Since different review methods can lead to very different conclusions, it is important to identify and use credible reviews to shape policy and practice.

It has been argued that we already know what works and that the problem is that effective interventions are underutilized. However, much of the conventional wisdom about what works—as represented by lists of evidence-based practices and prominent model programs— has been arrived at with haphazard review methods.

Haphazard reviews do not provide a firm foundation for practice or policy. An evidence base created with haphazard review methods is like a house of cards: an unstable structure built with the veneer of statistically significant results from selected, nonrepresentative samples of studies. Traditional narrative reviews do not stand up to close inspection because they do not meet current scientific standards for research synthesis. For these reasons, the practice of compiling evidence using haphazard traditional methods should be abandoned.

Systematic reviews and meta-analyses can use methods that correct common errors and biases in the selection, assessment, and synthesis of results across studies. Systematic reviews use detailed protocols, careful selection and analysis of studies, and state-of-the-art methods for research synthesis. They provide more accurate and reliable syntheses than other methods; hence, they should replace traditional narrative reviews and stand-alone meta-analyses that are conducted outside of the systematic review framework. To ensure their integrity, systematic reviews and meta-analyses should follow current guidelines and standards. These are contained in the Cochrane Handbook (Higgins & Green, 2008) and the PRISMA statement (Moher, Liberati, Tetzlaff, Altman, & The PRISMA Group, 2009; Liberati et al., 2009).

Systematic reviews and meta-analyses vary in scope. Narrowly focused reviews are useful for testing assumptions about the effects of model programs, like multisytemic therapy. Broader reviews can be used to identify common elements of effective programs and build better intervention theories to guide program development and evaluation design (Lipsey, 1997). For example, across a wide range of programs and practices in juvenile justice, Lipsey (2009) found that more positive outcomes were associated with a therapeutic intervention philosophy, work with high-risk offenders, and the quality of program implementation. However, systematic reviews and meta-analyses are not limited to questions about intervention effects. These reviews can assess the incidence and prevalence of various conditions, trends over time, associations between variables, and the accuracy of diagnostic and prognostic instruments.

Rigorous research synthesis is necessary but insufficient for EBP. A careful summary of research results will not tell decision makers what to do in light of the evidence. As Davies, Gibbs, Sackett, and others have noted, decision makers must consider other important factors, including policy goals, intervention goals, consumers' values and preferences (including cultural differences), clinical expertise, program costs and available resources, and legal and ethical constraints (Davies, 2004; Gibbs, 2003; Sackett et al., 1996; Straus et al., 2005). These factors will shape the ways in which research syntheses are used in practice and policy.

For example, in light of the evidence that multisystemic therapy is not consistently more or less effective than other alternative approaches, decision makers have a number of options. In Ontario, policy makers cancelled multisystemic therapy services because they were more costly and no more effective than regular juvenile justice services there. In Sweden, where equivalent outcomes were found for usual services and multisystemic therapy (Sundell et al., 2008), policy makers have retained multisystemic therapy, even though it entails increased service costs (Olsson, 2008), because clinicians and administrators value the structure and documentation that this intervention offers. Each of these decisions is based on the best available evidence and other important considerations. Given two interventions with comparable outcomes, defensible choices can be on the basis of consumer preferences, clinical expertise, resource constraints, cultural preferences, and other considerations.

Systematic reviews and meta-analyses need to be updated every few years to take into account growing bodies of evidence and to avoid premature closure of inquiry. Similarly, evidence about the reliability and accuracy of review methods is building, and new methodological reviews will help to shape the science and future of research synthesis.

References

Anzures-Cabrera, J., & Higgins, J. P. T. (2010). Graphical displays for meta-analysis: An overview with suggestions for practice. *Research Synthesis Methods* 1(1): 66–80.

APA Publications and Communications Board Working Group on Journal Article Reporting Standards. (2008). Reporting standards for research in psychology: Why do we need them? What might they be? *American Psychologist*, 63(9), 839–851.

Brunk, M., Henggeler, S. W., & Whelan, J. P. (1987). A comparison of multisystemic therapy and parent training in the brief treatment of child abuse and neglect. *Journal of Consulting and Clinical Psychology*, 55(2), 171–178.

Burns, B. J., Schoenwald, S. K., Burchard, J. D., Faw, L., & Santos, A. B. (2000). Comprehensive community-based interventions for youth with severe emotional disorders: Multisystemic therapy and the wraparound process. *Journal of Child and Family Studies*, 9(3), 283–314.

Chalmers, I., Hedges, L. V., and Cooper, H. (2002). A brief history of research synthesis. *Evaluation and the Health Professions, 25*(3), 12–37.

Chambless, D. L., Baker, M. J., Baucom, D. H., Beutler, L. E., Calhoun, K. S., Crits-Christoph, P., . . . Woody, S. R. (1998). Update on empirically validated therapies, II. *The Clinical Psychologist, 51*(1), 3–16.

Chambless, D. L., & Ollendick, T. H. (2001). Empirically supported psychological interventions: Controversies and evidence. *Annual Review of Psychology, 52,* 685–716.

Chan, A.-W., & Altman, D. G. (2005). Identifying outcome reporting bias in randomised trials on PubMed: Review of publications and survey of authors. *British Medical Journal, 330*(7494), 753.

Chan, A.-W., Hróbjartsson, A., Haar, M. T., Gøtzsche, P. C., & Altman, D. G. (2004). Empirical evidence for selective reporting of outcomes in randomized trials: Comparison of protocols to published articles. *JAMA, 291*(20), 2457–2465.

Chan, A.-W., Krleza-Jeric, K., Schmid, I., & Altman, D. (2004). Outcome reporting bias in randomized trials funded by the Canadian Institute of Health Research. *Canadian Medical Association Journal, 171*(4), 735–740.

Cooper, H. M., Hedges, L. V., & Valentine, J. C. (2009). *The handbook of research synthesis and meta-analysis* (2nd ed.). New York, NY: Russell Sage Foundation.

Davies, P. (2004). Is evidence-based government possible? Presented at the Fourth Annual Campbell Collaboration Colloquium, Washington, DC, February 19, 2004. Retrieved from http://www.nationalschool.gov.uk/policyhub/evidence_hotlinks/

Deeks, J. J., Dinnes, J., D'Amico, R., Sowden, A. J., Sakarovitch, C., Song, F., Petticrew, M., . . . Altman, D. G. (2003). Evaluating non-randomised intervention studies. *Health Technology Assessment, 7*(27), iii–x, 1–173.

Dickersin, K. (2005). Publication bias: Recognizing the problem, understanding its origins and scope, and preventing harm. In H. R. Rothstein, A. J. Sutton, & M. Borenstein (Eds.), *Publication bias in meta-analysis: Prevention, assessment, and adjustments* (pp. 11–33). Chichester, UK: John Wiley & Sons.

Dwan, K., Altman, D. G., Arnaiz, J. A., Bloom, J., Chan, A., Cronin, E., . . . Williamson, P. R. (2008). Systematic review of the empirical evidence of study publication bias and outcome reporting bias. *PLoS ONE, 3*(8), e3081.

Egger, M., & Smith, G. D. (1998). Bias in location and selection of studies. *British Medical Journal, 316*(7124), 61–66.

Egger, M., Zellweger-Zahner, T., Schneider, M., Junker, C., Lengeler, C., & Antes, G. (1997). Language bias in randomised controlled trials published in English and German. *The Lancet, 350*(9074), 326–329.

Flay, B. R., Biglan, A., Boruch, R. F., Castro, F. G., Gottfredson, D., Kellam, S., . . . Ji, P. (2005). Standards of evidence: Criteria for efficacy, effectiveness and dissemination. *Prevention Science, 6,* 151–175.

Fugelsang, J., Stein, C., Green, A., & Dunbar, K. (2004). Theory and data interactions of the scientific mind: Evidence from the molecular and the cognitive laboratory. *Canadian Journal of Experimental Psychology, 58,* 132–141.

Gandhi, A. G., Murphy-Graham, E., Petrosino, A., Chrismer, S. S., & Weiss, C. H. (2006). The devil is in the details: Examining the evidence for "proven" school-based drug abuse prevention programs. *Evaluation Review, 31*(1), 43–74.

Gibbs, L., & Gambrill, E. (2002). Evidence-based practice: Counterarguments to objections. *Research on Social Work Practice, 12*(3), 452–476.

Gibbs, L. E. (2003). *Evidence-based practice for the helping professions: A practical guide with integrated multimedia.* Pacific Grove, CA: Brooks/Cole–Thompson Learning.

Gorman, D. M. (2003). The best of practices, the worst of practices: The making of science-based primary prevention programs. *Psychiatric Services, 54*(8), 1087–1089.

Harden, A., Brunton, G., Fletcher, A., & Oakley, A. (2009). Teenage pregnancy and social disadvantage: Systematic review integrating controlled trials and qualitative studies. *British Medical Journal, 339,* b4254.

Henggeler, S. W., Schoenwald, S., Borduin, C., Rowland, M., & Cunningham, P. (1998). *Multisystemic treatment of antisocial behavior in children and adolescents.* New York, NY: Guilford.

Henggeler, S. W., Schoenwald, S. K., Rowland, M. D., & Cunningham, P. B. (2002). *Serious emotional disturbances in children and adolescents: Multisystemic therapy.* New York, NY: Guilford.

Higgins, J., & Green, S. (Eds.). (2008). *Cochrane handbook for systematic reviews of interventions.* Chichester, UK: John Wiley & Sons.

Hopewell, S., Clarke, M., Stewart, L., & Tierney, J. (2001). Time to publication for results of clinical trials. *Cochrane Database of Methodology Reviews 2001, Issue 3.* Art. No.: MR000011. DOI: 10.1002/14651858.MR000011.

Hopewell, S., Loudon, K., Clarke, M. J., Oxman, A. D., & Dickersin, K. (2009). Publication bias in clinical trials due to statistical significance or direction of trial results. *Cochrane Database of Systematic Reviews 2009, Issue 1.* Art. No.: MR000006. DOI: 10.1002/14651858.MR000006.pub3.

Hopewell, S., McDonald, S., Clarke, M., & Egger, M. (2007). Grey literature in meta-analyses of randomized trials of health care interventions. *The Cochrane Database of Systematic Reviews, 2007* (Issue 2), Art. No.: MR000010. DOI: 10.1002/14651858.MR000010.pub3.

Jensen, P. S., Weersing, R., Hoagwood, K. E., & Goldman, E. (2005). What is the evidence for evidence-based treatments? A hard look at our soft underbelly. *Mental Health Services Research, 7*(1), 53–74.

Jørgensen, A. W., Hilden, J., & Gøtzsche, P. C. (2006). Cochrane reviews compared with industry supported meta-analyses and other meta-analyses of the same drugs: Systematic review. *British Medical Journal, 333,* 782–785.

Kazdin, A. E., & Weisz, J. R. (1998). Identifying and developing empirically supported child and adolescent treatments. *Journal of Consulting and Clinical Psychology, 66*(1), 19–36.

Liberati, A., Altman, D. G., Tetzlaff, J., Mulrow, C., Gøtzsche, P. C., Ioannidis, J. P. A., . . . Moher, D. (2009). The PRISMA statement for reporting systematic reviews and meta-analyses of studies that evaluate health care interventions: Explanation and elaboration. *PLoS Med, 6*(7), e1000100.

Lipsey, M. W. (1997). What can you build with thousands of bricks? Musings on the cumulation of knowledge in program evaluation. *New Directions for Evaluation, 76,* 7–23.

Lipsey, M. W. (2009). The primary factors that characterize effective interventions with juvenile offenders: A meta-analytic overview. *Victims and Offenders, 4,* 124–147.

Lipsey, M. W., & Wilson, D. B. (2001a). *Practical meta-analysis.* Thousand Oaks, CA: Sage.

Lipsey, M. W., & Wilson, D. B. (2001b). The way in which intervention studies have "personality" and why it is important to meta-analysis. *Evaluation and the Health Professions, 24*(3), 236–254.

Littell, J. H. (2005). Lessons from a systematic review of effects of multisystemic therapy. *Children and Youth Services Review, 27,* 445–463.

Littell, J. H. (2008). Evidence-based or biased? The quality of published reviews of evidence-based practices. *Children and Youth Services Review, 30,* 1299–1317.

Littell, J. H., Corcoran, J., & Pillai, V. (2008). *Systematic reviews and meta-analysis.* New York, NY: Oxford University Press.

Littell, J. H., Popa, M., & Forsythe, B. (2005). Multisystemic therapy for social, emotional, and behavioral problems in youth aged 10–17. *Cochrane Database of Systematic Reviews* (4). & Sons, Ltd.

Luborsky, L., Diguer, L., Seligman, D. A., Rosenthal, R., Krause, E. D., Johnson, S., . . . Schweizer, E. (1999). The researcher's own therapy allegiances: A "wild card" in comparisons of treatment efficacy. *Clinical Psychology: Science and Practice, 6*(1), 95–106.

Mahoney, M. J. (1977). Publication prejudices: An experimental study of confirmatory bias in the peer review system. *Cognitive Therapy and Research, 1*(2), 161–175.

Mihalic, S., Fagan, A., Irwin, K., Ballard, D., & Elliott, D. (2004). *Blueprints for Violence Prevention* (No. NCJ 204274). Washington, DC: U.S. Department of Justice, Office of Juvenile Justice and Delinquency Prevention.

Moher, D., Hopewell, S., Montori, V., Gøtzsche, P., Devereaux, P. J., Elbourne, D., . . . Altman, D. G. (2010). CONSORT 2010 explanation and elaboration: Updated guidelines for reporting parallel group randomised trials. *British Medical Journal, 340,* c869.

Moher, D., Liberati, A., Tetzlaff, J., Altman, D. G., & The PRISMA Group. (2009). Preferred reporting items for systematic reviews and meta-analyses: The PRISMA statement. *PLoS Med, 6*(7), e1000097.

Nickerson, R. S. (1998). Confirmation bias: A ubiquitous phenomenon in many guises. *Review of General Psychology, 2,* 175–220.

Olsson, T. (2008). Crossing the quality chasm? The short-term effectiveness and efficiency of MST in Sweden: An example of evidence-based practice applied to social work. (Unpublished dissertation). Lund, Sweden: Lund University.

Patrick, T. B., Demiris, G., Folk, L., Moxley, D. E., Mitchell, J. A., & Tao, D. (2004). Evidence-based retrieval in evidence-based medicine. *Journal of the Medical Library Association, 92*(2), 196–199.

Petticrew, M., & Roberts, H. (2006). *Systematic reviews in the social sciences: A practical guide.* Oxford, UK: Blackwell.

Rosenthal, R., & DiMatteo, M. R. (2001). Meta-analysis: Recent developments in quantitative methods for literature reviews. *Annual Review of Psychology, 52,* 59–82.

Rothstein, H., Sutton, A. J., & Bornstein, M. (2005). *Publication bias in meta-analysis: Prevention, assessment, and adjustments.* Chichester, UK: John Wiley & Sons.

Sackett, D. L., Rosenberg, W. M. C., Gray, J. A. M., Haynes, R. B., & Richardson, W. S. (1996). Evidence based medicine: What it is and what it isn't. *British Medical Journal, 312,* 71–72.

Scherer, R. W., Langenberg, P., & von-Elm, E. (2007). Full publication of results initially presented in abstracts. *Cochrane Database of Systematic Reviews 2007,* Issue 2. Art. No.: MR000005. DOI: 10.1002/14651858.MR000005.pub3.

Schulz, K. F., Altman, D. G., & Moher, D. (2010). CONSORT 2010 statement: Updated guidelines for reporting parallel group randomised trials. *British Medical Journal, 340,* c332.

Schulz, K. F., & Grimes, D. A. (2002). Allocation concealment in randomised trials: Defending against deciphering. *The Lancet, 359,* 614–618.

Shadish, W. R., Cook, T. D., & Campbell, D. T. (2002). *Experimental and quasi-experimental designs for general causal inference.* Boston, MA: Houghton Mifflin.

Song, F., Parekh-Bhurke, S., Hooper, L., Loke, Y., Ryder, J., Sutton, A., . . . Harvey, I. (2009). Extent of publication bias in different categories of research cohorts: A meta-analysis of empirical studies. *BMC Medical Research Methodology, 9*(1), 79.

Straus, S. E., Richardson, W. S., Glasziou, P., & Haynes, R. B. (2005). *Evidence-based medicine: How to practice and teach EBM* (3rd ed.). Edinburgh, Scotland: Churchill Livingston.

Substance Abuse and Mental Health Services Administration. (2007). *National registry of evidence-based programs and practices.* Retrieved from http://www.nrepp.samhsa.gov/

Sundell, K., Hansson, K., Löfholm, C. A., Olsson, T., Gustle, L., & Kadesjo, C. (2008). The transportability of multisystemic therapy to Sweden: Short-term results from a randomized trial of conduct-disordered youth. *Journal of Family Psychology, 22*(3), 550–560.

Thomas, J., Harden, A., Oakley, A., Oliver, S., Sutcliffe, K., Rees, R., . . . Kavanagh, J. (2004). Integrating qualitative research with trials in systematic reviews: An example from public health. *British Medical Journal, 328,* 1010–1012.

Torgerson, C. J. (2006). Publication bias: The Achilles' heel of systematic reviews? *British Journal of Educational Studies, 54*(1), 89–102.

Wells, K., & Littell, J. H. (2009). Study quality assessment in systematic reviews of intervention effects. *Research on Social Work Practice, 19,* 53–62.

Williamson, P., Altman, D., Gamble, C., Dodd, S., Dwan, K., & Kirkham, J. (2006). Outcome reporting bias in meta-analysis. Presentation at the Fourteenth Cochrane Colloquium, Dublin, Ireland.

Wilson, D. B., & Lipsey, M. W. (2001). The role of method in treatment effectiveness research: Evidence from meta-analysis. *Psychological Methods, 6*(4), 413–429.

PART II

Dissemination and Implementation

CHAPTER SIX

Implementing and Sustaining Evidence-Based Practice: Case Example of Leadership, Organization, Infrastructure, and Consultation

Stanley G. McCracken, Elisabeth Kinnel, Fred Steffen,
Margaret Vimont, and Charlotte Mallon

A rapidly growing amount of well-designed treatment outcome research is available to inform clinical decision making. However there continues to be a significant lag between completion of the research and its use in clinical practice. Implementation has lagged behind evidence, and this is particularly true of evidence-based practice (EBP) as a process or as an approach to practice. There are few studies of sustaining EBP in community practice settings. This chapter will describe the effort to implement and sustain evidence-based practice in a large metropolitan social service agency.

Background and Literature Review

Some definitions of EBP describe it as a product consisting of evidence-supported interventions, guidelines, and treatments (e.g., Chambless, 1998; Eddy, 2005; Rosen & Proctor, 2003), and others present it as a process or an approach to practice (e.g., Mullen & Streiner, 2004; Sackett, Straus, Richardson, Rosenberg, & Haynes, 2000; Shlonsky & Gibbs, 2004). In our project, we sought to implement EBP as an orientation to practice that values evidence as a resource for clinical decision making, while recognizing that evidence alone is never sufficient for that purpose (Berlin & Marsh, 1993; Guyatt & Rennie, 2002; Weisz & Addis, 2006). Specifically, we viewed EBP as a process in which a practitioner or team of practitioners use their expertise to integrate client clinical states, needs, circumstances, preferences, culture, values, and actions with the best available evidence (for example, research literature and systematic data from practice) in a specific organizational and environmental (practice and community) context (Council for Training in Evidence-Based Behavioral Practice, 2008; Haynes, Devereaux, & Guyatt, 2002; Regehr, Stern, & Shlonsky, 2007).

We chose this conceptual definition for several reasons. First, it recognizes that EBP is not solely about the research, though it places a high value on locating and using the best available evidence, whatever the source (Gellis & Reid, 2004). Rather than focusing on implementation of one or more specific evidence-supported interventions, we sought to provide staff with the skills to locate such interventions that are relevant to their specific practice needs. Second, it recognizes the central role of the client system as a partner in the clinical decision-making process (Norcross, Hogan, & Koocher, 2008). Client clinical states, needs, and circumstances initiate the practice question, and client preferences, values, and actions determine the choice of intervention.

Third, this definition of EBP respects the expertise of practitioners at all stages, beginning with engagement, formation of the therapeutic alliance, and assessment of the client through all the steps of the EBP process and ending with termination (McCracken & Marsh, 2008). Finally, it acknowledges the fact that services will be provided in the context of a particular agency with specific organizational structures, community and stakeholder interests, funding and service priorities, and available resources (Denis, Hébert, Langley, Lozeau, & Trottier, 2002).

We followed Sackett and colleagues (2000) in operationalizing EBP as involving five steps:

1. Convert the need for information into an answerable question.
2. Track down with maximum efficiency the best evidence with which to answer that question.
3. Critically appraise that evidence for its validity and usefulness.
4. Integrate the critical appraisal with practitioner clinical expertise and with the client values, preferences, and clinical circumstances, and apply the results to practice.
5. Evaluate the outcome.

The literature on implementation has focused primarily on implementation of evidence-supported interventions (e.g., Carroll et al.,

2006; Fixsen, Naoom, Blase, Friedman, & Wallace, 2005; Greenhalgh, Robert, MacFarlane, Bate, & Kyriakidou, 2004), and the reactions of practitioners and others to the use of research and evidence-supported interventions in their practice (e.g., Aarons & Palinkas, 2007; Blasinsky, Goldman, & Unutzer, 2006; Dulcan, 2005; Nelson, Steele, & Mize, 2006; Proctor et al., 2007). Although the findings of specific studies have varied, several consistent themes and concerns have emerged. One set of concerns has to do with the interventions themselves. Key among these is whether efficacious interventions can be generalized to real-world clients and settings (Aarons & Palinkas, 2007; Nelson et al., 2006). A second set has to do with clinicians: their lack of knowledge or skills, insufficient time for learning and mastery of the approach, and a general hostility toward evidence-supported interventions (Cook, Biyanova, & Coyne, 2009; Rapp et al., 2008; Willenbring et al., 2004).

In general, provider attitudes toward evidence-supported interventions and EBP have been reported as both favorable and suspicious. McColl and colleagues (1998) reported that general medical practitioners welcomed evidence-based medicine and agreed that it improved patient care. On the other hand they saw lack of time and access to resources as barriers to practicing evidence-based medicine and felt that the best way to move toward it in general medical practice was to use evidence-based guidelines or proposals developed by colleagues (McColl, Smith, White, & Field, 1998). Guyatt and associates (2000) concluded that not all trainees are interested in obtaining advanced evidence-based medicine skills and that some would prefer using evidence-based summaries generated by others and evidence-based guidelines or protocols (Guyatt, Meade, Jaeschke, Cook, & Haynes, 2000). It has been reported that although guidelines are considered educational tools that can improve quality of care and provide structure to therapy, they are also seen as inflexible and as lacking adequate attention to the therapeutic relationship (Godley, White, Diamond, Passetti, & Titus, 2001; Nelson et al., 2006; Willenbring et al., 2004).

Finally, a variety of organizational and administrative concerns have been identified, such as lack of administrative support for the use of evidence-supported interventions, lack of staff previously trained in the interventions, and lack of funding for training and implementation (Aarons & Palinkas, 2007; Blasinsky et al., 2006; McCracken & Corrigan, 2004). Studies that have examined reactions to the process of EBP mirror concerns raised about evidence-supported interventions, such as lack of research relevant to real-world practice; lack of access to the full text of research articles; and lack of time and skills to formulate questions, conduct searches, and evaluate the evidence (e.g., Bellamy, Bledsoe, Mullen, Fang, & Manuel, 2008; Dulcan, 2005).

A number of authors have reviewed the implementation literature and have made recommendations about adoption of practice innovations, many of which may be applied to implementation of EBP (Backer, Liberman, & Kuehnel, 1986; Bradley et al., 2004; McCracken & Corrigan, 2004; Rosenheck, 2001). Ongoing, active, and visible support from agency leaders as well as buy-in from line-level staff are essential to successful implementation. Thus leaders need to model interest and enthusiasm in an innovation and to delegate the resources necessary for staff to learn and use it. There must be a fit between the innovation and agency values, mission, goals, needs, and patterns of practice. It must be clear to staff that the innovation makes sense for their agency and their practice. If the innovation does not fit with and help to further the mission of the agency, it is unlikely that either staff or administrators will believe that learning and implementing it is worth the expense and effort.

With respect to training, there is value in training staff in teams rather than individually (Bellamy et al., 2008; Corrigan & McCracken, 1997, 1999). Social service and health care agencies often deliver services in teams, and working in teams takes advantage of the fact that different staff have different areas of expertise. Training in teams divides tasks, time, and effort among several people. Finally, training staff in teams recognizes that staff turnover is a fact of life in social service agencies. If staff are trained as a team, several members of the team will have knowledge and skills to share with new staff members, and the work can progress.

It is also important to prepare the agency for change. Staff should be brought into the change process as early as possible, agency resources should be identified and allocated for the innovation, infrastructure to support and sustain the innovation should be put in place, and a mechanism for gathering and disseminating data on implementation and outcomes should be developed (Bradley et al., 2004; McCracken & Corrigan, 2004).

A number of models of dissemination and implementation have been proposed. Backer (1993) stated that the literature identifies four conditions necessary for effective technology transfer: appropriate innovations must be brought to the attention of the organization and must be accessible for dissemination, evidence must show that the innovation is both effective and feasible to implement, resources must be adequate for implementation, and interventions must be provided that encourage staff and organizations to change.

Simpson (2002) proposed a four-stage model for transferring research to practice. His stages are exposure to the technology through training; adoption, or an intention to try the innovation; implementation in a trial period to test the innovation's feasibility and potential;

and practice, in which the innovation is incorporated into regular use and sustained, perhaps even modified. Simpson notes that while adoption may be a formal decision by program leaders, it also includes a personal level of commitment on the part of individual staff about whether the innovation is appropriate and should be tried (2002).

Rosenheck (2001) began his four-stage model with an individual or group making a decision to implement the innovation in the organization. He distinguishes the scientific rationale for a new treatment from the broader set of systems factors (such as budget, politics, and organizational objectives) that influence the decision in a particular organization. The decision to implement is followed by initial implementation, sustained implementation, and either termination or transformation. Rosenheck states that effective implementation requires a clear, well-specified implementation decision with commitment of adequate resources; an operational definition of the target population, service delivery strategies, and desired outcomes; and objective monitoring and enforcement of adherence to program design (2001). A combination of internal and external developments can result in either transformation or termination of the intervention.

Rogers (2003) views diffusion as: "the process in which an innovation is communicated through certain channels over time among members of a social system," (p. 5). He proposed the diffusion of innovations theory to help practitioners to understand and organize this process. According to this theory, which is analogous to transtheoretical theory, or stages of change theory (Prochaska, DiClemente, & Norcross, 1992), the individual implementing the innovation progresses through five phases: the knowledge stage, in which an awareness and understanding of the innovation develops; the persuasion stage, in which leaders seek information so they can better understand the innovation and assess its compatibility with the organization and available resources; the decision stage, in which the individual or organization decides whether to adopt or reject the innovation; the implementation stage, in which the innovation is put into practice; and the confirmation stage, in which the innovation is integrated into routine practice, the benefits are assessed, and the innovation is promoted to others (Rogers, 2003). Reinvention, the modification of an innovation during the process of adoption and implementation, may occur during the implementation stage. Reinvention is not necessarily a bad thing, and it may lead to a faster rate of adoption and a higher level of sustainability (Rogers, 2003).

Each of these stages has potential barriers and solutions. For example, in the knowledge stage, a potential barrier to implementing EBP is the misconception that EBP advocates implementation of evidence-supported interventions as an alternative to clinical judgment or that it emphasizes technique while ignoring the therapeutic alliance (Dulcan, 2005; Pagoto et al., 2007).

Both theory and research on dissemination suggest that successful implementation of an innovation involves complex interaction of multiple sets of factors relating to the innovation, staff, leaders, the organization, and broad system and social contextual factors (Fitzgerald, Ferlie, Wood, & Hawkins, 2002). Several characteristics of EBP make dissemination difficult. For example, EBP requires a complex decision-making process involving a number of skills that may be unfamiliar to practitioners—for example, question formulation, electronic search, and research evaluation skills. Innovations that are perceived as complex and difficult to understand diffuse more slowly than those that do not require new skills and understanding (Rogers, 2003). This suggests that adopting and sustaining EBP will require addressing staff beliefs about the difficulty of doing EBP, developing user-friendly training to teach the new skills, and providing incentives to practice the skills until a basic level of proficiency is achieved.

Another characteristic that may make EBP difficult to disseminate is that there is no clear evidence that practitioners who use EBP in clinical decision making have better client outcomes or provide more efficient services than those who do not use EBP. Innovations with a greater perceived relative advantage diffuse more rapidly than those with less perceived relative advantage (Rogers, 2003). At this time, the perceived advantage of EBP may be less about demonstrated improvement in services (an empirical question yet to be answered) than about the perception that EBP may facilitate the process of program development, that it may facilitate critical thinking and problem solving among staff, and even that agencies who use EBP may be viewed more favorably by referral or funding sources. On the other hand, there are characteristics of EBP that could facilitate dissemination efforts in the right situation. For example, EBP may be well received in agencies in which staff and leaders have a strong commitment to being a learning organization or that see themselves as innovators on the cutting edge of new technologies and interventions.

EBP at Jewish Child and Family Services: A Case Study

Jewish Child and Family Services (JCFS) is a large metropolitan Chicago social service agency with many different programs that serve children, adults, and families with diverse health and mental health needs. Agency staff have differing levels of education and training, from bachelor's to doctoral level; come from many professional backgrounds, including social work, psychology, counseling, teaching, and occupational therapy); and have expertise in a variety of areas, including early childhood development, child and adult mental health, and education. Programs are similarly diverse and include counseling centers, a therapeutic day school, programs serving children with autism, and services for families with adopted and foster children.

JCFS was formed in 2006 from a merger of two agencies, the Jewish Children's Bureau and Jewish Family and Community Service. This merger took place shortly after the EBP training program was initiated at the Jewish Children's Bureau. It combined two agencies with a long-standing institutional commitment to learning and staff development and an extensive training program for psychology and social work students.

Shortly before initial contact in 2005 between the consultant (Stanley McCracken) and the agency's associate executive director (who will be referred to as the EBP champion), the Jewish Children's Bureau had instituted a Center for Practice Excellence, which was designed to link to the agency's utilization review and continuous quality improvement (CQI) groups and to agency-wide training coordination. Through this network, client outcome and staff data from within the agency, as well as research from external sources could be disseminated for use by staff in various programs. A variety of projects grew out of the new Center for Practice Excellence, including a grant to train staff to implement trauma-informed services (awarded by the state Department of Child and Family Services), a cognitive behavioral training project, and other ongoing training for students and new staff. Professional staff beginning employment at JCFS have a three-year training program through the Center for Practice Excellence that covers such topics as psychopharmacology, substance use, and diversity. The center functions in a constellation that includes multiple departments, with the intent to strengthen the EBP project's intra-agency connections.

INITIAL CONTACT AND EXPLORATION

Initial contact between the consultant and the EBP champion occurred during a daylong workshop on EBP that was conducted by the consultant in the spring of 2005. At the conclusion of the workshop, the champion indicated that he was considering whether EBP might be a useful component of the agency's clinical excellence project. After receiving approval from the agency director, the champion identified a staff person to be the project coordinator and to assist on the project, and the two attended a second EBP training session in the summer of 2005.

Following the second session, the consultant, the champion, and the project coordinator held a series of meetings in the summer and fall to plan implementation of EBP in the agency. The primary goals of the EBP project were to introduce a system in which emerging practices supported by empirical evidence would be identified and implemented and to organize and manualize the agency's own best practices. EBP was seen as a way to help practitioners choose empirically supported interventions and to identify situations in which there was a gap in the literature or in which the agency's own practices might be superior to what was currently supported by the literature. A series of leadership meetings and staff focus groups introduced the idea of EBP, linked it to the clinical excellence project and the training institute, and elicited staff reactions to and concerns about EBP.

Compatibility refers to the degree to which an innovation fits with the values, goals, past experiences, and needs of the organization. An innovation that is compatible with the values and norms of a social system will be adopted more readily than one that is incompatible (Rogers, 2003). Staff saw EBP as fitting well with the norms, values, and history of the Jewish Children's Bureau, such as the view of the agency as a learning organization and the goals of the clinical excellence project, and the agency's history of early adoption of evidence-supported interventions. EBP was seen as a way to identify evidence-supported interventions that could be adopted to improve service delivery. Finally, the Center for Practice Excellence and the agency's training system provided the foundation of an infrastructure for learning and implementing EBP.

In any dissemination project the questions that must be answered are: Why this innovation, at this time, in this setting? And what is the problem for which the innovation is the solution? For the EBP champion, there was a fit, but that didn't mean that other leaders or staff in the organization would agree. The next task in preparing the organization for change was to get buy-in from managers and staff. It was necessary to identify potential barriers to implementing EBP and to facilitate acceptance of change.

The impetus and resources for the EBP project came from within the agency. This situation differs from many agency-academic collaborations that are funded externally and in which the academic partner seeks out the agency partner. In this project, the first author was a consultant and trainer, not the project director; his role was to assist the EBP champion and others in implementing EBP at JCFS. At the same time he was interested in seeing whether EBP could be implemented on a large scale in a community agency, with resources that are available to practitioners working in real-world settings, and with minimal use of university resources (such as expensive search engines and electronic access to the full text of research articles). The consultant served as a trainer and was analogous to a linkage case manager rather than a direct provider of resources, unless the resources were otherwise unavailable. The concern was that if implementing and sustaining EBP in real-world settings relies on academic resources and external funds, it may have a poor chance of being widely used because the number of social service agencies far exceeds the capacity of universities to provide technical support.

PREPARING THE ORGANIZATION FOR CHANGE

The EBP champion presented his ideas to other senior administrators and team leaders and conducted a series of small-group meetings during the winter of 2005 to 2006. At these small-group meetings the champion and project coordinator elicited comments on the strengths and limitations of current programming, perceptions and concerns about EBP, and suggestions about what would be needed to do EBP (see figure 1).

In spite of the agency's history of implementing evidence-supported interventions, managers did not have a favorable impression of research. In addition to recalling that they disliked research courses

FIGURE 1   Staff Reactions to EBP Elicited during the Small-Group Meetings

Perceptions of research:
- Didn't like the research class in graduate school.
- Research is not connected to practice.
- Limited research on relevant questions, populations.
- Research skewed to certain kinds of interventions, unreliable and changing, and biased.

Perceptions of EBP:
- Fear that EBP would be rigid, stifle creativity, and be limited to one approach.
- Fear that EBP would be imposed without staff input.

Additional concerns about EBP:
- Lack of time and access to information.
- Loyalty to a particular theoretical perspective.
- Staff had a wish for EBP to be implemented in a thoughtful way that takes into account the work they already do and provides appropriate resources.
- Want EBP to guide, not control practice.
- Want depth, not overview.
- Want information and resource bank.

From McCracken, Steffen, & Hutchins, 2007,

during their professional training and being concerned that research was biased toward behavioral and cognitive behavioral interventions, they had reservations about the relevance and applicability of research to their agency. While team leaders did not actively oppose the EBP Project, they wanted their expertise to be respected. They did not want EBP to be narrowly focused on one approach or to be rigidly imposed without their input. Finally, team leaders were concerned about whether EBP was feasible, given limitations on time and on access to information, and whether they would receive the depth of training needed to implement EBP. A serendipitous event occurred during one of the group sessions. It turned out that one of the staff who participated in that session was a graduate of the first cohort of EBP master's students trained by the consultant. She had been hired after graduation and was an enthusiastic supporter of EBP.

Information gathered from these meetings was reflected in the plans for the training sessions, in terms of both the substance of the training and how the project was framed at the trainings. For example, principles of motivational interviewing were infused into the training, the central role of the therapeutic alliance and the therapist-client relationship was noted at the beginning of training, EBP was framed as a tool that could be used to identify interventions to augment existing practice methods, and the importance of practitioner expertise and client values and preferences were emphasized. Finally, the EBP grad was invited to present a case in which she had used EBP to identify an intervention to use with a family seen in the agency.

Two other events occurred at the same time these meetings and focus groups were being conducted. First, the EBP champion proposed including in the 2006 Jewish Children's Bureau annual plan an objective to incorporate the concepts, methods, and processes of EBP into the agency's ongoing operations and into the operations of the agency as a whole. Second, there was discussion of a merger between the Jewish Children's Bureau and the Jewish Family and Community Service—two agencies with different organizational characteristics, programs, and staff. One question that arose as a result of the merger proposal was whether to delay EBP training until after the merger had occurred or to move forward with the plan to train staff from the Jewish Children's Bureau. The decision was to move forward with training and to include staff from the Jewish Family and Community Service after the merger. A representative staff person from each of the key programs was chosen to participate in the first training cohort.

To be selected for participation in the training cohort, staff had to have been with the agency for several years; expect to stay in the agency for several more years; and be energetic, intellectually oriented, and likely to be interested. Because of the requirement that participants had been with the agency for several years, the first cohort were all graduate-level staff. The first training session was conducted in spring 2006, eleven months after initial contact between the consultant and the champion. Deciding to adopt the innovation, planning implementation, and preparing the organization for change lasted nearly a year.

The decision to implement EBP was made carefully and is best thought of as a process rather than an event. The process generally followed the sequence of stages outlined by Rogers (2003)—knowledge, persuasion, decision—though these stages often overlapped. Rather than a single decision being made about implementation, a number of decisions were involved and were made by several individuals or groups of individuals. The process reflected the "prolonged and negotiated process between individuals and groups" described by Fitzgerald and associates (Fitzgerald et al., 2002, p. 1441). The first decisions were about whether to gather more information or to continue with planning. Later decisions were about whether to move forward with implementation at the Jewish Children's Bureau or to delay until after the merger. The EBP champion and initiator of the process sought and received support from his superior and then from other administrators, managers, and team leaders. Even with support of leadership, buy-in from line-level staff was not assumed, it was solicited. Administrative support is necessary, but innovations have failed due to lack of support from those who ultimately are expected to use them.

The issues raised about research and EBP by the staff and leaders at the Jewish Children's Bureau were much the same as those identified in the research literature noted above. Staff and team leaders were concerned about the relevance of the research, the feasibility of EBP, a bias toward behavioral and cognitive approaches, and whether EBP would be imposed rigidly and without regard for their expertise. Providing staff and leaders with the opportunity to voice these concerns and to have them taken seriously was an important part of preparing the organization for change.

Care was taken in selecting the staff who would participate in the first training cohort. We were interested in identifying staff who had a commitment to the organization and who were energetic and interested in learning new approaches—characteristics of champions of change and of opinion leaders (Corrigan, Holmes, & Luchins, 1993; Rogers, 2003). Careful planning is important, but one should never underestimate the importance of being lucky. We were quite fortunate to have a recently trained graduate who supported EBP and was willing to be integrated into our early training.

Initial Training Sessions

We developed a curriculum to teach the first four steps of EBP in four three-hour sessions with homework between the sessions. In the first session we presented an overview of the EBP model, contrasted EBP with evidence-supported interventions, and formulated practice questions. In the second session we discussed planning and conducting an electronic search. In the third we covered evaluating the quality of evidence, and in the fourth, evaluating the usefulness of the evidence and applying it to practice. Initially the training was conducted in groups of about thirty, made up of teams from the major programs within the Jewish Children's Bureau, and training was done by the consultant, who used a combination of didactic and interactive methods and presented the material contextually. Training examples were taken from the agency itself, and participants were asked if they would consent to the use of their questions, electronic searches, and other products in the training of other staff and students.

Information gathered from the group meetings informed the content of training. For example, participants were asked at the beginning of the session what they had heard about EBP and what concerns they had about it both as an approach to practice and as an approach for their teams. It appeared that allowing people to vent concerns and skepticism carried over the pretraining discussions and may have calmed staff who either had felt similarly but hadn't said so or had wondered whether the subject or the sessions would become contentious.

We identified and discussed a number of common misconceptions about EBP: that EBP ignores the therapeutic relationship, that it is only about research and ignores practitioner expertise and client wishes, and that it is at odds with the realities of agency practice. Similarly, limitations of EBP were openly acknowledged and addressed, and solutions were discussed. For example:

> *Problem:* Learning and using EBP is time-consuming.
> *Solution:* EBP will be used primarily as a program development tool, and staff will work in teams to spread out the workload. EBP skills, like any other skills, take time to learn and become easier and more efficient with practice. The program coordinator will be available for consultation and assistance.
>
> *Problem:* It is difficult to obtain the full text of journal articles.
> *Solution:* The program coordinator will serve as a resource to obtain full text of articles from a local university. Student

interns may be asked to access papers from their school libraries. Local universities allow alumni to use the library. Community colleges allow public access to their libraries. Many community public libraries either subscribe to or can obtain through interlibrary loan copies of articles from professional journals. If necessary, the consultant will obtain a copy of the article.

Problem: There are many problem areas, populations, and settings for which there is minimal, if any, research.

Solution: EBP isn't limited only to large randomized controlled trials. Evidence may include other types of research. However, some problem-client combinations may require conducting more than one search. For example, it may be necessary to combine information from an effectiveness question about treatment of a particular problem with information from a descriptive or background question about a particular client group. In some cases, it may be necessary to acknowledge that there is no published research about a particular practice question.

Information from the meetings also influenced the style of training. the training was interactive, empowering, and infused with the principles of motivational interviewing. EBP was presented as a supplement to rather than a replacement for current decision-making models. The champion let the teams know that they would be given latitude to make decisions about their programs and that the goal was program excellence not rigid adherence to one specific model of practice. Finally, it was made clear that the teams would be provided with the resources and technical assistance needed to learn EBP.

Following the first session, teams were assigned to formulate practice questions from their programs. The project coordinator met with individual teams and provided assistance, as needed, with completing this and all future homework assignments.

Session two, on planning and conducting an electronic search, was logistically the most difficult of the sessions since we needed to conduct the training using computers with high-speed Internet access. Fortunately, we were able to arrange the first of these sessions at a location within the agency. We had staff work two to a computer, and we did our best to ensure that both people did some of the typing. This turned out to be a wise decision, since several participants who had little experience using the Internet to locate information found that they could use their newly learned search skills to find answers to personal questions as well as practice questions. In subsequent cohorts, we recommended that staff with more advanced search skills pair with staff who were less familiar with electronic searching so the more skilled partners could coach the less experienced staff members. We have relied on public-access databases (such as PubMed, ERIC, and Google Scholar) in trainings. Exceptions to this rule were when there were questions about subscription databases (such as PsychINFO, CINAHL, and Social Work Abstracts) from staff or students who were in school or had alumni access to online university library resources.

As part of session 2, we asked the staff person who was the EBP graduate to present the case in which she had used EBP to identify an intervention. She discussed all the elements of this case, including client assessment and question formulation, conducting an electronic search, evaluating the results of the search, involving the client in selecting the intervention, and finally implementing the intervention (for a detailed description of this case, see McCracken & Marsh, 2008). Being able to use a case from the agency made this process much less abstract for the participants.

The homework assignment from session two was for teams to prioritize their questions and to conduct an electronic search of the most important questions. Staff were free to use any database to which they had access, and some used subscription databases to locate and download articles. An additional homework assignment between sessions two and three was for everyone to read a research paper that was relevant to all the teams; this paper was selected by the project coordinator in conjunction with the team leaders.

Although session two was the most logistically challenging, session three (evaluating the quality of the evidence) was the most conceptually challenging for the staff. Many staff had stated during the small-group sessions that research was far from their favorite subject in graduate school and that they had little confidence in their ability to understand or critique research methodology. After we reviewed their homework assignments, we initiated the discussion of research by noting that extensive knowledge of statistics is not a prerequisite for evaluating the quality of research. Most staff were familiar with basic concepts like statistical significance; mean, median, and mode; and standard deviation. We introduced and discussed the importance of effect size and demonstrated effect size calculations as a group exercise. We reviewed the uses, strengths, and limitations of common research designs, such as randomized controlled trials and quasi-experimental, pre-experimental, and qualitative research designs. Part of this discussion included a recognition that which research design is best depends on the type of question being asked.

In session three we used a number of handouts from Gibbs (2003). In later cohorts we augmented these with other resources, including some from the Danya International's REACH-SW (Research and Empirical Applications for Curriculum Enhancement in Social Work) curriculum. Following the overview of research designs, we discussed the Quality of Study Rating Form (Gibbs, 2003), and teams used the form to rate an article that they had previously read. The homework assignment from session three was for teams to pick one or more interventions with high-quality research support that they might consider implementing.

For the initial cohorts, session four, evaluating the usefulness of the research and applying it to practice, was conducted with participants from several teams and programs. In later cohorts, we conducted this session with individual teams and programs because by this time many participants had narrowed their focus to specific interventions that they were considering for their own programs. Although the principles of evaluating the usefulness of research are the same across programs, the specific considerations are quite different for the diverse programs at the Jewish Children's Bureau due to their differing client populations, problem areas, and funding sources. Furthermore, one of our fundamental principles was for training to be contextual, which made it difficult to identify interventions that were appropriate across programs.

Reactions to the Initial Training Sessions

Teams expressed minimal resistance to EBP during the training sessions and their team meetings with the project coordinator and champion. Many staff left the training feeling stimulated and expressing enthusiasm for the project, though we weren't able to involve all of them in continuing, organized EBP activities. For some staff, the trainings were interesting informational events, and for others, they were the beginning of a substantive process. One of the factors that may have contributed to the generally favorable response was that they were energized by each other's company and by the diversity of programs and roles represented at the training. (The Jewish Children's Bureau was a large agency, and training events that involved multiple teams and programs were rare.) The director of the psychology training program requested a presentation for the interns and externs. Several staff with little prior experience searching the Internet for information were excited to learn how to use Boolean search language to construct more efficient and effective searches. These early attempts to seed basic EBP skills among directors and supervisors in many different programs formed the agency-wide roots of participation and support.

The merger between the Jewish Family and Community Service and the Jewish Children's Bureau was unfolding at the same time the initial training sessions were being conducted. Jewish Family and Community Service directors and supervisors and some Jewish Children's Bureau administrators who were unable to attend the earlier set of small-group meetings and focus groups were introduced to EBP in a meeting several months after the initial training sessions and after the merger talks were under way.

Jewish Child and Family Services (JCFS), the agency created from the merger and the EBP champion provided several infrastructure supports in addition to assistance to the teams from the project coordinator. For example, the agency intranet was available for participants to recommend papers and to share searches, web links, and other EBP resources among the teams and programs. This intranet had existed prior to the EBP project but had been used primarily for administrative and logistical purposes, such as accessing personnel forms and checking on room availability. After the project began, an EBP folder was added in which forms and reference material could be shared. About six months after the first training session, the first issue of an agency newsletter, *Supplies to the Clinical Trenches*, was released. This newsletter was overseen by the project coordinator, and a number of staff wrote articles and brief reports that were published. The first issue described the EBP project and had articles about evidence-supported interventions that were being implemented in some of the programs.

Information from the small-group meetings proved invaluable for putting together the initial training sessions and consequently gaining the support of staff for this process. The EBP champion and project coordinator carefully prepared the team leaders and staff for change by eliciting their opinions and concerns, by assuring them of administrative support, and most important, by respecting their opinions and expertise. Working in teams is often mentioned in the implementation literature (Bellamy et al., 2008). A team format allows responsibility for different activities to be shared and takes advantage of the fact that different team members have expertise in different areas. For example, recent graduates may have more advanced electronic search and research evaluation skills, and more experienced staff may have a better sense of what sorts of interventions may be acceptable to clients. Support from administrators and team leaders also contributed to staff accepting this project. The agency leadership did not just provide verbal support, they provided tangible support in the form of funding and other resources. The fact that this support continued even when the agency was involved in the merger indicated the level of administrative support for the project.

One of the most significant changes that occurred was that the EBP champion became incapacitated and eventually had to retire. As often happens when a well-liked and respected leader leaves, there is a period of adjustment and formation of new patterns of influence. Fortunately, he was able to continue to provide guidance to the project coordinator, and a new leader stepped in to provide support for the project and the project coordinator.

IMPLEMENTING AND SUSTAINING EBP

The EBP Project has had two main goals: teaching basic EBP skills to as many staff members as possible and embedding the evidence-based process in the life of the agency through the establishment of program EBP teams.

Progress on the First Goal

Over the past four years of the project over 140 staff have participated in basic EBP training. More staff have received training in the first two steps of EBP (question formulation and electronic search strategies) than have received training in subsequent steps (critical appraisal of the research; integration of the critical appraisal with practitioner clinical expertise and with client values, preferences, and clinical circumstances; and application of the results to practice). Evaluating the outcome was addressed in another project, conducted by JCFS's CQI system.

EBP training has been added to the agency's yearly training cycles. By the end of 2010 five cycles of new clinicians will have received this training. Refresher training has been offered to some staff, and there are plans to offer this to others. EBP training is mostly self-sustaining within the agency. The project coordinator has had responsibility for teaching the first two sessions for almost two years and is conducting the refresher training. The EBP newsletter has been reenvisioned to reflect agency goals, and four editions have been printed as of mid-2010. Current plans include conducting research discussions on articles and topics recommended by staff, and offering EBP activities in conjunction with larger events such as agency in-services.

EBP training sessions have thus far remained relatively unchanged in structure. However, leaders are considering offering three formats for training: the traditional format for new employees, joint student and staff training for student interns, and case-based learning for teams interested in more concentrated training around a specific program development priority. There have also been discussions about ways to shorten the training sessions and to simplify the third session on evaluating the quality of the evidence. Although most staff find that the majority of the items on the Quality of Study Rating Form are relatively straightforward, they find that using this form and conducting a detailed analysis of the research findings are very tedious. Staff were able to use the form to rate an article but did not like taking the extra time to answer all the questions. Similar to other practitioners (McColl et al., 1998; Guyatt et al., 2000), staff found evidence summaries and critical reviews prepared by colleagues more useful and efficient than single research articles.

Progress on the Second Goal

About a year and a half into the project the first individual program team was selected. The goal for this team was to identify and plan implementation of specific evidence-supported interventions identified through the EBP process. The team identified several practice questions and conducted group sessions to search and discuss the research literature. Shortly after this team began its work, the program lost funding. The funding was later reinstated, but by that time the program had already begun closing and most staff did not return. Consequently, work with this team was suspended.

The state budget problems that led to the initial loss of funding for the program generalized to other programs and led to changes in the EBP project for JCFS. One of the most significant is that rather than leaders identifying a program and designating an EBP team to pursue clinical questions, when a question was raised during the course of service delivery, it could become a crystallizing point around which staff would gather to formulate a specific question, conduct a search, examine evidence, and make decisions about implementation. This has resulted in EBP being increasingly integrated into program meetings. There are several indicators that this integration has actually taken place. Staff requested project coordinator assistance with conducting searches or locating articles 76 times in 2009 and 49 times during the first two quarters of 2010. Also, in a survey circulated in 2009, over 60 percent of respondents reported searching the Internet once or more a month for answers to clinical questions during the preceding six months. Nearly 20 percent reported searching once or more a week. Finally, it has become an agency-wide expectation that all new program proposals be supported by a review of research on effectiveness.

Staff are beginning to use the EBP process to explore the research basis of current programming. They begin by operationalizing the elements of the current program and then searching the literature for evidence on the effectiveness of these components. One program that recently completed this self-evaluation project eliminated or reduced treatment components with less empirical support and increased emphasis on components with more support. Overall, staff felt that this process resulted in more clearly focused programming. These activities overlap with the development department's efforts to develop and submit proposals for new and continuing funding.

Structurally, the EBP Project is now under the oversight of the treatment issues branch of the agency's CQI system. One of the first activities after this change was to develop the EBP survey, initially distributed in 2009, with a second round to be sent to staff in fall 2010. Data from this survey will shape future EBP project goals and methods and will be part of long-term project evaluation. The survey asked respondents to identify:

Empirically supported interventions that staff already use, whether or not they are labeled as such
EBP activities that are currently used by the team in the program
EBP activities that staff engage in individually
Preferred methods for sharing research
Presenting problems staff members feel least prepared to treat and in which training is needed, and what sort of help might be most useful

The response rate for the 2009 survey was 45 percent (81 respondents), and all but one of the JCFS programs were represented by at least one respondent. Not only did the majority of staff reported going to the Internet for information to answer a clinical question, over two-thirds of respondents reported discussing research with colleagues at least once a month, and over one-third reported that their program was required to demonstrate that its methods were evidence-based—often by a funder. Data from the 2010 survey will be used to monitor changes in the way that EBP is used by staff and programs and to shape EBP diffusion efforts going forward.

Lessons Learned

The EBP project is over four years old (five years, counting the planning and preparation phase) and has become a significant part of the training and program development process at JCFS. This effort has been sustained through the merger, major changes in service priorities and funding, significant staff turnover, and a change in leadership. The project is in the sustained implementation (Rosenheck, 2001) or implementation-reinvention stage (Rogers, 2003). Training in EBP has become standard practice for the organization and is fully integrated into core training for new employees. The EBP process initially appeared to be used less as a method for clinical decision making than as a general method for educating staff about research. However, at this time staff are increasingly using the EBP process to make program development decisions. Supporting proposals for funding and new programming with a review of the evidence has become an expectation.

The goals discussed in the previous section were the goals of the organization. The consultant's goal was to see whether EBP could be implemented on a large scale in a community agency using resources that are available to practitioners working in real-world settings and with as little use as possible of university resources that are available only through the consultant. The evidence to date suggests that widespread training in EBP can be implemented and sustained in community agencies using agency resources and outside consultation and that EBP can be implemented as a program development tool. Whether this process can be sustained for the making of program development decisions is yet to be determined.

Several factors appear to have contributed to the progress thus far. In the initial stages the most important factors were the presence of strong administrative support, an effective champion with solid transformational leadership skills, and a project coordinator with strong technical and interpersonal skills. The champion clearly understood the importance of eliciting, rather than assuming, support from senior administrators, middle management, and staff, as well as the need to prepare the organization for change. Initial small-group meetings elicited concerns about EBP and began building staff support for the project. Information gathered from these meetings helped to inform both the content and the structure of the subsequent trainings.

The period of preparation lasted nearly a year. It is possible that this stage could have been shortened if this had been a university-driven project with dedicated research staff. However, during this time the champion and the project coordinator, as well as other managers and staff, had the usual competing demands of running a social service program, as well as preparing for a pending merger. In any dissemination project there is a tension between allowing adequate time to prepare the organization for change and achieving and maintaining the momentum for change. Moving too fast carries the risk that planners will overlook key elements of preparation; moving too slowly can lead to management and staff getting bored and losing interest in the project.

One of the most important ways that administrators demonstrated their support for the project was by devoting resources both for training and for developing the infrastructure needed to implement and sustain the project. Without a project coordinator who has continued to provide support to the teams; computers, high-speed Internet access, and an intranet to share resources; and staff time to attend trainings, to meet about homework, and to engage in program development discussions, it is unlikely that the project would have succeeded as well as it has. In addition to the resources themselves, provision of the resources was a clear indication to the staff that agency administrators took the project very seriously and were invested in its success. Other indicators of administrative support for the project were the facts that the project was not suspended during the merger and that it was carried on after the champion became disabled. These kinds of indicators do not go unnoticed by staff.

Another key element was the fit between EBP and the goals, values, and practices of the agency. Although most staff were unfamiliar with the specifics of EBP, the agency prided itself in being a learning organization and had a tradition of providing good training to new employees and students, of engaging in reflective practice, and of being an innovator and early adopter. Finally, the EBP project fit well with the CQI project and utilization review committees. EBP training did require some restructuring of time and staff resources, but it did not require the sort of shift in organizational culture that might be needed in agencies that do not have the kinds of traditions and practices seen at JCFS and its predecessor agencies.

Training the staff in teams was also an important factor in implementing EBP. Different staff members have strengths in different areas. One of the concerns that arose in the small-group meetings, as well as in the literature, is about the time it takes to learn and use EBP skills. Training and working in teams allows the staff to divide the tasks and time demands among different individuals. Also, training and working in teams recognizes that staff turnover is a fact of life in community agencies and builds in a mechanism for team members to be replaced should they leave. Perhaps most important of all, working in teams is often more fun than working alone.

A final set of important factors were the relationships among the different people involved in the project. The relationship between the consultant, the champion, and the project coordinator, and the relationship between these three individuals and the leaders and staff who participated in the training were key to the outcome of this effort. At one level, dissemination is a social-influence activity, and relationships among the actors in this activity is important. The fact that the consultant, champion, and project coordinator liked and respected each other and enjoyed working together was important and, we expect, not unnoticed by the staff. We also believed that the relationship between these three and the other leaders and staff was important and was analogous to the therapeutic alliance. Although there is little research on this aspect of dissemination, these interpersonal factors are likely to be as important in organizational change as they are in therapeutic change; they warrant systematic investigation.

The process of adopting and implementing EBP is complex and multifaceted, as is true of any innovation. This project demonstrated that EBP can be implemented in the community, but the experience suggests that doing so requires a significant commitment of resources and effort by the adopting agency. It is possible that this project could have been implemented more efficiently, more rapidly, and with less cost and commitment of resources. We also propose that major events (agency reorganization, staff turnover, loss of funding, and changes of program priorities) be treated as expectations rather than exceptions. This means that flexibility needs to be built into the implementation process. Implementation models and even the innovations themselves are likely to need to be adapted in response to ongoing shifts in the circumstances of the agency. We cannot say with any degree of certainty which of the factors noted above were necessary for the progress that has been made so far. We continue to learn from the staff and from each other.

References

Aarons, G. A. & Palinkas, L. A. (2007). Implementation of evidence-based practice in child welfare: Service provider perspectives. *Administration and Policy in Mental Health and Mental Health Services Research, 34*, 411–419.

Backer, T. E. (1993). Information alchemy: Transforming information through knowledge utilization. *Journal of the American Society for Information Science, 44*, 217–221.

Backer, T. E., Liberman, R. P., & Kuehnel, T. G. (1986). Dissemination and adoption of innovative psychosocial interventions. *Journal of Consulting and Clinical Psychology, 54*, 111–118.

Bellamy, J. L., Bledsoe, S. E., Mullen, E. J., Fang, L., & Manuel, J. I. (2008). Agency-university partnership for evidence-based practice in social work. *Journal of Social Work Education, 44*, 55–75.

Berlin, S. B., & Marsh, J. C. (1993). *Informing practice decisions.* New York, NY: Macmillan.

Blasinsky, M., Goldman, H., & Unutzer, J. (2006). Project IMPACT: A report on barriers and facilitators to sustainability. *Administration and Policy in Mental Health and Mental Health Services Research, 33*, 718–729.

Bradley, E. H., Webster, T. R., Baker, D., Schlesinger, M., Inouye, S. K., Barth, M. C., . . . Koren, M. J. (2004). *Issue Brief: Translating research into practice: Speeding the adoption of innovative health care programs.* Yale University School of Medicine: The Commonwealth Fund.

Carroll, K. M., Ball, S. A., Nich, C., Martino, S., Frankforter, T. L., Farentinos, C., . . . Woody, G. E. (2006). Motivational interviewing to improve treatment engagement and outcome in individuals seeking treatment for substance abuse: A multisite effectiveness study. *Drug and Alcohol Dependence, 81,* 301–312.

Chambless, D. L. (1998). Empirically validated treatments. In G. P. Koocher, J. C. Norcross, & S. S. Hill (Eds.), *Psychologists' desk reference* (pp. 209–219). New York, NY: Oxford University Press.

Cook, J. M., Biyanova, T., & Coyne, J. C. (2009). Barriers to adoption of new treatments: An Internet study of practicing community psychotherapists. *Administration and Policy in Mental Health and Mental Health Services Research, 36,* 83–90.

Corrigan, P. W., Holmes, E. P., & Luchins, D. (1993). Identifying staff advocates of behavioral treatment innovations in state psychiatric hospitals. *Journal of Behavior Therapy and Experimental Psychiatry, 24,* 219–225.

Corrigan, P. W., & McCracken, S. G. (1997). *Interactive staff training: Rehabilitation teams that work.* New York, NY: Plenum.

Corrigan, P. W., & McCracken, S. G. (1999). Training teams to deliver better psychiatric rehabilitation programs. *Psychiatric Services, 50,* 43–45.

Council for Training in Evidence-Based Behavioral Practice. (2008). Definition and competencies for evidence-based behavioral practice (EBBP). http://ebbp.org/documents/EBBP_Competencies.pdf.

Denis, J., Hébert, Y., Langley, A., Lozeau, D., & Trottier, D. (2002). Explaining diffusion patterns for complex health care innovations. *Health Care Management Review, 27,* 60–73.

Dulcan, M. K. (2005). Practitioner perspectives on evidence-based practice. *Child and Adolescent Psychiatric Clinics of North America, 14,* 225–240.

Eddy, D. M. (2005). Evidence-based medicine: A unified approach. *Health Affairs, 24,* 9–17.

Fitzgerald, L., Ferlie, E., Wood, M., & Hawkins, C. (2002). Interlocking interactions, the diffusion of innovations in health care. *Human Relations, 55,* 1429–1449.

Fixsen, D. L., Naoom, S. F., Blase, K. A., Friedman, R. M., & Wallace, F. (2005). *Implementation research: A synthesis of the literature* (FMHI Publication No. 231). Tampa, FL: University of South Florida, Louis de la Parte Florida Mental Health Institute, National Implementation Research Network.

Gellis, Z. & Reid, W. J. (2004). Strengthening evidence-based practice. *Brief Treatment and Crisis Intervention, 4,* 155–165.

Gibbs, L. E. (2003). *Evidence-based practice for the helping professions.* Pacific Grove, CA: Brooks/Cole.

Godley, S. H., White, W. L., Diamond, G., Passetti, L., & Titus, J. C. (2001). Therapist reactions to manual-guided therapies for the treatment of adolescent marijuana users. *Clinical Psychology Science & Practice, 8,* 405–417.

Greenhalgh, T., Robert, G., MacFarlane, F., Bate, P., & Kyriakidou, O. (2004). Diffusion of innovations in service organizations: Systematic review and recommendations. *Milbank Quarterly, 82,* 581–629.

Guyatt, G. H., Meade, M. O., Jaeschke, R. Z., Cook, D. J., & Haynes, R. B. (2000). Practitioners of evidence based care: Not all clinicians need to appraise evidence from scratch but all need some skills. *British Medical Journal, 320,* 954–955.

Guyatt, G., & Rennie, D. (2002). *Users' guides to the medical literature: Essentials of evidence-based clinical practice.* Chicago, IL: American Medical Association.

Haynes, R. B., Devereaux, P. J., & Guyatt, G. H. (2002). Clinical expertise in the era of evidence-based medicine and patient choice. *Evidence-Based Medicine, 7,* 36–38.

McColl, A., Smith, H., White, P., & Field, J. (1998). General practitioners' perceptions of the route to evidence based medicine: A questionnaire survey. *British Medical Journal, 316,* 361–365.

McCracken, S. G., & Corrigan, P. W. (2004). Staff development in mental health. In H. E. Briggs & T. L. Rzepnicki (Eds.), *Using evidence in social work practice: Behavioral perspectives,* pp. 232–256. Chicago, IL: Lyceum.

McCracken, S., & Marsh, J. (2008). Practitioner expertise in evidence-based practice decision making. *Research on Social Work Practice, 18,* 301–310.

McCracken, S., Steffen, F., & Hutchins, E. (2007). Implementing EBP in a large metropolitan family service agency: Preparing the organization for change. Society for Social Work and Research Annual Conference.

Mullen, E. J., & Streiner, D. L. (2004). The evidence for and against evidence-based practice. *Brief Treatment and Crisis Intervention, 4,* 111–121.

Nelson, T. D., Steele, R. G., & Mize, J. A. (2006). Practitioner attitudes toward evidence-based practice: Themes and challenges. *Administration and Policy in Mental Health and Mental Health Services Research, 33,* 398–409.

Norcross, J. C., Hogan, T. P., & Koocher, G. P. (2008). *Clinician's guide to evidence-based practices: Mental health and addictions.* New York, NY: Oxford University Press.

Pagoto, S. I., Spring, B., Coups, E. J., Mulvaney, S., Coutu, M., & Ozakinci, G. (2007). Barriers and facilitators of evidence-based practice perceived by behavioral science health professionals. *Journal of Clinical Psychology, 63,* 695–705.

Prochaska, J. O., DiClemente, C. C., & Norcross, J. C. (1992). In search of how people change: Applications to addictive behavior. *American Psychologist, 47,* 1102–1114.

Proctor, E. K., Knudsen, K. J., Fedoravicius, N., Hovmand, P., Rosen, A., & Perron, B. (2007). Implementation of evidence-based practice in community behavioral health: Agency director perspectives. *Administration and Policy in Mental Health and Mental Health Services Research, 34,* 479–488.

Rapp, C. A., Etzel-Wise, D., Marty, D., Coffman, M., Carlson, L., Asher, D., Callaghan, J., & Whitley, R. (2008). Evidence-based practice implementation strategies: Results of a qualitative study. *Community Mental Health Journal, 44,* 213–224.

Regehr, C., Stern, S., & Shlonsky, A. (2007). Operationalizing evidence-based practice: The development of an institute for evidence-based social work. *Research on Social Work Practice, 17,* 408–416.

Rogers, E. M. (2003). *Diffusion of innovations,* (5th ed.). New York, NY: Free Press.

Rosen, A., & Proctor, E. K. (Eds.). (2003). *Developing practice guidelines for social work intervention: Issues, methods, and research agenda.* New York, NY: Columbia University Press.

Rosenheck, R. A. (2001). Organizational process: A missing link between research and practice. *Psychiatric Services, 52,* 1607–1612.

Sackett, D. L., Straus, S. E., Richardson, W. S., Rosenberg, W., & Haynes, R. B. (2000). *Evidence-based medicine: How to practice and teach EBM* (2nd ed.). New York, NY: Churchill Livingstone.

Shlonsky, A., & Gibbs, L. (2004). Will the real evidence-based practice please stand up? Teaching the process of evidence-based practice to the helping professions. *Brief Treatment and Crisis Intervention, 4,* 137–153.

Simpson, D. D. (2002). A conceptual framework for transferring research to practice. *Journal of Substance Abuse Treatment, 22,* 171–182.

Weisz, J. R., & Addis, M. E. (2006). The research-practice tango and other choreographic challenges: Using and testing evidence-based psychotherapies in clinical care settings. In C. D. Goodheart, A. E. Kazdin, & R. J. Sternberg (Eds.), *Evidence-based psychotherapy: Where practice and research meet* (pp. 179–206). Washington, DC: American Psychological Association.

Willenbring, M. I., Kivlahan, D., Kenny, M., Gillo, M., Hagedorn, H., & Postier, A. (2004). Beliefs about evidence-based practices in addiction treatment: A survey of Veterans Administration program leaders. *Journal of Substance Abuse Treatment, 26,* 79–85.

CHAPTER SEVEN

Addressing the Barriers to EBP Implementation in Social Work: Reflections from the BEST Project

Jennifer L. Bellamy, Sarah E. Bledsoe, Lin Fang,
Jennifer Manuel, and Edward J. Mullen

Despite numerous discussions, little is known about the use of evidence-based practice (EBP) in social service agencies beyond researcher, practitioner, and educator opinions (Bellamy, Bledsoe, Mullen, Fang, & Manuel, 2008). These discussions have often focused on the barriers to and validity of EBP in social work practice (e.g., Gibbs & Gambrill, 2002; Mullen & Streiner, 2004; Webb, 2001). The BEST (Bringing Evidence for Social Work Training) Project was an effort to begin to address this gap in knowledge by studying the implementation of the EBP process in three social service agencies through a hands-on, problem-based training model.

In this chapter we use data from BEST to revisit barriers to EBP in social work that were identified through a review of the literature at the project's earliest phase. These barriers were organized into four general categories: suspicion and distrust, lack of knowledge, limited resources, and lack of fit between research evidence and practice contexts (Bellamy, Bledsoe, & Traube, 2006). In this chapter we describe strategies that our team used to address each of these barriers as well as the challenges and limitations that we identified throughout the duration of the

This work was supported in part by the National Institute of Mental Health Training Grant 5T32MH014623 (S. E. Bledsoe, J. Bellamy, J. Manuel) and the Wilma and Albert Musher Program at Columbia University.

project. We will also discuss our reflections on possible directions for future efforts to implement EBP in social service agencies through university-agency partnerships, with an emphasis on implications for schools of social work.

Background and Significance

EBP is conceptualized here as a professional model of practice in social work and one of many possible strategies that have been proposed to bridge the gap between research and practice. This conceptualization is based on the work of Sackett and others who developed the concept of EBP in medicine (Sackett, Ronsenberg, Gray, Haynes, & Richardson, 1996; Sackett, Straus, Richardson, Rosenberg, & Haynes, 2000). The model was later translated for application in social service agency contexts by Gibbs (2003).

In this tradition, evidence includes empirical research, clinical wisdom and expertise, and client values and preferences (Haynes, Devereaux & Guyatt, 2002). The process of EBP involves a series of steps that include formulating practice-relevant questions, searching for research evidence to answer those questions, judging the quality of that research, and applying this research knowledge to practice through a collaborative exchange with clients that incorporates their values and preferences (Gibbs, 2003). EBP also includes a philosophical orientation that values client-centered practice, transparency, critical evaluation of practice, and a commitment to lifelong professional learning.

EBP as a professional model of practice has been characterized as a bottom-up approach whereby service providers and clinicians, working collaboratively, are the key actors in the implementation of EBP (Mullen, Bledsoe & Bellamy, 2008). Clinical decision making is informed by research evidence, but it is the social worker who organizes and integrates this evidence into daily practice within partnership with clients. This stands in contrast to a top-down approach to EBP, which is characterized by the implementation of select clinical practices identified as adequately supported by research evidence. The social worker in the top-down model is tasked with implementing the selected practices. An increasing number of studies have examined the implementation of a single empirically supported intervention, practice guideline, or program (e.g. Glisson & Schoenwald, 2005; Melzer, Hubbard, & Huang, 2003; Unützer et al., 2002). However, little research has examined the bottom-up approach used to guide the BEST project.

The discourse around EBP in social work has continued in spite of limited empirical evidence to inform its use in practice. We believe that the need to develop this evidence is pressing due to the growing demand for EBP, particularly in health and mental health settings. Increased interest in EBP is evident among the priorities of many organizations and agencies that fund initiatives and shape policies that impact both schools of social work and social service agencies, including government agencies, private foundations, and accreditation organizations.

Federal agencies such as the Substance Abuse and Mental Health Services Administration (SAMHSA), the Agency for Healthcare Research and Quality, and National Institutes of Health (NIH) now routinely link requests for proposals, contracts, workshops, conferences, and other efforts to concepts and topics related to EBP. One example is the NIH Conference on Building the Science of Dissemination and Implementation in the Service of Public Health. Another example is the SAMHSA National Registry of Evidence-Based Programs and Practices.

Private foundations have also increasingly emphasized accountability through rigorous research and the use of EBP. The William T. Grant foundation recently announced a request for research proposals that aims to increase understanding of the acquisition, interpretation, and use of research evidence in policy and practice. Important social work organizations have also prioritized EBP. The Council on Social Work Education's most recent accreditation standards specify that social workers should "employ evidence-based interventions" under Educational Policy 2.1.6. In the current social work practice context, where funding and standards are linked to the study and application of research evidence in policy and practice, we believe that both social service agencies and schools of social work would benefit from the development and testing of strategies to support the integration of EBP into social work education and practice.

Relatively little research directly informs the process by which new practice technologies are selected, adapted, and applied in practice while practice wisdom and clients' values and preference are taken into account (Addis, 2002; Gira, Kessler, & Poertner, 2004). We have chosen to use the phrase *practice technology* as an umbrella term to refer a broad range of innovations that might be identified by agencies through the EBP process, including interventions, programs, protocols, guidelines, and assessments. Social service agencies that seek to implement bottom-up EBP confront a complex and difficult process. A large body of literature has focused on barriers to using research evidence, EBP, and new practice technologies in social work practice. In the initial phase of the BEST Project we conducted an extensive review of this literature, focusing primarily on practitioner attitudes, along with interviews with experts in the field of EBP research, education, and implementation (Bellamy et al., 2006).

We maintain that social work practitioners and social service agencies will continue to struggle with the same barriers to EBP, and the gap between research and practice will persist without specific strategies designed to support the dissemination and implementation of EBP. One potential strategy for addressing this gap is the use of university-agency partnerships to support EBP. The combination of field placements, continuing education programs, and related activities make schools of social work natural hubs at the center of networks of social service agencies. These networks offer an existing platform on which to build university-agency partnerships to support EBP and to increase the translation of EBP to routine social work practice. By building the EBP capacity of social workers in the field and informing research with practice knowledge, these partnerships enhance the connection between classroom training and field experience.

Thus we believe that university-agency partnerships have great utility for advancing the use of EBP among social work practitioners, classroom and field educators, students, and researchers, and that this advancement of EBP can ultimately benefit social work clients. The BEST project is an example of a university-agency partnership aimed at beginning to address these barriers, and it provides an illustration of some of the challenges and limitations of this approach.

The BEST Project

The BEST project has been described in a number of publications that have explored different dimensions of the pilot study as it was developed over time (for a comprehensive list of publications related to the project, see the Columbia University Wilma and Albert Musher Program's Evidence Based Practice and Policy Online Resource Training Center website). BEST was anchored by a team-based hands-on training. The training was delivered in 10 modules that were designed using a seven-step process of EBP. Tools developed by Gibbs (2003) were integrated into the training to support each step of the process. Several themes and processes emerged before the training modules were finalized, and a description of them provides a context for understanding the conceptualization and evolution of the larger project.

A senior faculty member at the Columbia University School of Social Work led the BEST project. Two doctoral students (hereafter called the research team) served as project coordinators, developed the training resource materials, engaged directly with the agency teams to collect project data through focus groups and observation notes, and conducted the trainings. The research team partnered with a convenience sample of three New York City agencies that had expressed a willingness to collaborate with the research team on an EBP-focused project. Each agency team worked individually with the research team.

Descriptive process notes that were recorded by the research team members during meetings with agency participants, focus groups, and trainings throughout the duration of the project were collected and analyzed. Qualitative data were also collected through two rounds of focus groups, one conducted before the BEST project training was implemented at each agency, and one after. Finally, the participants provided demographic data through structured questionnaires that were completed before participating in the training. Details regarding the specific methods used in the BEST project, including the qualitative methodology, have been described in greater detail elsewhere (Bellamy et al., 2008). The study was approved by the Columbia University institutional review board for human participant research.

A review of the research revealed that the bulk of literature focused on EBP in social work describes the lack of EBP in the field and the barriers to using the EBP process. The barriers that were identified through this review were organized into four general themes: 1) social workers' suspicion and distrust of research evidence, researchers, or the research process in general, including objections to EBP due to political, ethical, or professional-autonomy concerns; 2) social workers' limited training and knowledge about how to access, critically evaluate, and use research evidence to serve clients; 3) the paucity of resources available to social work agencies and practitioners; and 4) lack of fit— that is, the gap between currently available research evidence and practice contexts, including the diverse problems, populations, and settings common to social work practice that are not fully reflected in existing research evidence. (For more detail see Bellamy et al., 2006).

We use these four themes as a framework to describe our efforts to break down some of these barriers in partnerships with agencies through the BEST project. We also describe the barriers that are important to address in future university-agency EBP partnerships. Table 1 presents these themes, as well as the strategies used in BEST. Many of these strategies were neither static nor developed in advance, but were iterative in nature and the product of a combination of conversations with agency participants, our ongoing review of the existing literature, and research team discussions that evolved over time.

ADDRESSING SUSPICION AND DISTRUST

Given the exploratory nature of this study and the need to address practitioners' potential skepticism about researchers and research, the research team placed an emphasis on partnership as a strategy to reach out to agencies as collaborators rather than subjects. Similarly, the

TABLE 1 BEST Project Barriers and Strategies

Barriers	Suspicion and distrust of research and researchers	Lack of knowledge	Limited resources	Lack of fit between research evidence and practice contexts
Strategies	1. Engagement of agencies in the early project planning stage	1. Use of hands-on EBP training experience	1. Flexible modular training design	1. Training content on application of research evidence and planning for evaluation
	2. Emphasis on partnership and collaboration	2. Engagement of agencies through teams	2. Protection of participant time through scheduled training	2. Team discussions on assessing generalizability
	3. Inclusion of team members who are open to change	3. Participation of researchers as team members	3. Contribution of researcher time and research skills	
	4. Integration of training content on motivation to use EBP		4. Access to search engines and other resources through the university	

inclusion of agencies in the initial decision-making processes at the earliest stages of the project was also an explicit effort to address suspicion and distrust.

In initial meetings with agencies that occurred prior to the implementation of the EBP training, senior administrators and the research team discussed results of the literature review, explored ideas about how the partnership might proceed, and ultimately agreed to enter into a partnership focused on EBP. During the initial meetings, both top-down and bottom-up approaches to the partnership were discussed (Mullen et al., 2008). Top-down approaches that would incorporate research evidence rather than engaging the agency in the process of EBP included strategies to implement a particular empirically supported intervention, program, protocol, or other practice technology in each agency. In this top-down approach, a practice technology would be selected by administrators or other agency decision makers. Bottom-up approaches, by contrast, were described as strategies that would include clinicians, supervisors, and other staff at each step and incorporate an EBP practice model to bring research evidence to social work practice, from question formulation to application.

Administrators at all three agencies indicated that they preferred a bottom-up EBP approach. This preference was later confirmed by project participants in the pretraining focus groups. Agency partners voiced their interest in working with researchers to engage in the process of EBP, rather than implementing a preselected empirically supported intervention, program, protocol, or other practice through a top-down procedure. Administrators were reluctant to demand that staff implement new practices without including supervisors and practitioners in the process, and agency participants were reluctant to implement new practices without examining and assessing the quality and nature of any supporting research for themselves.

Another product of these early conversations was the decision to ground the partnership in EBP training. Given the preference for a bottom-up versus a top-down approach, the identification of a lack of knowledge as a barrier to EBP, and the appeal of providing no-cost professional development training to agencies led to the decision to develop the project training model. A total of ten training modules were developed to cover the seven steps of EBP as outlined by Gibbs (2003). The modules were designed to provide agency teams with hands-on problem-based training, tools, and real-time technical assistance from the research team, which would actively collaborate with each agency team at every step of the EBP process, rather than simply instruct or guide. These modules are available for download from the project website (Columbia University Wilma and Albert Musher Program, n.d.), and detailed participant and investigator feedback on each module has been published elsewhere (Bledsoe, et al., under review).

After a bottom-up training approach was selected, teams of four to six project participants were formed at each agency. Because this was an exploratory study, the selection of agency team members was not random. One consideration that informed the selection of members of two of the agency teams was the perception by administrators that the potential participants were motivated to participate and open to exploring new models of practice. Team participants included a mix of front-line social workers and clinicians, supervisors, administrators, and in one case an MSW student intern.

The research team held initial meetings with supervisors and staff who would compose the agency teams to discuss the project details, answer questions, seek their input as to the frequency and duration of the training sessions, and begin to identify which programs or areas of practice might be of interest to each of the agency teams. The research and agency team members worked together to select a practice-relevant target problem through discussions about current challenges facing the agency and the population they served. After a practice-relevant problem was selected, the research team used this problem as the focus of the training and research-question formulation.

The first training module was designed to increase participants' motivation to use EBP by engaging the agency team members in a discussion about common barriers to and misconceptions about EBP that were identified in the literature review. Some of these same concerns were voiced by participants in the pretraining focus groups, so the module content and discussion gave the research team the opportunity to acknowledge the concerns and correct any misinformation. This module also included a discussion of EBP as more than a process of using research to inform practice, but also a commitment to values congruent with social work, including client-centered practice, transparency, critical evaluation of practice, and a commitment to lifelong professional learning.

In sum, BEST addressed the issue of suspicion and distrust through four general strategies: 1) consulting agency administrators and participants at the earliest stages of the project about their needs and preferences as to how the partnership would proceed; 2) joining with agency participants as team members and collaborators focused on cooperatively solving a problem or concern of interest to the agency; 3) inclusion of team members who are open to change; and 4) integrating content into the training modules on the motivation for using EBP, including a discussion about its values that are congruent with social work and about perceived barriers to and misconceptions about EBP. These strategies appear to have been successful in allaying suspicions and distrust, particularly toward our specific research team and project. However, participants retained concerns that EBP could be used in a way that would negatively and inappropriately limit practice, as indicated in the post-training focus groups (Bellamy et al., 2008).

ADDRESSING LACK OF KNOWLEDGE

The bulk of the BEST training modules focus on providing skills and tools that were designed to guide the agency teams through the process of question formulation, the search for evidence, the evaluation of the quality of evidence found, and planning for the implementation of any indicated changes to practice. These tools included worksheets that were designed to walk practitioners through step-by-step processes and could be retained and used for reference and downloaded from the project website. For example, one worksheet provided a format within which participants could brainstorm and organize search terms that would be used to locate research evidence in electronic databases. Other tools included tip sheets for evaluating the quality of evidence, a glossary of common research terms, and lists of EBP websites and search engines that include information about the associated costs and content. The hands-on process gave the agency participants the opportunity to use these tools with the support of the research team during the training. Participants generally responded positively to the interactive nature of the training and liked many of the tools (Bellamy et al., 2008).

Another preference conveyed in both initial meetings with agency participants and later in focus groups was to work in agency-based teams throughout the process of EBP (Bellamy et al., 2008). Although EBP was originally conceptualized in medicine as a process carried out at the individual practitioner level, each of the agency partners was skeptical about being able to apply the process without the support of a team. They felt strongly that they wanted to work with their colleagues when engaging in the EBP process.

Similarly, the participants voiced doubt that they would be able to transfer what they learned in the training and continue to apply the process of EBP on their own without the support of the research team members. In particular, agency team members felt ill-equipped to confidently and critically interpret complex research designs and statistics. Throughout the training the research team members provided a great deal of assistance. This assistance included help with brainstorming potential practice problems, live demonstration of techniques used to systematically search electronic databases, coaching through the use of each of the worksheets and tools, provision of examples and illustrations, search assistance and contributions to the discussions to supplement the work of the agency team members. During the training discussions the research team members answered agency team members' questions and informed the discussion around any methodological and statistical issues that arose.

After participating in the training process each of the agency teams identified potential practice technologies that they could implement at their agencies. Interventions were not the only practice technologies they considered. For example, one agency was interested in improving assessment strategies to more effectively match participants to their program at intake. Following the training, the agency teams felt as though they had a better grasp of the research that informed their practice decisions related to the problem each team had chosen as their focus for the project. Participation in the training and the EBP process appeared to increase the teams' readiness to implement new practice technologies on the basis of research evidence. However, none of the three teams felt that they had the capacity to implement the practice changes that they identified through the training.

Although the agency teams were able to identify research evidence, important implementation questions were not addressed in the training. For example, the modules do not cover issues related to estimating cost, finding training, structuring supervision, or seeking consultation to support the implementation of new practice technologies. In general, participants felt unsure of how to move forward. Bottom-up EBP includes steps related to the application of research evidence and the evaluation of this application, and the training briefly addressed follow-up plans for each agency team, but development of this part of the training was limited.

The three general strategies that were used to address lack of knowledge in BEST were providing hands-on training and skill development on the process of EBP, working with teams of practitioners, and supporting the process by providing in-person technical assistance from the research team. Overall, practitioners reported that they gained some skills and knowledge essential to critically engaging in the EBP process, but that once the training was concluded they were unlikely to engage in the same process on their own. Participants described using parts of the process or certain tools, rather than implementing the full EBP process as a model of practice in their agencies (Bellamy et al., 2008).

ADDRESSING LIMITED AGENCY RESOURCES

Time is one of the most limited agency resources, and difficult to address. To attend to this barrier, the training was made flexible through a modular design to suit different agency constraints. For example, two agency teams chose to work through one or two modules at a time over many weeks, whereas the third agency participated in the entire training over two full days. For one agency, the trainings were integrated into an existing supervisors' meeting schedule, whereas the others reserved dates and times specifically for the EBP training. Despite the different schedules, each agency still struggled to protect the training time. Interruptions due to immediate and often unforeseen issues, such as client crises, were common; and each of the agencies had to reschedule training at least once due to competing demands.

Another theme related to the protection of time, and more specifically to the span of time over which the trainings were conducted, emerged during the BEST project. The agency that chose to spread the training over a greater span of weeks also had to reschedule the training most often, sometimes expanding the time between meetings to over a month; by contrast, the agency that chose to fit the training into two full days expressed a desire to have more time to absorb and engage with the materials. While the trainings were designed to respond to each agency's scheduling preferences, the pace of the training materials may have an impact on the participants' ability to maintain momentum and retain the information they are learning through the training.

Despite the challenges related to determining the optimum distribution of the training modules over time, we found that the protection of agency participants' time through the scheduled trainings was essential to working through the EBP training process. Although they were invited to carry out searches and other activities between trainings, very few participants were able to engage in any work related to the EBP process outside of the training. On the basis of our experience, it may be unrealistic to expect social work practitioners to simply fit EBP-related activities into their schedules. It is likely a better approach to reserve worker time, through workgroup meetings or other approaches, specifically for engaging in EBP.

Because the BEST model included the participation of the research team members not only as trainers, but also as full collaborators in the work of the group, the teams benefited from resources that may be less accessible to agencies working on their own. For example, the research team enjoyed greater and easier access to the university library, including search engines and other resources that are not easily accessed by agencies, particularly when fees for use are involved. Agency team members had access to free search engines through the Internet, as well as search engines available through public libraries. Some of them also had access to search engines through university libraries that they were affiliated with as students or field instructors. However, as compared to the research team, participants generally had much more limited access to a broad variety of resources and databases, particularly those that provide access to the full text of journal articles.

The training taught agency team members strategies to more efficiently search for research evidence, and the process of searching seemed less burdensome to the participants as they gained these skills (Bellamy et al., 2008). However, the research team members also contributed time and expertise that enhanced the depth and efficiency of the process by participating in the search for and evaluation of evidence as part of the team.

The lack of resources to support agency efforts to engage in EBP was addressed through the use of a flexible, modular training design; the protection of agency participant time to engage in the EBP process through scheduled trainings; the contribution of research team members' time and research skills; and access to search engines and other research resources through the university. While social service agencies are engaging in EBP, resources are pulled away from direct services to clients and engaged in other important tasks. Unfortunately, the EBP process is costly in terms of the amount of time and expertise needed to execute each of the steps. Researchers are generally better equipped to search for and evaluate research evidence efficiently and confidently, due to their training and their access to research evidence, than are social workers in the field.

ADDRESSING THE LACK OF FIT BETWEEN RESEARCH EVIDENCE AND PRACTICE CONTEXTS

The BEST training module content includes some tools that were designed to help participants plan to apply the research evidence identified in the evidence search and critical evaluation. Team discussions during the trainings also focused on planned changes to current practices, as well as the need to evaluate the impact of these efforts in order to monitor whether the practice changes resulted in the desired outcomes and should be maintained. During these discussions, important issues such as assessment of the clinical significance of study outcomes and the generalizability of study findings were discussed within the training. The agency team members likewise debated key questions about the fit between the body of research evidence that was identified and their own practice contexts.

Most agency participants were disappointed with the some aspect of the research evidence. Participants observed the mismatch between the questions that they were interested in asking of the research, and the research questions addressed in available studies. Few studies were found that precisely informed the practice decisions that the agency teams were trying to make. Disappointingly few studies were identified overall, and there was especially a lack of high-quality intervention studies, meta-analyses, and systematic reviews that addressed problems of interest identified by each team. Participants also raised concerns about the differences between the samples included in the studies that they identified and the populations that their agencies served. The lack of assessments and interventions that have been specifically crafted for or tested with minority and immigrant populations were highlighted by many agency team members (Bellamy et al., 2008).

The two strategies employed in BEST to address the mismatch between best available evidence and the practice contexts of the three agencies were training content on planning for the application of research evidence and team discussions on issues related to assessing the generalizability of research evidence. The BEST training did not, however, address in great detail important and complex issues related to implementation. For example, factors that have been empirically linked to the successful implementation of innovations were not reviewed in the training, including organizational factors, such as culture and climate; practitioner factors, such as training and attitudes; and innovation factors, such as complexity and adaptability (Greenhalgh, Robert, Macfarlane, Bate, & Kyriakidou, 2004). Strategies designed to improve or support implementation efforts, such as the adaptation of research technologies to better fit diverse practice contexts and client populations, were not addressed in the training modules.

Evaluation

Overall, it appears as though the strategies employed in the BEST project were generally most successful at decreasing barriers related to mistrust and suspicion of research and researchers; increasing knowledge of the EBP process and of skills for searching and judging evidence; and providing some of the resources that are needed to formulate questions, search the evidence, and critically evaluate the quality of the evidence. However, it was clear that the agency teams felt that they needed ongoing support, particularly for judging the quality of more sophisticated or complicated research evidence, in order to feel as though they could fully engage in the EBP process from start to finish. Also, the training fell short in addressing implementation issues. The agency teams arrived at the end of the BEST training feeling motivated to engage in EBP, but also ill-equipped to implement new practice technologies that were identified during the process and unprepared to fully engage in bottom-up EBP on their own.

The BEST project serves as a helpful illustration of the complexity involved in efforts to use EBP as a professional model of practice in social work. We believe that many of the strategies used in BEST, as well as lessons learned about the limitations of this approach, serve to inform future efforts to implement EBP in social service agencies through university-agency partnerships based in schools of social work. We now turn to a discussion of our reflections on possible strategies for future efforts and implications for social work education and partnerships with agencies. This discussion is organized around three themes: approaching EBP as a team or organizational process, taking a long-term approach to university-agency partnerships, and supporting an EBP culture of practice.

APPROACHING EBP AS A TEAM AND ORGANIZATIONAL PROCESS

Although we believe that it is important that individual practitioners receive training in EBP-related skills, we also feel that a more team-oriented approach to EBP has a number of benefits. First, BEST project participants reported that they preferred this approach. The agency participants also explicitly indicated their preference for engaging in the process as a team and their intentions to continue to work on EBP as a team. Some of the benefits of this approach were related to the mutual support provided by the team. Using the collective talents and skills of the team members, sharing the burden of engaging in the process, and using the group discussions to manage team members' feelings of being intimidated by the complexity of the EBP process were all benefits of using teams.

Furthermore, because individual agencies and practitioners often work in practice contexts with limited funding and resources, it is also likely to be a more cost effective approach to implement bottom-up EBP at the organizational, program, or team level, rather than at the individual practitioner level. The training and other resources needed to integrate new practice technologies into an agency can be costly, but the cost implementation per clinician can be reduced when resources are shared and these costs are spread across multiple individuals. Given these benefits, the team approach may be a more realistic format for engaging in EBP in social work than the individual approach as proposed and described in evidence-based medicine (Sackett et al., 1996; Sackett et al., 2000).

Other models and strategies have recently been described that target the implementation of EBP at the service system and organizational levels and utilize teams that include both practitioners and researchers (e.g. Glisson & Schoenwald, 2005; Curran, Mukherjee, Allee, & Owen, 2008), but this area of research is still in its infancy. Although there is currently no definitive model for training and implementation of EBP in social work, integrating group and organizational processes with EBP education and training for social workers may be necessary to support the skills and strategies needed to implement EBP, particularly in the context of current funding and practice restraints. Future university-agency partnerships to implement EBP may also benefit from a combined team and organizational approach.

TAKING A LONG-TERM APPROACH TO UNIVERSITY-AGENCY PARTNERSHIPS

The BEST project was built around a time-limited training project. During the course of the training and active university-agency partnership, the agency teams were able to participate in the EBP process. However, once the protected time for training ended and research team members were no longer available to agency teams, agency participants did not feel adequately prepared to engage in the process fully on their own, nor did they feel as though they had the skills and tools to implement the practice technologies that they had identified. Findings from this study suggest that time-limited approaches to university-agency partnerships are unlikely to result in the sustained use of EBP in partner agencies.

There are a number of reasons why long-term partnership models may be needed to implement EBP in social work agencies. First, a firm grasp of research methodology and statistics is needed to critically evaluate research, which is an essential step in the EBP process. Given that this is highly specialized knowledge and that methodological and statistical approaches become increasingly sophisticated over time, it seems unreasonable to expect clinicians to become research experts and remain abreast of this knowledge across their careers. Longstanding university-agency partnerships could alternatively provide a more stable forum for teams of researchers and clinicians to engage more continuously and to bring their unique and evolving expertise to the group process.

Taking a long-term approach to university-agency partnerships may not only support the implementation of research evidence into practice, but also provide a helpful feedback loop from practice back to research. A common complaint from practitioners and a barrier that was identified during the BEST training study were the discrepancies between the questions that are important to practitioners and the questions that are studied by researchers. These discrepancies impede the translation of EBP in agency practice, regardless of whether they reflect the poor match between study samples and client populations or the differences between practice and research contexts. Research that poorly reflects practice realities can contribute to suspicion and mistrust of the value of research evidence and presents some practical barriers to the identification and application of research evidence.

Practitioners may feel compelled to make adaptations to practice technologies that they perceive as poorly matched to their context of practice.

Fortunately, there is an ever-increasing body of research on a host of diverse practice technologies that could potentially correct some of the problems that arise from the mismatch between practice and research. Still, relatively little is known about how to integrate these technologies into practice. The BEST training, likewise, did not include strong content on implementation, yet participants clearly voiced a desire for support in the implementation process. A nascent body of research dedicated to the study of the translation and implementation of practice technologies into agency contexts has begun to build in recent years (e.g., Glisson & Schoenwald, 2005; Melzer, Hubbard, & Huang, 2003; Unützer, et al., 2002). However, there is a great deal yet to learn about translation and implementation in a variety of social work contexts. Others have noted the need for synergistic social work partnerships between researchers, practitioners, and consumers that have the potential to provide a platform from which to contribute to the development of translation and implementation science (Brekke, Ell, & Palinkas, 2007). Long-standing university-agency partnerships could provide such a platform.

SUPPORTING AN EBP CULTURE IN SOCIAL WORK

The BEST project was conducted in partnership with three agencies that had expressed a particular interest in partnering with university researchers on an EBP project, and utilized teams that included members who were perceived by their administrators to be particularly motivated and open to change. Therefore BEST may reflect ideal agency partners and participants. Even though our agency partners were interested and motivated, the implementation EBP as a model of practice represented a distinct departure from usual practice on multiple levels for the BEST teams. EBP, as we have conceptualized it here, involves not only the execution of a series of complex and time-consuming steps, but a commitment to a certain philosophy, or values and priorities that may or may not be congruent with existing agency culture and practice. For example, participants at one agency indicated that they would not consider the incorporation of any interventions, regardless of how compelling the research evidence, that were not consistent with the agency's mission to work with families rather than individuals.

Engaging in EBP may clash not only with the explicitly stated mission or philosophy of an agency, but with numerous other characteristics as well, such as power dynamics, routine, climate, and culture (Rosenheck, 2001). Few studies have examined how the forces that maintain current practices impact efforts to implement the EBP process generally, or specific practice technologies, but some studies do provide compelling evidence for the importance of organizational climate and culture to the success of implementing specific interventions (e.g., Glisson, 2007).

Johnson and Austin (2005) have described the general absence of evidence-based organizational culture within human service agencies, and recommend the use of agency-university partnerships as part of a broader strategy to help create this culture. The BEST training did incorporate some module content related to the motivation to use EBP in social work practice, including the EBP values relating to transparency, client-centered practice, an evaluation or outcomes orientation, and a commitment to lifelong professional learning. However, the bulk of the training was dedicated to the more technical steps of the EBP process. We did find that BEST participant attitudes changed from baseline to follow-up, as indicated by the focus group data, but it is hard to say what impact, if any, this change had on the broader agency context.

Future university-agency partnerships may benefit from a more balanced emphasis on both the philosophy of EBP, including how to create an agency culture that is supportive of EBP, and from the knowledge or skill building needed to participate in the steps of the EBP process. We feel that this broader philosophy of EBP as envisioned by its originators (Sackett et al., 1996; Sackett et al., 2000), and explored in detail by Gambrill and others in the context of social work (Gambrill, 2006), is also congruent with social work ethics and values as described in important documents such as the Council on Social Work Education accreditation standards and the National Association of Social Workers Code of Ethics.

Increasing the application of EBP in social work agencies and sustaining a culture that is supportive of EBP could also benefit social work education. The gold standard of professional education includes didactic training, such as classroom instruction, coordinated with field supervision (Davis et al., 1999). Field learning is a central component of master's level student training experiences; however, the extent to which students' field experiences support learning new evidence-supported practice technologies or the process of EBP is unknown. Indeed, the realities of social work practice could negate the impact of EBP-related skills taught in the classroom (Bellamy et al., 2006; Mullen, Bellamy, Bledsoe, Jean Francois, 2007). Without better coordination between agencies and schools of social work, the rift between what is taught and what is practiced can result in a sense of disjointedness and frustration for students, newly trained social workers, and field educators (Mullen et al., 2007). University-agency partnerships could be used as one strategy to better coordinate the classroom and training experiences of the next generation of social workers.

Conclusion

This chapter builds on earlier work from this project by describing specific strategies and core components of the BEST training to better facilitate university-agency partnerships as a mechanism to use EBP. There are multiple strategies, formats, and tools that can be used to increase the use of EBP in social work. According to pilot data from the BEST project, university-agency partnerships appear to offer a flexible and promising vehicle to implement and support EBP; however, this approach is limited, and barriers to EBP remain.

There is a need for the development of additional models, tools, and strategies designed to support each of the steps of the EBP process in both educational and practice contexts. For example, empirically supported EBP training programs are needed in schools of social work to prepare future social workers for the use of EBP in social work practice. Likewise, professional education and training is needed to develop the capacity of agencies to engage in and sustain EBP, as well as to supervise and support EBP field placements for students.

Because social work is practiced in a broad variety of contexts, has a longstanding history of research in community contexts, and has a tradition of providing services with limited resources, social work is particularly well poised to contribute to the development of creative and feasible approaches to EBP. University-agency partnerships can build on these strengths and improve outcomes for clients and communities by increasing the communication, flow of feedback, and synergistic learning between research and practice. We believe that it is in the best interest of both schools of social work and social service agencies to partner together to design these models, break down barriers to EBP, and reduce the longstanding gap between research and practice.

References

Addis, M. E. (2002). Methods for disseminating research products and increasing evidence-based practice: Promises, obstacles, and future directions. *Clinical Psychology: Science & Practice, 9*(4), 367–378.

Bellamy, J., Bledsoe, S. E., & Traube, D. (2006). The current state of evidence-based practice in social work: A review of the literature and qualitative analysis of expert interviews. *Journal of Evidence-Based Social Work, 3*(1), 23–48.

Bellamy, J. L., Bledsoe, S. E., Mullen, E. J., Fang, L. & Manuel, J. (2008). Learning from agency-university partnership for evidence-based practice in social work: Participant voices from the BEST project. *Journal of Social Work Education. 44*(3), 55–75.

Bledsoe, S. E., Manuel, J., Bellamy, J. L., Fang, L., Dinata, E., & Mullen, E. for the BEST Team. (under review). Implementing evidence-based practice in social agencies: An overview of the BEST training with practitioner responses. Under review for the *Journal of Evidence-Based Social Work.*

Brekke, J. S., Ell, K., & Palinkas, L. A. (2007). Translational science at the National Institutes of Mental Health: Can social work take its rightful place? *Research on Social Work Practice, 17,* 123–133

Columbia University Wilma and Albert Musher Program. (n.d.). *The Evidence Based Policy and Practice Online Resource Center.* www.columbia.edu/cu/musher/Website/Website/index.htm.

Curran, G. M., Mukherjee, S., Allee, E., & Owen, R. R. (2008). A process for developing an implementation intervention: QUERI Series. *Implementation Science, 3*(17), n.p.

Davis, D., O'Brien, M. A., Freemantle, N., Wolf, F. M., Mazmanian, P., Taylor-Vaisey A. (1999). Impact of formal continuing medical education: Do conferences, workshops, rounds, and other traditional continuing education activities change physician behavior or health care outcomes? *Journal of the American Medical Association, 282*(9), 867–874.

Gambrill, E. (2006). *Social work practice: A critical thinker's guide* (2nd ed.). New York, NY: Oxford University Press.

Gibbs, L. E. (2003). *Evidence-based practice for the helping professions: A practical guide with integrated multimedia.* Pacific Grove, CA: Brooks/Cole–Thompson Learning.

Gibbs, L. E., & Gambrill, E. (2002). Evidence-based practice: Counterarguments to objections. *Research on Social Work Practice, 12,* 452–476.

Gira, E. C., Kessler, M. L., & Poertner, J. (2004). Influencing social workers to use research evidence in practice: Lessons from medicine and the allied health professions. *Research on Social Work Practice, 14,* 68–79.

Glisson, C. (2007). Assessing and changing organizational culture and climate for effective services. *Research on Social Work Practice, 17*(6), 736–747.

Glisson, C. & Schoenwald, S. K. (2005). The ARC organizational and community intervention strategy for implementing evidence-based children's mental health treatments. *Mental Health Services Research, 7*(4), 243–259.

Greenhalgh, T., Robert, G., Macfarlane, F., Bate, P., & Kyriakidou, O. (2004). Diffusion of innovations in service organizations: Systematic review and recommendations. *The Milbank Quarterly, 82,* 581–629.

Haynes, R. B., Devereaux, P. J., & Guyatt, G. H. (2002). Clinical expertise in the era of evidence-based medicine and patient choice. *Evidence Based Medicine, 7,* 36–38.

Johnson, M., & Austin, M. (2005). Evidence-based practice in the social services: Implications for organizational change. *Journal of Administration in Social Work, 30*(3), 75–104.

Melzer, B. A., Hubbard S., & Huang J. Y. (2003). TIPs evaluation project prospective study. *Evaluation and Program Planning, 26,* 81–89.

Mullen, E. J., Bellamy, J. L., Bledsoe, S. E., & Francois, J. J. (2007). Teaching evidence-based practice. *Research on Social Work Practice 17*(5), 574–582.

Mullen, E., Bledsoe, S. E., & Bellamy, J. L. (2008). Implementing evidence-based social work practice. *Research on Social Work Practice, 18,* 325–338.

Mullen, E. J. & Streiner, D. L. (2004). The evidence for and against evidence-based practice. *Brief Treatment and Crisis Intervention, 4*(2), 111–121.

Rosenheck, R. A. (2001). Organizational process: A missing link between research and practice. *Psychiatric Services, 52*(12), 1607–1612.

Sackett, D. L., Rosenberg, W. M. C., Gray, J. A. M., Haynes, R. B., & Richardson, W. S. (1996). Evidence based medicine: What it is and what it isn't. *British Medical Journal, 312,* 71–72.

Sackett, D. L., Straus, S. E., Richardson, W. S., Rosenberg, W., & Haynes, R. B. (2000). *Evidence based medicine: How to practice and teach EBM* (2nd ed.). New York, NY: Churchill Livingstone.

Unützer, J., Katon, W. J., Callahan, C. M., Williams, J. W., Hunkeler, E., Harpole, L., . . . IMPACT Investigators. (2002). Collaborative care management of late-life depression in the primary care setting: A randomized controlled trial. *Journal of the American Medical Association, 288,* 2836–2845.

Webb, S. A. (2001). Some considerations on the validity of evidence-based practice in social work. *British Journal of Social Work, 31,* 57–79.

CHAPTER EIGHT

Implementing Evidence-Based Management and Evidence-Based Practice in Community Agencies: Lessons from a Case Study

Harold E. Briggs and Stephen Edward McMillin

Underfunded and under-resourced social service agencies that serve disadvantaged populations are vulnerable to experiencing declines in service delivery quality. Such declines often adversely affect agency reputation and reduce an organization's ability to lobby funders and regulators for adequate support, while frequently alienating stakeholders such as consumers and consumer families. The typical result can be a vicious circle in which a social service agency perceived as bad continues to lose the support it needs to launch a turnaround effort and regain the credibility and resources it needs to function well.

At the same time local, regional, and federal policymakers are increasingly looking for evidence-based practice (EBP) in the delivery of health and human services to justify public funding. Given mounting pressure for better-quality services by consumer and ally interest groups, professions such as social work are increasingly expected to demonstrate accountability and responsiveness (Gioia, 2007; Jenson, 2005; Silberman & Hansburg, 2005). The trends and innovations that have occurred in nursing, medicine, health care administration, and business are now reaching social work. The Council on Social Work Education is undergoing a change in its Educational Policy and Accreditation Standards that places greater emphasis on educating direct practice and administrative student practitioners to use empirically well-supported practices. The concept of evidence-based management is not mentioned in the standards, but its assumptions are addressed as major requirements for social work curricula. Evidence-based practice and management have also been identified as an important curricular theme in other social work arenas (Briggs & McBeath, 2009).

Thus practicing administrators are increasingly being held to higher standards of direct care. They are expected to manage for results in care settings by using sound, effective, and ethical management practice (Ovretveit, 1998). This expectation for agency management accountability is occurring at the same time that lawmakers and policy administrators are demanding increased accountability. In the state of Oregon, for example, funding of social and human services requires that agencies provide services that meet a high evidentiary standard. The implicit assumption is that these services are also expected to maintain costs at acceptable levels. The conflation of cost-savings with evidence-based practice is a potentially misguided assumption that is not supported by any research, yet it is chief among the reasons motivating governmental decision makers to require the use of empirically supported interventions (McBeath, Briggs, & Aisenberg, in press).

Agency administrators and program managers seeking to provide high-quality services through the use of evidence-based management will find guidelines for and case studies of such management helpful, especially since major implementation issues have continued to affect community agencies, and these issues can impede successful outcomes. This chapter offers a case study focusing on the establishment and evaluation of independent group homes serving persons with developmental disabilities to examine how successful implementation of evidence-based management and EBP in a community-based social service agency can assist turnaround efforts in troubled organizations that have experienced declining service outcomes. One of the aims of the study was to increase consumers' adjustment to the community setting and to decrease their behavioral problems, and this successful clinical outcome was at the forefront of the organizational restructuring and turnaround discussed below.

This chapter also posits that the science on EBP and empirically supported interventions is still quite new and incapable of guaranteeing or promising treatment effectiveness (McBeath, Briggs, & Aisenberg, in press). Merely implementing a well-tested program model or treatment product is far from enough to guarantee success in service delivery if the organization as a whole has not been able to incorporate critical thinking and responsiveness in its leadership and daily operations.

Given these major concerns, it is important to broaden the scope of the use of evidence to address the management structure (or lack of management structure) in community social service agencies, especially those that are experiencing a variety of troubles and are in need of a turnaround. Agency management that can develop an organizational culture that thoroughly pursues problem solving, strategic decision making, teaching, and staff learning (Briggs & McBeath, 2009) will be able to maintain the entire EBP process rather than merely implementing a single successful treatment or program. Furthermore, making decisions on the basis of research findings alone or merely implementing a single packaged treatment without fusing research evidence to other types of contextual knowledge and expertise may disqualify the contributions of culture, client knowledge, professional expertise, and experience as a filter for pursuing service effectiveness (Briggs, 2009).

Definition of Evidence-Based Management

Evidence-based management involves the strategic use of evidence and reasoning in the decision making of agency managers in order to resolve a host of administrative dilemmas. Like EBP in social work, evidence-based management can be seen as having both bottom-up and top-down dimensions. The bottom-up approach in evidence-based management mirrors the five-step process of EBP: develop an answerable management question, search electronic databases of agency and program management research, sift through the options and conduct a comparison of options, select an option that best fits the situation, and apply and evaluate the selection. The top-down approach to evidence-based management often involves implementing a specific model of decision analysis for the agency or organization. Kovner and Rundall (2006) note that two evidence-based management models, an eight-item decision-making process and the Shewhart Plan, Do, Study, Act (PDSA) approach, which relies on internal data as evidence for planning responses to and solving agency management dilemmas, have become especially popular for quality assurance management in health organizations.

Other top-down approaches to evidence-based management include restructuring the organization through new staffing and the use of external consultation in an effort to help a learning culture take root in the organization. This case study used a top-down evidence-based management approach that restructured the agency to include a new position (organizational development manager), and ongoing consultation to help the agency become data-driven and to supervise the transition to a comprehensive EBP process for daily operations. While the type of evidence-based management in this study is characterized as top-down because of the high-level staff restructuring it involved, the process of change in the agency was driven by participatory management in which staff at all levels were trained and empowered to be critical thinkers and questioners in an egalitarian learning environment. As Gambrill (2006) has pointed out, the EBP process is profoundly egalitarian when it is implemented as its founders intended; this should not be obscured by the emphasis on management and leadership decision making in this case study.

Case Study

This case study illustrates the benefits of successful implementation of EBP and evidence-based management through an academic-community partnership between a large center of higher learning and a family-driven nonprofit based in an African-American community, and it demonstrates a fusion between culture and science (Briggs, 2009). The study highlights organizational changes that result from the use of behavioral approaches to EBP processes, as well as incorporation of the principles of family-driven practice.

In this case, the executive committee of the agency's policy board, as well as executive management, were convinced by the results of an organizational management study that highlighted the need for planned organizational change to enhance the agency's system of service delivery. The organizational objectives for the study included the establishment of a university-community partnership as a training and consultation context for agency staff to learn ways to transfer research knowledge into agency practice effectively and to transform the crisis-management style of organizational management into an agency culture and operational process that embraced the use of evidence in administrative and clinical decision making by agency management and direct-care personnel.

In conceptualizing the fusion of research utilization, participatory management, and behavioral methods for use by staff, administration, and management, the agency adopted a task-centered, evidence-based, performance management model. The first author, Harold Briggs, having been trained in task-centered practice and performance management for social service administration, was hired to lead this change process in the newly created position of organizational development manager. This organizational case study involved administrators, managers, staff, consumers, the community, and university partners in a planned change effort to develop an accountable community organization with more effective service delivery.

SETTING

The study was set in an inner-city neighborhood of a major Midwestern city, in an agency that we give the pseudonym CSI. CSI provided clinical community-based services focusing on the total development of the individual, family, and community, with an additional emphasis on enhancing the functional capacity of those systems through the implementation of operant theory, social learning behavior interventions, and various empowerment strategies.

At the outset of the study, the organization functioned as a collection of seven autonomous divisions situated within a four-mile radius of CSI headquarters and employing approximately a hundred African-American professionals, paraprofessionals, and community volunteers. CSI operated a large array of programs, such as a community transitional housing and case management program for adults with chronic and persistent mental illness, an outpatient substance abuse program for adults, two private schools for school-age youth with developmental disabilities and serious emotional disorders, a supportive employment program, and two group homes for adults with developmental disabilities. The executive director was politically well-connected and charismatic. The chair of the agency board of directors was a community leader, politically resourceful, and widely popular. The majority of board members were community residents, family members of adults with developmental disabilities, and family members representing youth with serious emotional disturbances. The remainder of the board included philanthropic and civic leaders.

There was no central operating management framework prior to the hiring of the organizational development manager, and the mission of the organization was quite broad and difficult to define. There were no regularly scheduled meetings of the executive and program management staff, and neither communications nor services were coordinated across service divisions or through support functions. All budgets, however, were systematically tracked through division and program fiscal activities by the business management office. Funding was not based on agency performance in service provision, but was tied to personal and political relationships and previous working alliances. Agency programs managed to survive and remain funded in this political context, but stakeholders were increasingly dissatisfied with and concerned about service delivery quality.

Strengths of the organization included the administrative sanction voiced by the community, consumer and family input in activity planning, and the family-driven quality of CSI's board of directors. The sanction of these groups was essential in the process of designing and implementing a collection of behavior change interventions.

STAKEHOLDERS

The stakeholders in this case study included community members, the agency, agency staff, the involved families of consumers, and the consumers themselves. Community members did not want group homes in their neighborhood, which would provide an alternative to institutionalization. In general, they were not very knowledgeable about the community-based group-home program or the population it would serve. The agency had received poor performance evaluations from its state program auditor, who would not certify the agency's new community-based group homes for occupancy. CSI's existing group-home program design for persons with developmental disabilities was heavy on skilled nursing, occupational therapy, and case management rather than community integration and a less restrictive, more home-like setting. No client behavioral habilitation program was possible given budget constraints, so a custodial model and community nursing-home standard of care was implemented with limited resources, and little age-appropriate community-adjustment training was occurring. The consumers were largely passive recipients of services and had many opportunities for boredom and conflict. The families were concerned about the safety of their relatives and were skeptical that the agency's community residential program would give them the kind of secure care that a larger state facility seemed to guarantee.

The agency staff serving consumers with developmental disabilities was primarily made up of part-time workers who had full-time jobs elsewhere, and staff turnover was high. They had no training in human behavior, behavior modification, or management of small residential group-home programs, and did not know the differences between mental illness and developmental disabilities. The consumers whom the state wanted to refer to the new community-based group homes were those who experienced difficulties in state care and did not seem to be well suited for less intensive care in community-based living. Some consumers were apprehensive about moving to a smaller setting with a lower level of care. They had made alliances with people in state care that they would lose. They would have to meet strangers whom they did not trust and with whom they had no relationship, and they would have to turn over their established privileges to them. The consumers had inadequate self-care skills, and a number of them had behavior management issues. Finding a level of care that met client needs in the least restrictive setting possible while decreasing behavioral problems would be crucial to the success of any program changes.

APPROACH

The organizational development manager did a careful internal audit that noted strengths in the organization, but also cited infrastructure problems. He devised a plan of correction and made use of doctoral students and academics trained in the philosophy and process of EBP from a behavioral perspective. Strategies described by Rzepnicki and Briggs (2004) and Pinkston, Green, Linsk, and Young (2001) were the primary guides on transferring research to practice through strategic meetings with the board of directors, upper management, program supervisors, direct care staff, and families.

In order to facilitate organizational change and sustain program implementation strategies aimed at promoting service effectiveness and optimal performance of key stakeholders such as staff, management, families, and consumers, the organizational development manager devised an approach combining the EBP process and task-centered practice (Reid, 1979; Bailey-Dempsey & Reid, 1996). This approach incorporated elements of problem-solving empirical research and the use of science-based change processes to promote broadly defined behavioral change. In this chapter, the management components are delineated. The consumer interventions and behavioral reactions to them, reported as numerical outcome data, were highlighted in a previously published study (Briggs, 1996).

Monthly management meetings were held at the agency and program levels to establish general and specific organizational and programmatic outcomes and service-effectiveness indicators. This resulted in regular, institutionalized examination of program data. A newly hired operations manager, who possessed a keen ability for writing both process and decision-making notes and working through participatory team management approaches, took the minutes of the management meetings. The operations manager was responsible for managing the seven formerly near-autonomous service division directors. The business manager, fundraiser, political affairs officer, and community representative all reported directly to the CEO, who in turn reported to the board of directors.

From this case study, five strategies for organizational change emerged: engagement, assessment, planning, intervention or action, and evaluation.

FIVE STRATEGIES FOR PLANNING AND IMPLEMENTING ORGANIZATIONAL CHANGE

First, administrators, managers, and staff engaged in discussions about their perceptions regarding the success of the agency's functioning in relation to its mission, and about whether there was any need for organizational change.

Second, discussions regarding current agency challenges and the strategic vision were based on an assessment of change potential across all levels of the organization. This assessment directly examined the level of commitment to the change effort and the willingness to involve line staff in the development and implementation of the planned organizational change. During this assessment phase and during activities related to the planned change effort, natural leaders with a clear talent for relationship management emerged, and they were supported and empowered within the agency culture to accept appropriate responsibilities and demonstrate their leadership abilities. Top-down change efforts driven by only one leader are unlikely to last longer than that leader's tenure, but the amount of time necessary to allow change to spread across all levels of the organization can be considerable. For CSI this strategy of involving staff at all levels and supporting emergent leaders helped create a sense of group ownership of the change process.

Third, planned organizational change required clear goals that related to the agency's mission and were consistent with long-term values and the organization's core competencies—what the organization could do well that distinguished it from other organizations. CSI was known for its use of research-based methods and political influence as a context for advancing optimal consumer functioning, community and economic development, and the self-sufficiency and competencies of its stakeholders. To reinforce and uphold this organizational capability, the CEO hired a cadre of middle managers and the organizational development director, who were trained in the use of evidence in administration and direct practice. These staff members were highly skilled in working in teams, leveraging politics, and mobilizing their broad social networks to secure resources to ensure exposure of the consumers to as many opportunities for community integration and social reinforcement as possible. For example, through the various connections of the middle managers, CSI was often the recipient of tickets to attend NBA and NFL games, field trips to a pottery factory, organized cabarets, community block club events, concerts, plays, and theatre presentations. These opportunities were used for programming and reinforcement purposes with the consumers. As part of the planning effort, it was very important to analyze agency culture to determine the most effective change strategies to encourage staff to align their personal and professional values with organizational values because congruency reduces resistance to change. This approach to values clarification also assisted in the development of staff openness to participating and collaborating with others in the change effort.

Fourth, structural changes—such as the hiring of a new intra-agency cross-division manager and program supervisors, and the creation of a direct-care staff buddy support system—permitted the agency to plan and track change efforts while integrating inputs from all agency levels: bottom-up as well as top-down. This system developed, targeted, and mobilized appropriate resources, adequate funding, and support from both within and outside of the organization to keep change strategies under evaluation and accountable to CSI's primary aim. The implementation of this support system included the use of strengths-based participatory management techniques as part of monthly and quarterly collaborative management enhancement, professional and organizational development efforts that contributed to the development of a culture of learning, clear performance expectations, and the use of sound management approaches through trial and error.

Fifth, evaluation of the impact of the change effort on program and service effectiveness was transparent and was used as the impetus and model to launch planned organizational change in other CSI service divisions through collaborative action. The success of this effort reinforced the success of staff and personnel in the community residential program, which provided them opportunities to serve as trainers for managers and staff in other CSI departments seeking to achieve mutually agreed upon goals and objectives. In addition, a body of program and service evaluation documentation had been gathered throughout the project that supported overall organizational accountability and credibility. For example, the staff used weekly shift reports, individualized client treatment checklists, and detailed group activity checklists, while the program supervisor and organizational development manager used a supervisory checklist and a quality assurance task analysis format as mixed and multiple data collection sources to monitor service delivery and ensure that it was of high quality.

As mentioned above, one of the clinical aims of the study was to increase consumers' adjustment to the community setting and to decrease their behavioral problems. A participatory management approach was used in order to secure the collective strength and motivation of the program staff and management and to empower staff, consumers' families, and consumers to become equal participants and allies in planning habilitation services.

Adjustment to the community setting was defined as the ability to live successfully in a community setting, which included participation in community-based programming in areas such as activities of daily life, learning and using community-living skills such as grocery shopping and taking public transportation, and engaging in out-of-home leisure activities and visits to the homes of family members. In terms of community programming, staff were involved in meetings designed to teach staff members methods of engaging consumers and motivating them to participate in group-home services. Staff were also trained in methods for involving consumers in the planning of service delivery and for increasing out-of-home activities, and in techniques to improve both family participation and strategies to teach community survival skills.

RESULTS

A number of positive outcomes resulted from the evidence-based management strategies employed in this study.

Program Improvements

One of the fundamental objectives of the study was enhancement of staff performance in managing consumer behavior issues. This was accomplished by increasing staff opportunities for positive reinforcement, such as preferred work schedules, increased salaries, positive performance evaluations, and indirect feedback published throughout the agency by the CEO and board of directors as program operations, staff behavior, and client behavior improved over time.

It was hoped that the consumers' community stay would be enhanced by an increase in their participation in outdoor activities and by the frequency of their use of relevant cultural and social institutions. Another major objective was for consumers to access and use community services as independently and frequently as practical to demonstrate that they were benefiting from community-integrated residency. In initiating increased contact with the community at large, the consumers would be expected to visit places and function in settings not typically available to institutionalized patients. An initial activity program, involving planned changes in consumers' environments to include more community integration, was begun in Month 5 and continued throughout the study period.

Staff Stability

Between Months 1 and 6, baseline data were collected that demonstrated that staff performance and interactions with consumers were issues of concern to management and included roughly four critical incidents each day (for example, physical altercations between staff and consumers or consumer elopement from staff supervision). During Month 7 a new supervisor was hired and a revised personnel policy was put in place with an emphasis on hiring staff with more family management experience. Seven staff members were hired through attrition as other staff members left. A change in hiring policy allowed for flexibility to transition from hiring part-time staff who were predominantly younger men who were perceived as uncaring but strong enough to do a job framed as potentially dangerous, to hiring older women experienced with working with large families and perceived as caring and maternal. The program supervisor was promoted to division director of residential services in Month 24. No other staff changes occurred during the study period. This incremental change in staffing prevented a dramatic changing of the guard that might have been disruptive. Using the existing high staff turnover and hiring carefully vetted new staff through attrition resulted in real staffing change that enhanced rather than disrupted daily operations.

Client Movement to Least Restrictive Setting

At the beginning of the project, the total client population for the agency's two community-based homes was four male and four female adults with developmental disabilities, seven of whom were discharged to community-training foster homes (a less restrictive setting) within thirty days of the study completion date. This unanticipated outcome pointed to a potentially even broader effect for the group-home intervention and suggested the great potential of increasing community integration. Only one client continued to require group-home care, and this was because of a seizure disorder that necessitated ongoing staff assistance. The quality of daily activities in which the residents engaged changed over the course of the study from a routine that included indoor games and crafts to a greatly increased rate of out-of-home activities, such as sightseeing tours, picnics, parties, movies, festivals, and walks; visits to amusement parks, museums, the zoo, and aquariums; and leisure activities supervised by a recreation consultant.

Change in Administrative Structure

Changes in administrative structure were overlaid with training opportunities to help staff at all levels feel involved and unsurprised by structural developments. These changes unfolded over a relatively linear timeline.

In Months 5 and 6, training was implemented to help prepare staff for anticipated administrative changes. For example, a number of meetings were held with the staff of each group home to provide orientation to the change in their duties and work schedules, and meetings between staff and consumers were held to achieve buy-in and consumer choice and participation in group-home activity planning.

During Month 7, a new operating structure and chain of command were developed for the group-home program. The program was organizationally removed from one division and placed in a newly established residential division, and the program supervisor now reported directly to the operations manager for direction and supervision. During Month

7, a management task analysis and planning team was established in two settings, residential and vocational services.

Between Months 7 and 14, staff from both residential and developmental training centers met separately to establish integration of treatment planning and staff training and to plan opportunities for reinforcement of client behavior in more than one setting.

Although meetings are sometimes seen as the bane of organizational life, as this project unfolded, five types of productive meetings were scheduled that ensured that communication was maintained across all levels of the organization. These meetings combined communication of news and developments with coaching and educational opportunities.

In one weekly meeting, the supervisor of residential services met with a behavioral consultant to establish habilitation and behavior management plans for each client. A second weekly gathering was a joint meeting between staff and supervisors from vocational training, the residential program supervisor, and the behavioral consultant. The operations manager participated in some of the meetings. In the joint meeting an integrated training and administrative topical schedule was used to teach effective staff behaviors, target problem behaviors, and define tasks and measures for evaluating achievement of desired behaviors.

A third meeting was held biweekly between the behavioral consultant, the residential program supervisor, and the organizational development manager. The purpose of this meeting was to define expected performance, provide feedback, and set benchmarks in selected areas (such as client habilitation skills, physical plant issues, staff activities, staff concerns, and family input and concerns).

In Month 9, the program supervisor and organizational development manager began to meet weekly. The program supervisor brought in literature on effective strategies for addressing program, family, and consumer interests and needs and discussed the feedback and input from consumers. Resources were arranged to assist in implementing these and other choices of consumers for programming. Data collection procedures in residential services were changed from narrative progress notes to a checklist system that demarcated client skills in selected areas, including activities of daily living, home care, and community-living skills. This change was made to help staff to efficiently and effectively document the broad range of consumers' reactions to a series of changes in processes and activity programming.

An additional meeting was held weekly between the CEO and the operations manager. The purpose of this meeting was to review client and staff activities, examine program operations, discuss financial and material resource needs, and provide an opportunity for performance feedback. As the behavioral consultant phased out of the schedule, the organizational development manager began taking on some of the consultant's role while providing weekly supervision of the program, supervisor, and staff.

Agency Changes

The program went from being known for missteps (such as staff failing to properly secure and handle medication, or letting consumers jaywalk across the street without consideration for their limited intellectual functioning) to a program that transitioned consumers in less than three years to semi-independent adult living arrangements. The transition from group-home to semi-independent living arrangements was not anticipated by the program funding source or consumers' families as a realistic outcome; it came as a complete surprise. This project's consultants later provided services in CSI's child welfare division that had a carryover effect on development in the rest of the agency. The processes and methods tested in the group homes and in the child welfare study were transferred to the entire agency as a learning-and-results-focused framework for designing and delivering services and for ensuring the continuous quality control needed to accommodate client preferences and achieve service aims.

The mantra adopted by executive staff and passed throughout the agency was "What gets monitored gets done!" Among the areas that external and internal auditors most noted for improvement was the use of data in decision making, program design, quality control, evaluation, and development efforts. The research culture and the focus on performance management became mainstays of agency operations.

Community and Interagency Levels

The CEO favorably resolved the dispute over the location of group homes and supported the agency's family association in additional political advocacy, which were important to all of the consumers' parents. As a result of advocacy work across multiple levels of the organization, institutional care was redefined. Other community agencies began to refer their clients to CSI's new group-home facilities as extensions of their own programs; this enabled those agencies to provide a form of residential therapeutic care they previously had not been able to offer.

CSI was able to disseminate scientific, research-based interventions and use them, along with cultural knowledge and family input, benchmarking, and performance management, to help the vulnerable, the racially disadvantaged, and the politically fragile to become self-actualized and self-sustaining by participating in the agency's culture-specific programs and services. The community has accepted

CSI as a valued community resource. CSI has received the respect of academic centers of higher learning and state and national credentialing agencies. As a result of this work, the agency now has its own institutional review board for conducting more intervention and survey research. Furthermore, the program now operates community residential apartments in a congregate setting funded by the federal Department of Housing and Urban Development.

Analysis

The case study at CSI yielded a number of lessons about facilitating change and about accountability in community organizations. First, agency leaders will likely meet with less resistance from employees and co-workers and with more openness and willingness to collaborate and work in partnership with others during the change process if the process is open, transparent, and respectful of all stakeholders. Although evidence-based management may at first glance seem system- and process-focused, relationship management skills are also an essential quality for contemporary social work leaders and are an essential part of evidence-based management as well.

In this study, the organizational development manager engaged all the participants in discussions about the agency's mission and the need for change. Additionally, the he explored the feasibility of developing plans to improve service delivery and accountability. During assessment activities, it was decided that the priorities for change ought to be client-centered and focused on service effectiveness through a new emphasis on enhancement of the significant relationships of the agency and its caseworkers with the consumers and their families. These empowerment strategies strengthened family involvement and staff performance. Prioritizing these changes in the key areas of program management allowed the staff and management to work collaboratively to reinforce and support positive and integrated relationships and behavioral changes in community group homes. These same strategies were being used with other service areas of the agency, including child welfare (Briggs, 1994).

Planned organizational change as illustrated in this study was made gradually, allowing people time to adapt, grow, and move forward. The action plan had a feasible time schedule for implementation of changes in various areas in order to allow for overall program and service integration. By Month 21, the management and staff were ready for the integration of all phases of the system-wide organizational behavior modification strategy. This point highlights the futility of considering

EBP and evidence-based management as short-term or automatic cost-cutting measures. An agency's journey to EBP and evidence-based management may take months or even years. The financial pay-off can be substantial, as seen in the growing budgets of CSI during this case study, but it takes time and patience to see such results.

Assisting agencies to change practices to include use of program data and sound intervention methods that promote accountability involves many key elements. It is an iterative process that requires frequent evaluation of the change process to determine whether the planned organizational change is progressing as intended and to identify the lessons that were not considered in the original program design. It requires replacing a crisis management approach with the systematic use of key behavioral strategies and giving them time to work. It also involves supportive styles of communication between management, staff, and family members, followed by contributions to the development of increased community interaction and support, then by consequent improvement in service effectiveness and programmatic performance. In this study, education and staff training were key elements in maintaining the momentum of change.

For management, staff, consumers, and consumer families, having opportunities to learn new ways of communicating, behaving, and working in partnership with others contributed to enhanced productivity and accountability. In future studies of facilitating change and accountability in community organizations, investigators may want to differentiate the types of training needed for staff. This would include distinguishing between the need for technical training in client programming involving the EBP process and the need for training in cultural competency within group, interpersonal, leadership, and team building skills. The results of this case study suggest that an agency can achieve change by using a combination of the task-centered, traditional problem-solving perspective and evidence-based management and performance management strategies that incorporate personal knowledge and relationship management skills.

LESSONS FOR USING EVIDENCE IN ADMINISTRATION AND CHANGING AGENCY PRACTICE

Although Gambrill (2004, 2007), Rzepnicki and Briggs (2004), McCracken and Corrigan (2004), and others have documented the objections, challenges, organizational constraints and implementation issues involved with the EBP philosophy and process, this case study has identified seven themes or practice lessons that can serve as guides for administrators to use as key drivers for leading organizational change.

Commitment from Administrators and Managers

Utilizing EBP in agency cultures requires a commitment on the part of social work administrators and managers to think differently about the organization and the role and uses of program data.

The agency in this case study is not like most agencies. It had management staff with moderate to strong research skills and ties to academics well-versed in the philosophy and process of EBP. In nursing the EBP process is used by fewer than half of practitioners because most of them are unfamiliar with "the steps of the EBP process" (*Nursing News*, 2006, p. 607). Walshe and Rundall indicate that managers have been slow to adopt the ideas of EBP process "to their own managerial practice" (2001, pp. 429–430) and describe the need for a culture of experimentation, research, and critical thinking among management to facilitate improved decision making that is based in evidence. Melnyk and Fineout-Overholt (2006) indicate that client preferences and values are essential to the EBP process. Their ideas are consistent with those of Sackett, Straus, Richardson, Rosenberg, and Haynes (2000); Gibbs (2003); Gambrill (2004, 2007); and Hamilton (2005).

Organizational Culture

Despite the potential increase in costs, it is sensible to foster a culture of rigor, monitoring, training, consultation, and interdisciplinary collaboration with families.

As Gambrill (2007) notes, resource issues are certainly a concern, as is general uncertainty about treatment effectiveness. Rzepnicki and Briggs (2004) describe the challenges and benefits of using the philosophy and process of EBP in actual practice. Benefits include an emphasis on the clients' cultural customs, values, and needs. The process incorporates professional standards of ethical behaviors, assists in reducing practice errors, involves research and critical thinking, and contributes to the practice and research base of the profession. CSI benefits today because of its rich foundation and training in evidence-based management, an approach that succeeded in reducing community opposition to the group-home project and eventually helped to reestablish the agency's reputation and standing before the community, funders, and regulators.

Time and Resources

Time and resource needs may tax agency capacity to independently use the EBP process as a driver of the agency's performance-management culture. The agency may have to integrate researchers into their work to assist as scholars in residence.

Rzepnicki and Briggs (2004) identify a number of challenges for implementing the EBP process, including time to engage in research utilization, translation of evidence for use by consumers, and resources such as management-information databases that are sufficient to address the agency's data needs. Accessing computerized databases may not be as user friendly for staff with less than a college education, such as the group-home staff in this case study. The organizational development manager, the consultant, and field students collected literature and translated it into user-friendly language that staff could understand and use as a basis for decisions about the type of training they were interested in receiving. Thus the team transferred literature into training, and used previous research in planning individual and group behavior programming for habilitation. Field students and interns can be especially valuable as part of a regular agency-university partnership in which the agencies reserve a certain number of spots each academic year for social work student interns in an EBP concentration. Such agency-university partnerships not only give the agencies research assistance for a considerable part of every year, but may also be a win-win situation if some interns are hired by the agencies as employees after graduation.

Critics note that very few community-based social service agencies have on-staff researchers, and these are only the largest organizations with significant resources. In other cases, agency quality assurance coordinators are often experienced clinicians with clinical expertise, but are far removed from contemporary research. This is a challenge for social work curricula, which is often divided into silos so some students are trained to use research evidence as clinicians and others to use data analysis and statistical benchmarking as administrators, sometimes with little crossover. Agencies that can hire social workers who are well-trained in EBP and can supplement this preparation with in-house training programs that can expand on evidence-based management emphases will be well-situated to have staff who can handle some of the research load while still being involved in the work of service delivery and supervision. The organizational development manager position at CSI is an example of a position that combines research provision and supervision with broader consulting and operations responsibilities. Other such hybrid positions may be suitable for small agencies and may be attractive to early-career social work graduates who have been well-trained in EBP and also seek career advancement.

Workforce Development

The need for workforce development for existing managers may far exceed agency capacity, so the agency may require assistance from faculty as trainers and from student interns as temporary staff members and support resources.

According to Rzepnicki and Briggs (2004), social work faculty roles may have to change. Both practice and research teachers may have to assist field instructors with the growing demands on agencies to use research training in preparing their staff and management for using the EBP process. At CSI, the organizational development manager's personal and political connections to university researchers and specialists made it easier for him to transfer these relationships to staff and to maintain some relationship with both staff and researchers. Field students were used as EBP trainers of consumers and staff of the group home, teaching them task-centered practice to aid them in establishing a social leisure program and a behavior modification program for addressing critical incidents.

Critics have pointed out that it is likely that there will always be far greater agency demand for assistance with EBP than academic capacity to assist, and there is likely to be little incentive for tenure track academic faculty to provide more consistent assistance without academic incentives. Agency-university partnerships are a promising way to build research opportunities for faculty into community agencies' daily work, but as Holosko, Thyer, and Danner (2009) have suggested, this may require a new tolerance for the open and transparent scholarly reporting of agency evaluation outcomes, including the reporting of agencies' clinical outcome data in academic journals.

Diffusion of Evidence-Based Management

Diffusing evidence based management evidence-based management throughout agency culture is challenging but worthwhile.

According to Stewart (1998), evidence-based management is a state of mind that regards a "questioning approach as acceptable and encouraged" (p. 29). The barriers to using it are workload, inadequate time, poor work skills, poor attitudes of peers and superiors, and the belief that "management is intuitive" and not a function of experimentation and research. Incentives for the use of evidence-based management include a focus on research that recognizes that management can also be a science, that learning from the practices of others is essential (Rzepnicki & Briggs, 2004), and that effective time management and self-regulation are important management skills that can be improved by research consumption.

All in all, management research is complex and is harder to measure or transfer to decision making than clinical research is for EBP (Blumenthal & Their, 2003). It involves highly complex settings, with few comparable data sets across agencies, and managers who are not trained in research are less likely to "encounter the products of management research when they appear in journals outside the mainstream of scholarship" (Blumenthal & Their, 2003, p. 368).

Evidence-based management was used in this case study to reform a struggling program and increasingly was diffused agency-wide. The benefits accrued to all levels of the organization, including the families, the consumers, the staff, and the management of the organization. The state gave the agency high praise, and CSI has remained a nationally recognized social service agency with strong quality assurance and performance management capabilities.

Experimentation

It is beneficial to establish a culture of experimentation. Settings where evidence-based management and the EBP process are effective are in health care and medical industries, which value research culture and scientific rigor as drivers of improvement.

Pfeffer and Sutton (2006) indicate there are a few things managers can do to keep an evidence-based management mind-set. They believe that managers should view their agencies "as an unfinished prototype" (p. 35), should use evidence from reliable and valid measures, and should use outside reputable opinions as markers. They believe that everyone in the organization should collect and use data and should educate each other about the new knowledge they have acquired. Engaging in social marketing involves selling peers on the evidence. It allows staff and managers to expose bad practices and disqualify them for future use, and to learn from errors and remember failures so they will not be repeated. The success of the staff and residents in this case study were publicized weekly, program audits were handled smoothly by program supervisors, and regulatory bodies certified that the agency's operations and program functioning were a model for other agencies to follow. As seen in this case study, when program evaluation data comes back to program managers and treatment teams so they can use it in daily clinical decision making, a high level of rigor and critical thinking infuse the agency as a whole.

A Glossary of Terminology

A glossary of evidence-based management terminology can create a common language for all participants and encompasses evidence-based management as a quality-improvement system, a problem-solving method, and a rational decision-making process.

Evidence-based management is a mind-set that encompasses a culture of research, experimentation, and usage of evidence in decision making. In this case study, such a culture of research and critical thinking was shared across all levels of the infrastructure. Ovretveit (1998) perhaps put it best: "Using evaluation in different ways to inform management and policy decisions is the exception rather than the norm, in most places other than the United Kingdom" (p. 381). He goes on to say that in the electronic age, with its better educated and informed consumers, managers will have to use research knowledge to support their professional interests because other peers will be advocating and leveraging their perspectives with the information they collect.

In this case study, evidence-based management occurred with the administrative support of research partnerships, but also with the cooperation of staff, families, and consumers. In order for staff to buy into the process agency-wide, they developed a glossary of terms and reached consensus about every definition. The glossary of concepts formed a common language for staff and management to aid in the implementation of the agency's performance management system. Academic consultants who are familiar with writing codebooks for research projects may be useful in helping agency staff write a glossary, but the utility of having stakeholders share terms and concepts in their own words cannot be overemphasized.

IMPLICATIONS

Future research investigating the effects of an agency culture of questioning, trial and error experimentation, and research utilization on key staff, management and client performance variables needs to be conducted. Such investigation should track the measurable extent of evidence-based management and EBP broadly and identify its specific impact on agency and client aims. Future studies need to include evaluation methodologies such as single-case designs as well as aggregate data analysis methods that staff can use to track agency management and direct practice processes and outcomes systematically.

Little research has been conducted on the optimal agency conditions and circumstances needed for staff to use EBP and evidence-based management effectively in social service agencies. It is not clear whether mandated or voluntary conditions provide better incentives or disincentives for effectively using EBP and evidence-based management. Further examination is needed of specific ways managers on the ground engage in internal marketing and otherwise seek to influence staff to accept and faithfully use an innovation. Rothschild (1999) offers a conceptual framework for how public and social service managers use education, marketing, and law or mandates as ways to influence targeted behavior; Rothschild's notions of education, marketing, and law refer back to Charles Lindblom's categorization in *Politics and Markets*

(1977) of persuasion, exchange, and authority. Education or persuasion seek to gain voluntary compliance, with the knowledge gained as its own (and often the only) reward. Marketing or exchange seeks to elicit desired behavior by explicitly touting benefits the behavioral target would like to see and motivating self-monitoring of compliance for ongoing behavioral participation. Law or authority uses coercion and the threat of consequences to achieve desired behavior, adding external monitoring to the self-monitoring implied in marketing.

While most translational research frameworks heavily emphasize training and education components; the role of marketing and mandating in the translation of evidence-based practice is much less examined. Rothschild (1999) uses the metaphor of an insurance risk premium to suggest that people targeted for behavioral change will engage in change resistance behavior that depends on how risky the desired behavioral change seems to them; behavioral targets will be willing to pay a higher risk premium in the form of resisting or obstructing change the more the desired change seems risky or threatening. Rothschild suggests that education efforts alone are likely to be successful only when fear of change is low or nearly absent, while moderate fear of change may be dissipated by internal marketing efforts. Relatively high fear of change may respond only to the imposition of a mandate or law that seeks involuntary compliance.

Rubin (2007) argues that EBP "expects too much of busy practitioners with limited time and perhaps limited access to literature databases" (p. 542). Agency-wide implementation of EBP and evidence-based management processes and agency-university partnerships such as those discussed in this case study are attempts to mitigate the individual practitioner's burden. Practitioners seeking to use EBP and evidence-based management in agency practice should collect data on the realities and unintended consequences of doing so. As participants in this case study remind us, what gets monitored gets done. Agency-level implementation of EBP and evidence-based management, in partnership with university researchers, offers an exciting possibility to see how systematic and scientific management can help create better outcomes for communities, families, and individuals.

References

Bailey-Dempsey, C., & Reid, W. J. (1996). Intervention design and development: A case study. *Research on Social Work Practice, 6*(2), pp. 208–228.

Blumenthal, D., & Their, S. O. (2003). Improving the generation, dissemination, and use of management research. *Health Care Management Review, 28*(4), pp. 366–375.

Briggs, H. E. (1994). Promoting adoptions by foster parents through an inner-city organization. *Research on Social Work Practice, 4,* 497–509.

Briggs, H. E. (1996). Enhancing community adjustment of persons with developmental disabilities: Transferring multilevel behavioral technology to an inner-city community organization. *The Journal of Applied Social Sciences, 20,* 177–190.

Briggs, H. E. (2009). The fusion of culture and science: Challenges and controversies of cultural competency and evidence-based practice with an African American family advocacy network. *Children and Youth Services Review, 31*(11), 1172–1179.

Briggs, H. E., & McBeath, B. (2009). Evidence-based management: Origins, challenges, and implications for social service administration. *Administration in Social Work, 33,* 242–261.

Gambrill, E. (2004). Contributions of critical thinking and evidence-based practice to the fulfillment of the ethical obligations of professionals. In H. E. Briggs & T. L. Rzepnicki (Eds.). *Using evidence in social work practice: Behavioral perspectives* (pp. 3–19). Chicago, IL: Lyceum.

Gambrill, E. (2006). Evidence-based practice and policy: Choices ahead. *Research on Social Work Practice, 16*(3), 338–357.

Gambrill, E. (2007). Book review. Norcross, J. C., Beutler, L. E., & Levant, R. F. Evidence-based practices in mental health: Debate and dialogue on the fundamental questions. *Research on Social Work Practice, 17*(3), pp. 428–434.

Gibbs, L.E., (2003). *Evidence-based practice for the helping professions: A practical guide with integrated multimedia.* Pacific Grove, CA: Thomson/Brook/Cole.

Gioia, D., (2007). Using an organizational change model to qualitatively understand practitioner adoption of evidence-based practice in community mental health. *Best Practice in Mental Health, 3*(1), pp. 1–15.

Hamilton, J., (2005). Clinicians' guide to evidence-based practice. *Journal of the American Academy of Child and Adolescent Psychiatry, 44*(5), pp. 494–498.

Holosko, M. J., Thyer, B. A., & Danner, J. E. H. (2009). Ethical guidelines for designing and conducting evaluations of social work practice. *Journal of Evidence-Based Social Work, 6*(4), 348–360.

Jenson, J.M., (2005). Connecting science to intervention: Advances, challenges, and the promise of evidence-based practice. *Social Work Research, 29*(3), pp. 131–135.

Kovner, A. R., & Rundall, T. G. (2006). Evidence-based management reconsidered. *Frontiers of Health Services Management, 22*(3), 3–22.

Lindblom, C. E. (1977). *Politics and markets: The world's political-economic systems.* New York, NY: Basic Books.

McBeath, B., Briggs, H.E., & Aisenberg, E. (in press). Examining the premise supporting the empirically supported intervention approach to social work practice. To be published in *Social Work.*

McCracken, S. G., & Corrigan, P. W. (2004). Staff development in mental health. In H. E. Briggs & T. L. Rzepnicki (Eds.), *Using evidence in social work practice: Behavioral perspectives* (pp. 232–256). Chicago, IL: Lyceum.

Melnyk, B. M., & Fineout-Overholt, E. (2006). Consumer preferences and values as an integral key to evidence-based practice. *Nursing Administration Quarterly, 30*(2), pp. 123–127.

Nursing News. (2006). Dermatology nursing. *Nursing News, 18*(6), p. 607.

Ovretveit, J. (1998). Medical managers can make research-based management decisions. *Journal of Management in Medicine, 12*(6), pp. 391–397.

Pfeffer, J., & Sutton, R. I., (2006). Profiting from evidence-based management. *Strategy and Leadership, 34*(2), pp. 35–42.

Pinkston, E. M., Green, G. R., Linsk, N. L., & Young, R. N. (2001). A family eco-behavioral approach for elders with mental illness. In H. E. Briggs & K. Corcoran (Eds.), *Social work practice: Treating common problems* (pp. 339–370). Chicago, IL: Lyceum.

Reid, W. J. (1979). The model development dissertation. *Journal of Social Research, 3*, pp. 215–225.

Rothschild, M. L. (1999). Carrots, sticks, and promises: A conceptual framework for the management of public health and social issue behaviors. *The Journal of Marketing, 63*(4), 24–37.

Rubin, A. (2007). Improving the teaching of evidence-based practice: Introduction to the special issue. *Research on Social Work Practice, 17*, 541–547.

Rzepnicki, T. L., & Briggs, H. E., (2004). Using evidence in your practice. In H. E. Briggs & T. L. Rzepnicki (eds.), *Using evidence in social work practice: Behavioral perspectives.* Chicago, IL: Lyceum.

Sackett, D. L., Straus, S. E., Richardson, W. S., Rosenberg, W., & Haynes, R. B. (2000). *Evidence-based medicine: How to practice and teach EBM* (2nd ed.). New York, NY: Churchill Livingstone.

Silberman, M., & Hansburg, F. (2005). Defining knowledge management. *Strategic Direction, 21*(10), pp. 22–24.

Stewart, R. (1998). Management theory: More art than science. *Health Service Journal, 108*, pp. 28–29.

Walshe, K., & Rundall, T. G., (2001). Evidence-based management: From theory to practice in health care. *The Milbank Quarterly, 79*(3), pp. 429–457.

CHAPTER NINE

Learning from Data: The Beginning of Error Reduction in Illinois Child Welfare

*Tina L. Rzepnicki, Penny R. Johnson, Denise Q. Kane,
Diane Moncher, Lisa Coconato, and Barbara Shulman*

This chapter describes a newly legislated initiative in Illinois meant to identify common patterns of case decision error and to develop a systemic response to improve the state's ability to protect children in families where there have been allegations of abuse or neglect. These efforts were born out of a deep interest in making the best use of evidence to support good practice and improve child welfare outcomes. We begin by describing a framework for understanding human error in an organizational context and then apply the framework to examples in child protection uncovered during investigations conducted by the Illinois Department of Children and Family Services' Office of the Inspector General. Drawing on evidence from both the social science knowledge base and data collected by the inspector general's office on child protection practices, a model of error reduction was designed that is currently in the beginning stages of development and implementation. We offer examples of incremental changes that are being attempted, along with plans for their evaluation. It is hoped that a series of such changes

This project is supported in part by a contract between the Illinois Department of Children and Family Services and the University of Chicago School of Social Service Administration. The authors thank the DCFS Office of the Inspector General staff, Quality Assurance staff, and Ashley Curry, Erick Guerrero, Huong Nguyen, and John Smagner for their contributions to data collection and analysis.

can be built into practice statewide to improve the safety of children and create a work environment for child protection staff that supports sound practice and encourages learning from mistakes.

A Framework for Understanding Error
in Case Decision Making

It is widely understood that child protection decision making typically occurs in highly stressful, complex environments. Many barriers to sound case decision making exist, including time constraints, limited and uncertain information regarding case events, the need to accommodate other systems (such as the courts, police, and other service providers), lack of adequate supervision, and policies and procedures that do not provide clear guidelines for practice. Together, these factors produce organizational pressures that may encourage child protection workers to circumvent some procedural mandates in the interest of closing cases in a timely manner. Mistakes in judgment leading to inaccurate assessments of risk are inevitable under such difficult circumstances. Decisions about risk and removal involve difficult appraisals of family functioning; a key question is what degree of poor parenting is better than the trauma of foster care. An excellent risk assessment may conclude that there is a low probability of harm, but low probability events do happen.

Unfortunately, errors[1] occasionally result in tragic case outcomes, such as the serious injury or death of a child. While individual caseworkers may suffer the blame for poor decision making, it is increasingly recognized that mistakes are likely to result as much from problems with organizational processes as from individual misjudgments. Although such events occur infrequently, a child's death in a family known to child protective services is a tragedy for the family and community. After a death the agency may experience collateral consequences, including loss of public trust, loss of credibility, and negative media attention resulting in reputational damage. Given the high cost of error, child welfare belongs in a special set of organizations that must be highly reliable. Theories and practices that have been developed in the context of organizations that have shown a high degree of reliability (that is, minimal error) in high-risk environments have powerful application to child welfare.

---

[1] For the purposes of this chapter and on the basis of the work of James Reason (J. Reason, 1990), errors include mistakes in gathering or assessing available information, mistakes in planning, unintended failures of execution, and rule violations. Actions of sabotage—that is, violations with malicious intent—are excluded from our definition.

In the last thirty years social scientists have made great strides in studying errors in the context of organizational processes, developing ways of predicting their occurrence, and creating strategies for preventing similar errors in the future. Moving away from individual psychology and a strictly human-factors approach, a systems perspective has been adopted for understanding human error. The systems perspective assumes that errors occur in a dynamic rather than static organizational environment and takes into account the contributions of individual behavior, interaction and communication patterns, organizational culture, and administrative and policy factors. In this model, decision error is the result of the increasing complexity of a system that isn't flexible enough to adapt to changing conditions. Multiple weaknesses in organizational processes occasionally line up to create a tragic outcome. While it is recognized that occasional accidents can't be avoided, a systems perspective makes it possible to introduce a systematic and comprehensive approach to investigation and prevention efforts with the goal of decreasing their occurrence (Dekker, 2002; Rasmussen, 1990b; Reason, 1990, 1997).

A systems perspective, based on the theoretical advances of Charles Perrow (Perrow, 1984), Jens Rasmussen (Rasmussen, 1990b), James Reason (Reason, 1990), and others was first introduced as an approach for examining industrial and engineering accidents that had catastrophic outcomes including loss of life. The nuclear power plant accidents at Three Mile Island (1979) and Chernobyl (1986), Union Carbide's chemical plant tragedy at Bhopal (1984), the space shuttle Challenger disaster (1986), and major airline crashes have all set the stage for the development and refinement of methods to uncover contributing factors. Scholars investigating these events concluded that human error is rarely a sufficient explanation for negative outcomes.

For example, Shrivastava's investigation of the Bhopal accident determined that the catastrophe resulted from a combination of "HOT" factors. HOT factors call to attention the unique roles played by human failings (H), inadequate organizational processes (O), and technological problems (T) that can result in decision errors and the need to examine all three domains in searching for causes (Shrivastava, 1987). A parallel can be drawn in the field of child welfare, where practice is adapted to conform to insufficient worker skill and experience, staff shortages, time limits prescribed by state mandates, caseload size, imperfect software programs that don't provide staff with timely information, and other factors that impinge upon job performance.

Reason (Reason, 1997) further refined the systems perspective on organizational failure (errors and accidents) when he introduced the related concepts of active failure and latent failure to express the multi-level nature of incident causation. He maintained that active failure is

usually associated with the errors and rule violations of frontline opera-
tors (in child welfare, child protection investigators or direct-service
staff) and has an immediate impact upon the system. Latent failure is
most often generated by individuals more distant from the incident, at
the upper levels of the system (policy makers, program designers, or
managers) and may lie dormant indefinitely. Examples of latent failure
in child welfare might include errors that occur as a result of chronic
staff shortages and when there is pressure to complete child protection
investigations within thirty days. Most active failures are not sufficient
in and of themselves to cause an accident; other conditions are necessary to set the stage.

Reason created the "Swiss cheese" model to describe how organizations are built with layers of defense against active failures, but with
holes at each level representing weaknesses and gaps (latent failures).
The layers are in constant flux, but holes occasionally line up perfectly,
allowing an accident to occur (for example, when a child is severely
injured while an abuse investigation is underway). This model offers
insights into system dynamics that can produce a tragic outcome in a
child protection case. Understanding potential sources of error provides a foundation upon which to build better organizational processes
that will reduce the likelihood of similar mistakes occurring in the
future.

A Strategy for Uncovering Error

Establishing detailed procedures and frequent training for the operational level (child protection investigators and direct-service staff) are
two ways management typically attempts to reduce the occurrence of
serious errors. In child protection we have seen a proliferation of
detailed procedural guidelines, forms, assessment tools, and related
training, all of which are intended to limit worker autonomy and
enhance accountability, reliability, and good decision making (Munro,
1999). Despite these strategies, underestimations of the level of risk to a
child continues to occur, suggesting perhaps that a culture of compliance is not effectively meeting the needs of the family or the organizational goal of child protection.

A number of explanations are consistent with the Swiss cheese
model. Perhaps in-service training lacks support for generalizing new
skills to the specific job. Policies, written procedures, or incentives may
discourage sound practice and encourage staff to engage in task shortcuts that then become routinized within their work units. There may be
a lack of support for exploring alternative explanations and hypotheses.
Faulty processes such as these illustrate the "dynamic interrelationship

between organizational structure, environmental contingency, and practitioner experience" (Dekker & Suparamanian, 2005, p. 2).

Practitioners can establish preventive actions by first understanding the elements of failure. However, merely classifying error is not the same as taking effective corrective action. It is also important to understand common patterns of failure across cases, including contextual factors that create hospitable conditions for error. Finally, identification of organizational processes likely to produce a more effective and supportive work environment provide the final step leading to the selection of effective actions.

In an effort to understand problems with the Illinois child protection risk assessment protocol, we applied root cause analysis. Our goal was to collect and analyze data on a sample of cases to guide efforts aimed at improving the child protection investigation system and increasing the safety of children.

A structured investigative and analytic tool, root cause analysis grew out of the theory and accident investigations in high-risk industries referenced earlier. The central aim of root cause analysis is to find points in a system where improvements are feasible that will reduce the likelihood of a similar incident or negative event in the future. As a general approach to the investigation of error, root cause analysis follows the principles of logic.

Root cause analysis is the systematic examination of multiple systems and causes that may contribute to an adverse event. The safety of a child who comes into contact with a public child welfare organization is a product of the interaction of multiple players and a complex system of supports and constraints, each of which has a role in promoting child well-being. Root cause analysis moves beyond assignment of individual culpability to the identification of organizational or system problems that lead to individual errors. It prompts examination of larger system failures, some of which may result from organizational culture and seeks solutions that may prevent future incidents. At each step, the analyst considers events and contextual factors in a systematic way.

The problem to be analyzed begins with the negative outcome or sentinel event—in this case, the fatality of a child during or soon after involvement by the child welfare system. The immediate cause is identified as an action (for example, the father stuffed baby wipes in the child's mouth) which itself is the result of another action or set of conditions (the father was responsible for child care; the child was crying). For each event in the chain, the investigator asks, "What led to this event? What allowed it to happen?" This process is repeated a number of times in a single investigation, resulting in the creation of a complex event tree with many branches and multiple root causes.

This approach reduces the influence of hindsight bias by requiring careful consideration of the information that was available and known at specific points in time, rather than assuming that what was known at the end of the case was also known early on and disregarded. In this way, the analyst attempts to step back in time to accurately understand the full context in which staff actions were or were not taken.

Due to the complexity of human service organizations and their operations, identifying contributing factors and root causes of a tragic outcome, such as the fatality of a child, can take a great deal of time and much digging for facts. The results, however, are only as good as the data available from the fatality investigation. It was essential to make every effort to obtain corroborating information on the facts of the case and to be mindful of the dangers of cognitive biases and assumptions. We next turn to an example of how root cause analysis was used to uncover risk assessment errors in child protection cases and to provide a direction for a statewide initiative to improve child maltreatment investigations.

The Illinois Investigation

In Illinois, the Department of Children and Family Services' (DCFS) Office of the Inspector General (OIG) was created by the Illinois General Assembly in 1993 to investigate complaints against the department and private child welfare agencies in cases where children were seriously injured or died within a year of child welfare involvement. A key goal was to identify areas in the child welfare system that are in need of improvement and to recommend change.

A special project[2] was developed in 2005 to uncover common patterns of error across cases and to provide to the state director of DCFS additional data to inform recommendations for the improvement of child protection investigations and agency practice. The OIG had previously noted concerns with implementation of the Child Endangerment and Risk Analysis Protocol (CERAP) by DCFS investigators in their examination of child deaths. The goal of this special project was to identify common factors that led to inaccurate assessments of risk and to ineffective safety plans during child maltreatment investigations. For this examination, we considered not only child protection investigator behavior, but also the broader context in which safety and risk assessment decisions are made. Our effort to find a method for sorting out the multiple and specific causes of CERAP errors led to the selection of

---

[2] The description of this project is adapted from Office of the Inspector General, Illinois Department of Children and Family Services, 2007.

an analytic approach based on root cause analysis. This permitted us both to highlight problems and their context and to identify ways the CERAP process and tool might be improved.

METHODS

The root cause analysis method was adapted to examine CERAP errors in cases of death or serious injury of a child whose family had been known to DCFS through child protection investigations or services within the previous year. Although the sample of cases was not representative of cases served by DCFS, subsequent data collection focusing on a sample of cases that did not involve near-lethal child injury or death confirmed that such errors were widespread and, under certain conditions, could have had tragic outcomes.

Below we present a brief description of the data collection and analytic strategies applied to each of several samples obtained from the OIG. We examined overlapping samples of cases by applying three case review strategies: a software tool for examining individual cases using root cause analysis (DECISION Systems, Inc., 2003a) and two additional analyses using the logic of root cause analysis but not the software: one an analysis of cases using data from OIG investigations and the other an analysis of original case material. The team's primary interest in root cause analysis was its potential for offering a framework that would help ensure that all avenues of an investigation were exhausted in comprehensive case reviews. We reviewed ten cases with at least one of the methods and subjected some of the cases to multiple reviews (see table 1). The use of overlapping samples and multiple data sources and analyses permitted us to compare results and increased our confidence in the findings.

OIG Examination of Cases

A team of OIG staff worked together to analyze four cases of child death. The cases that were selected had been involved with DCFS within the previous year, were currently under investigation by the OIG, and had provoked questions about the quality of case decision making pertaining to allegations of child maltreatment. Each case was analyzed separately. The analysis began with the creation of a timeline of events leading to the child's death or injury, and this timeline served as a general guide for the rest of the analysis. Key elements of the root cause analysis method included creating a causal tree that incorporated the following: 1) a statement of the sentinel event or adverse outcome; 2) a backward chaining of events, conditions, and inactions; 3) identification of causal sets; 4) logic testing for accuracy of each causal set; 5)

TABLE 1 Root Cause Analysis Sample

		Analytic Method		
Case Number	OIG Investigation Type	REASON®	OIG investigation reviewed	Original case material reviewed
1	Death of medically complex child		X	
2	Inadequate services to substance-exposed infant		X	
3	Child death in an open family case with serious home safety hazards		X	X
4	Death of a teen ward's infant due to physical abuse		X	
5	Serious physical injury to medically complex child after unnecessary protective custody taken		X	X
6	Child death by physical abuse in family with open case	X		
7	Serious injury to child during pending child protection investigation	X	X	
8	Child death due to lack of parental supervision following child protection investigation		X	
9	Death of substance-exposed infant in family with open case	X	X	X
10	Death of child from physical abuse during pending child protection investigation	X		

termination of cause-effect chains; and 6) identification of prevention principles (DECISION Systems, Inc., 2003b; Rzepnicki & Johnson, 2005).

Analysis of the four cases benefited from the multiple perspectives generated through the team's group process. The combination of group discussion and introduction of multiple perspectives may have helped the team to monitor and control biases, especially hindsight bias, which is the most common. Backward tracking of case events by a group was aimed at preventing the use of information that became available only during the death investigation and was not known to child welfare staff while the family was being investigated by protective services. The group process also aided in modeling an accurate sequence of events because reconstructing a chronology typically becomes increasingly difficult as the analysis moves back in time. Multiple perspectives represented by practitioners, lawyers, administrators, and child welfare experts provided a safeguard against groupthink.

Although the root cause analysis facilitated judgments about what was important and what was not, it was still possible to overlook factors that had contributed to faulty decision making regarding a child's level of safety and risk of harm. Intimate knowledge of the organizational environment permitted the group to expose factors that may have reduced the effectiveness of child protection efforts. This knowledge facilitated the identification of latent errors, such as hidden disincentives for following agency protocol regarding the CERAP. Despite the safeguards against bias, however, it was still possible that team members' personal biases may have influenced the selection of some factors.

Case Analyses Using OIG Investigation Reports

Eight cases were selected for analysis using completed OIG investigation reports. From a pool of twenty-three cases in which it had been noted that at least one element of the CERAP protocol had not been followed, a range of cases was selected to ensure a wide variety of circumstances, complexities, and case variables. The goal was to have a diverse pool of cases to analyze and then to generalize basic thematic findings.

Using the logic, philosophy, and key principles of root cause analysis, this analysis aggregated the causes of CERAP failures on different levels to increase the power of the findings from individual cases. For each case, we examined CERAP-related actions on the part of staff; conditions or contextual factors that set the occasion for particular actions to occur; and inactions—actions that didn't happen, but should have—at the policy, supervisory, and individual worker levels (adapted from DECISION Systems, Inc., 2003a). Cases were coded in this way to obtain a multifaceted understanding of organizational processes and individual worker behavior that led to errors in safety and risk assessment. Each case was then reviewed with the OIG staff responsible for the original investigation of the child's death or serious injury, to evaluate the results of the analysis for accuracy and completeness, to reduce the likelihood of introducing hindsight bias, and to discuss potential implications of the findings.

Case Analyses Using Original Case Material

Three cases were selected randomly from the sample subjected to the case analysis of OIG investigations and project staff analyzed them thoroughly using a data collection instrument that surveyed the most relevant factors in child protection investigations, as informed by the literature on risk assessment and decision making.[3] The analysis of contributing factors covered a limited period of time, from the hotline call to the completion of the initial safety and risk assessment. This time frame was selected because it would provide a realistic sense of what information and resources were available to the child protection investigator at that particular time. This reduced the opportunity for hindsight bias to influence the analysis.

MAJOR FINDINGS

The analysis uncovered decision-making errors and contextual conditions that made such errors more likely.

Level 1 Qualitative Findings: Decision-Making Errors

Child maltreatment investigations frequently require complex decision making under uncertain conditions. The child protection investigator is expected to seek out and make use of all relevant sources of information, but our analysis revealed several problems with data collection. These included a failure to seek information from multiple sources or to access available information, failure to recognize cumulative risk, and failure to develop and monitor a safety plan. Although these problems represent weaknesses in investigation practices, the context in which they occur offers opportunities for potential remedies at other levels within the agency.

Failure to Use Multiple Sources of Information or to Access Available Information. This was one of the most frequent errors identified in our

---

[3] Individual Case Review Form available from first author.

individual case analyses, occurring in 80 percent of the cases examined. Collateral contacts who should have been consulted, but were not, included treatment providers (doctors, nurses, therapists, residential staff, homemakers, foster parents, social workers, and so on), the police, the other parent, teachers, neighbors, friends and relatives, and the person who made the report.

Gathering information from multiple sources increases the probability of an accurate assessment of the family situation. First, interviewing multiple sources allows the investigator to get a clear and complete picture of the problem. Second, it is important to corroborate information provided by the parent, other caregivers, family members, and service providers. Contradictory reports must be pursued until the child protection investigator is confident that complete and accurate information has been obtained.

Collecting data on persons in the home who have a criminal background, on alleged perpetrators who have access to the child, and on other adults with access to the child who have histories of violence or substance abuse must be part of the risk assessment and safety plan. Although a parent may profess that the alleged perpetrator no longer has access to the child, corroborating that information with professionals and family members is essential, and obtaining a protective order could provide more confidence in the parent's compliance.

Failure to Recognize Cumulative Risk. During an investigation of a specific allegation, the investigator may learn of contextual or other factors that create additional risk of harm. In our sample child protection investigators frequently failed to recognize cumulative risks posed by a combination of historical and current circumstances, such as previous injuries, substance abuse, domestic violence, and mental health problems that posed additional danger to the child.

In half of the cases examined, substance abuse was a significant problem that went unrecognized when it was not the allegation that was reported to the child abuse hotline. For example, in a case of alleged medical neglect of an infant, the mother suffered from poly–substance dependence and had tested positive for cocaine at a previous birth, but she was investigated only on the allegation of medical neglect. The investigator did not recognize the presence of substance abuse as an additional risk, despite knowing that the mother was addicted to drugs and had moved in with another addict. A change of circumstances, such as the return home of an abusive partner in a violent relationship, the cessation of medication in a parent with a psychiatric diagnosis, or entrustment of the care of a previously abused infant to a parent who has a long history of alcohol abuse, are other examples of situations that should have been, but frequently were not assessed for cumulative risk.

Failure to Develop and Monitor a Realistic Safety Plan. The development and monitoring of a safety plan is the most critical part of a safety assessment because it occurs in the context of an existing, identified safety concern. Our analysis found that investigators sometimes developed plans that lacked clarity and clear consequences. Mitigating factors that permitted children to remain in the home despite safety concerns were not verified to ensure that the underlying assumptions were correct, nor were contingency plans developed for situations in which circumstances in the home deteriorated; all of which suggest that child protection staff may not have planned details of implementation or anticipated obstacles to completion. For example, children might have been considered safe because the alleged perpetrator was incarcerated at the time of the investigation, but the plan did not provide for the contingency of the alleged perpetrator's release or the consequences of contact with him or her. Our examination of staff performance determined that there was inadequate guidance for child protection staff on how to develop realistic and effective safety plans that could be monitored and targeted to the identified safety concern. Directions on how to address specific components of the safety plan, such as violence, were also lacking.

When a safety concern has been identified, consideration of involving family resources is critical. When family members present as viable support and show concern about the child's well-being, their inclusion in the safety plan may mean the difference between protection and harm. If violence is the presenting issue, as it is in all physical abuse cases, a safety plan should include specific components that will increase surveillance and opportunities to better protect the child. Strategies might include daily observation of the child by an individual outside the immediate family whom the child trusts and who has demonstrated concern for the child. In addition, persons outside the immediate family such as daycare providers or extended family members can be included in the safety plan and can agree to notify the child protection agency if circumstances change.

Level 2 Qualitative Findings: Contextual Factors

The project team also took account of contextual factors that could have contributed to case-decision errors.

Supervisory Responsibility. It is the responsibility of the supervisor to monitor the investigation and the completion of the CERAP protocol before the sixty-day time limit has been reached. The case studies indicated problems with supervisory monitoring in three major areas: approving the assessment without all needed information, poor judgment and decision making, and failure to ensure that the child protection investigator conducted an adequate risk assessment, completing all required steps.

The supervisory function in identifying safety concerns and developing safety plans is critical to the agency's ability to effectively protect children. It is the responsibility of the supervisor to identify areas of inconsistency and of inadequate fact finding and corroboration; to ensure that all sources of available information, such as child abuse records and criminal history have been obtained; and to ensure monitoring of safety plans once they have been established. The supervisor is responsible for oversight that ensures that the investigator verifies medical information through interviews with medical professionals and contacts the person reporting the abuse, police investigators, and child care professionals and other service providers. Prompts or checklists to ensure that all available critical information was accessed and a requirement that the investigator document sources for a particular safety factor would enable supervisors to perform a meaningful review of the safety assessment.

Other Systemic Factors. The review of cases and OIG recommendations revealed problems with the translation of policy into practice. The analyses revealed that some child maltreatment investigation policies did not clearly designate to whom, where, and when they should apply; were not clearly communicated; and were inadequately monitored at the staff and supervisory levels. The development of policies regarding caseload coverage and case management seem particularly critical. In one-half of the case studies, problems were evident due to inadequate staffing practices. Failures to fill open positions within the child protection team and failures to develop adequate plans for covering unstaffed caseloads resulted in insufficient supervisory support in understaffed teams and offices. Problems that originate at this level are best addressed by improvement in the communication of policies to staff and by marshaling of means to improve practice, such as additional training, staff, materials, or other resources, particularly with respect to problems in investigative practices. Problem-solving actions to address these workplace factors are important for maintaining sound practice in a less than ideal work environment.

Our efforts to identify common patterns of error pointed to a number of weaknesses in practice stemming from a lack of critical thinking, a stressful work environment that included staff shortages and informal incentives for practice and supervisory shortcuts, and an organizational culture that did not make use of mistakes as opportunities for learning.

Corroboration of Qualitative Findings

In conducting the qualitative analyses, we noted that the homicides of a number of children were preceded by a child protection investigation for cuts, welts, and bruises. In an effort to corroborate our findings and to learn how to best target remedial actions relevant to specific types of cases, we reviewed a new sample of 300 recent child protection investigations involving allegations of cuts, welts, and bruises to children. The stratified random sample of cases included those in which there were no serious injuries and an oversampling of cases involving infants five months of age or younger (N = 100), due to their overrepresentation in homicides. Recurrent errors and system weaknesses identified for this category of cases included an overall lack of critical thinking, inadequate knowledge of normal childhood bruising, failure to involve medical professionals in diagnosis and prevention, the lack of a requirement that investigators interview child-centered collaterals, problems in developing effective safety plans, and lack of management support. Each of these issues was consistent with the general problems found in the earlier analyses. A curriculum to address risk assessment and safety planning principles was developed, and training was initiated.

INITIAL STRATEGIES TO REDUCE ERROR

One of the results of this work was the promulgation of legislation (20 ILCS 505/35.7) that requires the OIG to remedy patterns of errors or problematic practices that compromise or threaten the safety of children, as those patterns are identified in the inspector general's death and serious injury investigations and by child death review teams.[4] Although the findings from our analyses suggested that intervention was required at multiple levels in the organization, incremental change was viewed as having the greatest chance of success. As a first step, the inspector general developed a training curriculum related to cuts, welts, and bruises, and completed the first round of comprehensive trainings of all child protection workers and supervisors by the end of 2009.

Critical Thinking

The basic principle of the cuts, welts, and bruises error-reduction training included the application of critical thinking skills to investigations

---

[4] Discussion of content areas is largely adapted from Office of the Inspector General, Illinois Department of Children and Family Services, 2009.

to counteract the tendency to oversimplify and overlook relevant information, and to inform decisions regarding safety and imminent risk of harm. Critical thinking, the ability to consider all available information and actively seek disconfirming evidence, should underpin all important case decisions.

Common errors included investigators' overreliance on self-report and failure to objectively weigh the credibility of informants. The CERAP analyses found that when some child protection investigators encountered cases involving cuts, welts, and bruises, they did not contact multiple sources or seek corroboration of information provided by collaterals and other informants. At times, investigators became prematurely anchored to their initial impressions and rejected evidence that contradicted their first impressions, particularly when they did not perceive initial injuries to the child as serious. Others operated under a "Rule of Optimism," misinterpreting and overlooking harmful behaviors and discrediting facts that contradicted their optimism (Dingwall, Eekelaar, & Murray, 1983; Gambrill, 2006). For example, in one case the investigator relied on the mother's self-report that she was responsible for injuring her child despite contradictory information given by another family member that her boyfriend had abused the child. To reduce the effect of these biases and to lower the reliance on self-report, investigators must gather enough information to provide a fair and accurate account of the events leading to the child's injuries.

The training curriculum was designed to review key components of investigations, which include conducting a scene investigation and a mock reenactment of the incident, creating a timeline of events, and identifying key informants. Our analysis of cases pointed to other important areas warranting attention as well, all of which would enhance the investigator's ability to think critically about a cuts, welts, and bruises investigation.

Knowledge of Normal Childhood Bruising. A review of the literature on childhood bruising revealed that children who do not cruise do not bruise. It is rare for infants to suffer a bruise before they are crawling or walking. Those who do cruise tend to suffer accidental bruises on bony areas, such as the forehead and shins. Bruises on soft-tissue areas, such as cheeks, ears, the stomach, and buttocks, should cause concern (Carpenter, 1998; Sugar, Taylor, & Feldman, 1999). Because there were many cases in which child protection investigators ignored signs of mild bruising on young infants and on soft-tissue areas of older children, as well as failing to recognize the problem of multiple episodes of bruising, especially when the individual incidents were not perceived as serious, the research articles were shared with staff, reviewed, and discussed during the training.

Collaboration with Medical Professionals. The cuts, welts, and bruises sample showed that in 65 percent of the investigations, child protection investigators did not record a professional exchange of information with medical providers. Vital information was not shared with the pediatrician or family physicians. For example, in 31 percent of investigations of bruising in children two years old or younger, the parents or caretakers had a history of domestic violence, but this information was never shared with the doctors (Office of the Inspector General, Illinois Department of Children and Family Services, 2009).

Medical professionals are in a unique position to prevent child maltreatment because they can monitor children's well-being during doctor visits after child protection services conclude their investigations, but pediatricians are rarely provided information vital to children's follow-up care, even in substantiated cases of abuse, and tend to exist on the periphery of the child protection system.[5] Child protection needs the expertise of physicians to lower risk of harm to infants and children, and knowing that a child has had prior injuries may cause the physician to pay closer attention to later injuries. Also, the physician needs to know whether to provide guidance to the family if the family has domestic violence or substance abuse problems.

Investigators were trained on how to talk with a doctor and to exchange relevant facts so the physician can render an opinion of whether the injury is more likely to be the result of abuse than an accident (this is the standard of evidence for upholding an indicated finding of abuse or neglect on administrative appeal). Relevant case information includes, but is not limited to, the caretaker's explanation for the injury, a description of the scene, and whether there are domestic violence or substance abuse problems in the home.

Many investigators operated under the misconception that investigators could not exchange information with a doctor because it biased the doctor's opinion or violated confidentiality. To help dissipate this misconception, a DCFS attorney attended each of the trainings to clarify that the law allows investigators to obtain medical information from the physician and that when requesting a medical opinion, the investigator can share relevant information with the physician. A form was developed to guide workers in conducting a more systematic assessment and to assist in the documentation of risks as seen by the investigator and as seen by the physician. Data are being collected to determine the efficacy of this new protocol.

---

[5] Testimony of Kent Hymel, MD, FAAP, on behalf of the American Academy of Pediatrics, House Ways and Means Subcommittee on Human Resources Hearing: Improving Child Protection Services, May 23, 2006.

Identification of Child-Centered Collaterals. Although investigators are required to interview persons identified by the parent, they previously were not specifically required to talk to other persons whom the child identifies as trustworthy and who may have important information based on frequent opportunities to observe and interact with the child. The analysis of cuts, welts, and bruises cases found that relatives or professionals invested in the child's well-being often were not interviewed and that sometimes investigators minimized the importance of these collaterals. On the basis of these findings, several procedural changes for child protection investigators have been initiated. One of the key changes was the addition of child-centered collateral contacts, including fathers. The goal is to ascertain who in the family network has demonstrated concern for the child's well-being. Older children are asked "Who do you feel safe with?" For nonverbal children, investigators were trained to ask older siblings, if available, to identify those to whom the baby is special. Once identified, child-centered collaterals can be an important resource for safety planning and monitoring.

Safety Planning. The foundation of an effective safety plan is a solid investigation. Our review of CERAP cases revealed that there was often a failure to develop or monitor a realistic safety plan and a failure to recognize cumulative risks (Office of the Inspector General, Illinois Department of Children and Family Services, 2007). In the course of an investigation around a specific allegation, an investigator may learn of contextual factors that compound the risk of harm. As was found in the CERAP cases, risks posed by a combination of historical and current circumstances may increase the potential for future harm. The error reduction training emphasized the concern that when there is physical abuse to infants and young children, the future of safety in the household is unpredictable. These dangerous situations call for a safety plan, with an alternate caregiver, orders of protection, or protective custody. Full information must be shared with the alternate caregiver regarding the need for a safety plan, the parameters of the safety plan, and an agreement to contact the worker if critical identified circumstances change.

Establishing the Support of Managers and Supervisors

One of the biggest challenges of a successful error reduction plan is to involve administrators at multiple levels to ensure that allegations are properly investigated. Strategies to establish trust and improve morale so frontline staff can do their best work are essential to these efforts. In Illinois, actions are being planned to improve the communication and problem-solving skills of managers, to encourage flexibility when cases require it due to their complexity, to find creative ways to reward good performance, and to enhance team building. As with the frontline staff, initial efforts have been aimed at improving managers' and supervisors' critical thinking skills. Additional steps will be taken to create an environment in which managers and supervisors are better able to help their staff learn from mistakes and improve case outcomes. Although the effort has been slow to get under way due to personnel shortages and uncertainty regarding the state budget, these strategies are currently being developed.

Follow-Up

As staff from the Office of the Inspector General and Quality Assurance collect and analyze data on child abuse investigation practices, performance results provide feedback for ongoing practice improvement efforts. Additional rounds of training are based not only on performance data on investigative tasks, but also on needs expressed by the regional managers, as well as data on other job tasks found to be problematic. Following all trainings, child protection personnel are invited to submit comments and questions, and a newsletter that includes responses to frequently asked questions is emailed to all participants.

With training that addresses specific problems that are found to contribute to errors in the field at multiple levels of the organization, it is hoped that incremental improvements will be made and that the work environment will become more conducive to sound practice and improved child safety. Good supervision and ongoing collection and use of relevant data to provide performance feedback are keys to success.

Conclusion

The use of a systems perspective and root cause analysis in organizations that must manage high-risk situations has allowed for development of programs to reduce errors, especially errors that may result in tragic outcomes. Child welfare agencies, with their duty to ensure protection of children, are organizations where development of efforts toward error reduction is essential.

The Illinois initiative to identify and address failures in the state's child protection system is aimed at building better organizational processes and reducing the incidence of child injury and death. Although the initial focus was on case decision making, it was recognized that errors are frequently the result of multiple contributing factors in a complex system. Methods of remedial training, limitations on practice, and disciplinary actions will not be sufficient to improve practice. Changes will need to be made at multiple levels of the organization to create a work environment that can cope with complexity. Nevertheless, a starting point had to be chosen. The starting point of this change initiative was selected on the basis of a set of case analyses that highlighted specific patterns of error and opportunities to intervene.

Using data from multiple sources, the OIG identified practice errors in child protection investigations, including departures from the protocol guidelines and uninformed decision making. Because the work environment contains competing demands, pressures, and uncertainties, it is not surprising that practice does not always conform to formal expectations or agency policy. It was important to understand informal incentives for practice deviations and to develop supports that reinforce good practice. This meant developing practice aids and training staff to improve reasoning skills.

Applying an incremental approach to the development of a safety culture conducive to reducing errors, the OIG developed a training curriculum focused on critical thinking, the use of multiple sources of data, and analysis of alternative hypotheses as tools for decisions. A further step will be to work with supervisors to help them provide substantive supervision rather than focusing only on management of their workers, and to make use of critical reflection and discussion to improve staff performance. Efforts will also be made to establish a work environment where mistakes are viewed as opportunities for learning. Without a climate that supports open discussion and team building, it is unlikely that substantial improvements can be made in practice.

A learning culture supports flexible practice that adapts to uncertainty. The creation of a learning environment involves training and teambuilding for a common goal and enhanced communication across levels of the organization. It incorporates an incentive system that encourages open discussion of operations, errors of judgment, and near misses (instances in which serious mistakes in judgment either don't lead to a bad outcome or lead to a minor injury rather than a major injury). The use of incident reviews to examine close calls and data to provide continuous evaluation and feedback help ensure that valued processes are leading to valued outcomes.

One of the difficulties of establishing a culture of learning is that there is an inherent conflict between establishing a blame-free environment and responding to the legitimate need for accountability. Until we can better address that inherent conflict, creating a work environment in which staff feel supported in revealing major mistakes will continue to be a major challenge. Furthermore, how staff members are held accountable for case decisions is likely to influence the quality of decision making (Woods, 2005). Staff will be reluctant to discuss issues in their practice if they believe they will be punished. Near misses may not be revealed, and opportunities to identify potential paths to failure before serious injuries occur can be lost. Some actions require disciplinary action, however until definitions of nonpunishable errors are established, it is unlikely that workers will report them. On the other hand, it can be difficult to make a strong case that specific staff decisions or behaviors are directly linked to specific child outcomes, good or bad (Munro, 2008).

Administrative investment in reducing errors provides the leadership support critical to organizational change. Time and resources are essential for creating programs that incorporate feedback based on data regarding common practices that may represent system failures or weaknesses. Training supervisors to openly discuss errors and staff misperceptions without blame is essential to create an atmosphere of trust. Group supervision provides opportunities for collaborative cross-checking, where individuals can examine each others' assumptions and actions (Patterson, Woods, Cook, & Render, 2007). It can also provide opportunities for sharing successful problem-solving techniques, offering expertise and support to colleagues, and anticipating and planning to address new obstacles to effectiveness in the face of ongoing performance pressures and change. Such practices build a climate of shared vision, commitment, flexibility, and resilience as teams work together to solve problems with the goal of increased safety for children (Weick & Sutcliffe, 2007).

Developing strategies to identify and correct patterns of error is only a starting point. Research on organizations that engage in high-risk operations has demonstrated that reducing errors alone is not related to success (Rasmussen 1990a, 1990b; Rochlin, 1997). What is equally important is the anticipation of pathways to new errors before injuries occur. It is crucial to remain constantly aware of the potential for new failures and to take steps to prevent them.

The need to anticipate future issues is why the development of new protocols or procedural rules can go only so far in creating system improvements. Although protocols and rules can serve as rough guides to practice, new and novel situations arise, including new pressures, constraints, and informal incentives that fall outside the guidelines. Supervisors and staff must be prepared to think critically and to examine their assumptions, knowledge, and case data to plan and implement their work effectively.

References

Carpenter, R. F. (1998). The prevalence and distribution of bruising in babies. *Archives of Disease in Childhood, 80,* 363–366.

DECISION Systems, Inc. (2003a). REASON® root cause analysis software. Long-view, TX: DECISION Systems, Inc.

DECISION Systems, Inc. (2003b). *REASON®: Root cause analysis training-operations improvement.* Longview, TX: DECISION Systems, Inc.

Dekker, S. (2002). *The field guide to human error investigations.* Surrey, UK: Ashgate.

Dekker, S., & Suparamaniam, N. (2005). *Divergent images of decision making in international disaster relief work.* Ljungbyhed, Sweden: Lund University School of Aviation.

Dingwall, R., Eekelaar, J., & Murray, T. (1983). *The protection of children: State intervention and family life.* Oxford, UK: Blackwell.

Gambrill, E. D. (2006). *Critical thinking in clinical practice: Improving the quality of judgments and decisions* (2nd ed.). Hoboken, NJ: Wiley.

Munro, E. (1999). Protecting children in an anxious society. *Health, Risk and Society, 1*(1), 117–127.

Munro, E. (2008). *Effective child protection* (2nd ed.). Los Angeles, CA: Sage.

Office of the Inspector General, Illinois Department of Children and Family Services. (2007). *Child endangerment risk assessment protocol (CERAP) report* (Report to the Governor and the General Assembly. Chicago, IL: Department of Children and Family Services.

Office of the Inspector General, Illinois Department of Children and Family Services. (2009). *Error reduction* (Report to the Governor and the General Assembly). Chicago, IL: Department of Children and Family Services.

Patterson, E. S., Woods, D. D., Cook, R. I., & Render, M. L. (2007). Collaborative cross-checking to enhance resilience. *Cognition, Technology, and Work, 9,* 155–162.

Perrow, C. (1984). *Normal accidents: Living with high-risk technologies.* Princeton, NJ: Princeton University Press.

Rasmussen, J. (1990a). The role of error in organizing behavior. *Ergonomics, 33,* 1185–1199.

Rasmussen, J. (1990b). Human error and the problem of causality in analysis of accidents. *Philosophical Transactions of the Royal Society of London, Series B: Biological Sciences, 327*(1241), 449–460.

Reason, J. T. (1990). *Human error.* Cambridge, UK: Cambridge University Press.

Reason, J. T. (1997). *Managing the risks of organizational accidents.* Surrey, UK: Ashgate.

Rochlin, G. I. (1997). *Trapped in the net : The unanticipated consequences of computerization.* Princeton, NJ: Princeton University Press.

Rzepnicki, T. L., & Johnson, P. R. (2005). Examining decision errors in child protection: A new application of root cause analysis. *Children and Youth Services Review, 27*(4), 393–407.

Shrivastava, P. (1987). *Bhopal: Anatomy of a crisis.* Cambridge, MA: Ballinger.

Sugar, N. F., Taylor, J. A., & Feldman, K. W. (1999). Bruises in infants and toddlers: Those who don't cruise rarely bruise. *Archives of Pediatrics and Adolescent Medicine, 153*(4), 399–403.

Weick, K. E., & Sutcliffe, K. M. (2007). *Managing the unexpected : Resilient performance in an age of uncertainty* (2nd ed.). San Francisco, CA: Jossey-Bass.

Woods, D. D. (2005). Conflicts between learning and accountability in patient safety. *DePaul Law Review, 54,* 485–502.

CHAPTER TEN

From Deficits to Appreciative Inquiry: Uncovering Promising Practices in Work with Teen Parents

Ronald H. Rooney and Michael DeJong

This chapter describes the evolution of a five-year university-agency collaboration that uses data to inform practice to assist adolescent parents who are wards of the state. That evolution included modification of goals, objectives, and interventions including a shift in focus from deficits to strengths influenced by appreciative inquiry (see table 1).

Adolescent Parenting

Adolescent parenting can be a frequent and accepted rite of passage into adulthood in some cultural communities (Roosa, 1986). However, adolescents who become parents face challenging obstacles in managing conflicting demands.

All adolescents must cope with developmental changes, completing education, and preparing for employment, and those who are parents do so while assuming responsibility for caring for a child. It is not surprising, therefore, that teen parents often face educational challenges in completing a GED or high school education. The consequences of not completing a GED or high school are significant for the parent's future capacity to care for his or her children. For example, the mean income in 2008 for a female who does not complete high school is

Phase and year	Purpose/goal	Initiatives	Result	Plan for next phase
1:2006	• To enhance engagement of teen parents	• Training of case managers and supervisors in task-centered approach	• Training delivered with small, nonsignificant results • Fidelity study of records conducted	• Immersion into agency culture for consultant • Exploration for emerging promising practices
2:2007	• To immerse the consultant with teams to learn culture • To explore for emerging practices	• Examination of records • Meetings with teams • Study of closed cases • Development of videos	• Assessment of strengths and weaknesses completed • Videos developed • Analysis of collaboration and engagement conducted	• Focus on educational achievement
3:2008	• To prepare a training product focused on enhancing educational attainment • To solicit promising practices from clients and workers	• Elaborate role play video focused on educational achievement taped and edited • Focus groups with emancipated teen parents and TPSN workers	• Video tapes edited • Preliminary versions of video shared in training	• Presentation of elaborated model to staff
4:2009	• To present training focused on educational achievement with staff cotrainer	• Training delivered to staff in four presentations	• Generally positive response • No linkage back to educational achievement • Edited training product produced	

$14,494 a year, while those with a high school diploma earn about $21,856. Those with some college earn $27,555 and those with a college degree earn $39,346 (Census Bureau, 2008).

Teen parents experience particular stresses in attempting to reconnect to education after the birth of a child. Among the inhibitors to educational attainment are large, impersonal educational settings in which they feel awkward or out of place. They often feel stigmatized as teen parents or for participating in a low-status part of the curriculum such as a GED program (Bickel, Weaver, Williams, & Lange, 1997). Having a second child poses additional obstacles to educational success.

Individualized case management services can play a key role in facilitating educational success. Resources are needed to assist the adolescent in parenting and simultaneously attending school. Such resources include prenatal care, access to transportation, time off from school to attend medical appointments, home tutoring during the weeks after birth, day care, counseling about daily living needs, and information about wise parenting. Case management is more successful if multiple resources are coordinated (Solomon & Liefeld, 1998). Such coordination should include linkage to hospitals, clinics, mental health care, recreational activities, community involvement, and mentoring.

Intensive, individualized case management services can provide some of the needed support network that may be absent from a teen parent's life. These services can provide some of the supports that a parent, if available, might provide the adolescent. Working with and encouraging families, especially grandmothers, to support teen parents is also critical. Teen parents are unlikely to overcome the multiple barriers to school success without focused intervention that involves family members, school staff, and external resources.

Without such resources, teen parents are at risk of isolation, and they need to feel connected in order to stay in school. Discussions with other teen parents can be bonding experiences and opportunities to discuss topics of common interest. Another factor in school retention is the viability of employment postgraduation (Bickel et al., 1997).

Teen parents are more likely to remain in programs that have flexible attendance policies and are located near where they live. If the teen has not experienced educational success prior to the pregnancy, special concerns are raised about development of an appropriate support network. Assistance programs are most successful with adolescent parents who already have educational aspirations, support networks, and access to transportation.

Teen parents who are also wards of the state through placement out of the home face the same obstacles and challenges, and the state must assume some of the responsibilities that family members would otherwise have taken on.

Introduction to the Collaboration

The first author (Ronald Rooney) was contacted by staff of the Illinois Department of Children and Family Services' Office of the Inspector General (OIG) in 2006 to provide training in the task-centered approach to case managers and supervisors providing services to teen parents who were wards of the state of Illinois. Teen parent wards are entitled to supportive services and to be recognized as a family (Circuit Court of Cook County, Illinois, 2009). Those services included contact with a case manager who assisted them with steps toward independence, including educational attainment, acquisition of job skills, and preparation for parenting. Case managers from the Teen Parent Services Network (TPSN) met with teen parents for five hours per month. Such contacts had not been guided by a specific practice model but rather by the goal of best equipping teen parents to be relatively independent by their date of emancipation. Teen parents who participate in this program are voluntary in the sense that they can decline TPSN services. On the other hand, they can gain access to key resources such as housing and educational support by choosing to participate.

Examination of case records by OIG staff and TPSN agency administrators suggested that contact between case managers and clients tended to focus on crises, with little ongoing collaboration toward the teen parent's goals. It was therefore determined that the task-centered approach could be useful in providing a structure for coming to agreement with teen parents on measurable goals and for developing tasks for teen parents and workers to accomplish to reach those goals (Reid, 1992, 2000; Epstein & Brown, 2002). The approach has a basis of empirical support developed through extensive testing with various populations and in varied settings (Fortune, McCallion, & Briar-Lawson, 2010), including public social services and child welfare (Reid & Beard, 1980; Goldberg, Gibbons, & Sinclair, 1985). It also includes a clear structure for monitoring progress, linking with resources, and exploring obstacles (Reid, 1992). In addition, the involuntary-client perspective was expected to provide structure to make sure that the teens' goals for themselves were addressed (Rooney, 2009).

Although the teen parents' participation was legally voluntary, sometimes teens participated so they could access resources that were combined with the program in a sort of package deal. That is, they might participate in parent training or agree to return to school not because they desired to do these things, but because these activities were expected in order for them to receive the desired reward of support for living independently. Not-quite-voluntary contacts between case managers and clients are more likely to be successful if there is a fit between the motivation of the clients and the priorities of the case manager or agency; if clients attribute their success to their own motivation rather than to the effects of rewards or punishments; and if they perceive that they are making choices, even if those choices are constrained (Rooney, 2009).

PHASE 1, 2006: TRAINING IN THE TASK-CENTERED APPROACH AND EVALUATION OF TRAINING

In pursuit of the goal of enhanced engagement of teen parents, over a period of three months the first author provided sixteen hours of training in the task-centered approach (Reid, 2000) and perspectives for work with involuntary clients (Rooney, 1992, 2009). In addition, an adaptation of the training in the task-centered approach for supervisors was delivered in eight hours over this same time period (Caspi & Reid, 2002).

A twofold evaluation plan was developed to assess the impact of training on practice, including a paper-and-pencil test of training content knowledge and an assessment of case records, both of which were completed both pre- and post-training. Staff and supervisors selected a significantly higher number of correct answers after the training. The review of case records was an assessment of treatment fidelity to determine whether training content was found in records completed after training. Use of case records has mixed advantages and disadvantages for assessing the impact of training on actual practice (Reid & Beard, 1980). Reid and Beard (1980) looked at agency records to discern whether case records contained noticeably consistent task-centered referents after training in the task-centered approach. That analysis suggested that case records could render a good account of worker-client interactions, but that language common to both generic social work and task-centered approaches made distinctions about activities pre- and post-training difficult to assess. For example, case recordings may emphasize not process or practice, but decisions and outcomes. That is, recording may be guided more by accountability priorities of funders and managers than by the interactional processes in sessions.

A primary theme of training was the significance of engaging teen parents around their own goals, so a coding format was developed that reflected a variety of ways that efforts to engage clients might be detected. The coding format was tried on a small, convenience sample of files from before and after the training as a way of determining whether the coding format might be useful for tracking evidence of training impact. The sampled records contained little evidence of efforts to engage teens both before and after training. Hence, although the knowledge test indicated that the training might be having an impact, training effects were not immediately discerned from an assessment of case records.

In consultation with TPSN and OIG staff, these conflicting results led to a series of tentative interpretations. It could be that the trainer lacked an in-depth knowledge of the working and interactional environment of the program. Consequently, it was decided that the first author would next become more immersed in the culture of the organization and its patterns of practice interactions. This would be done through further examination of current records, meetings with teams, and a more specific study of prior case records.

PHASE 2, 2007: REVIEW OF CURRENT RECORDS, CONSULTATION WITH TEAMS, EVALUATION STUDY, AND DEVELOPMENT OF MODEL VIDEOS

Phase 2 was designed to gain greater immersion into the culture, as well as knowledge about the practice environment of TPSN. This plan took the form of four initiatives. The first author would review selected case records from all of the team members. Then he would meet with members of each of the four teams for a case consultation. Third, an in-depth study of case records was planned for further exploration of client engagement. Finally, a fourth initiative emerged from the first three: training videos would be developed, and they would feature agency staff modeling desired practice modes.

Review of Records

The first author was to meet with supervisors and staff of each of four TPSN teams in January through March 2007. In preparation for these meetings, each TPSN worker was asked to select two cases for consultation. For the first, they were to select a client with whom they were experiencing some success. For the second, they were to select a case with which they had been less successful. This request was designed to elicit areas of strength or promising practice in the former cases and possible gaps in skills and resources in the latter.

The first author read fifty case files in preparation for the team consultations. Several patterns emerged in these case files. The strengths of practice appeared to be that TPSN workers monitored child safety in almost every contact. They did so carefully, noting any potential hazards and often writing "no hazards noted." The TPSN workers also often provided needed resources to the teen parents. Indeed, the heart of many contacts appeared to be an exchange of resources that teen parents wanted and needed to support their children and their own independence. Such resources were often tangible items such as gift certificates and bus passes. Small incentive payments were made available for activities such as taking children to the doctor for shots and bringing in a shot record. How these resources were made available varied across teams and staff members. Some TSPN staff used such resources as rewards to be made available only upon client compliance with worker requests. In other teams, TPSN staff appeared to treat the items as entitlements.

The case records indicated that generally teen parents were motivated by what might be best for their children. Even when the TPSN worker's relationship with an adolescent parent appeared tenuous, they generally collaborated well around resources and the child's safety and well-being. Some TPSN workers appeared able to develop trusting relationships with the teen parents. They appeared to do so through activities such as taking teen clients shopping or going skating with them. For example, one TPSN staff member took a teen parent to the WIC store to get milk for her baby. During that trip, the worker observed how the baby had grown and complimented the mother on this.

Some TPSN workers were skillful in selectively supporting clients' rights to self-determination by providing information but respecting the teen parent's right to choose. Many TPSN staff workers were adept at helping clients manage crises. Some noted and supported client strengths and advocated for client goals. Staff workers frequently completed ecomaps with their clients.

In addition to these areas of promising practice, other practices reported in the case records raised questions. TPSN staff and teen parents were frequently in conflict about goals. Many TPSN staff members appeared to make assumptions about the teen parents' goals rather than seeking to understand what the teen parents identified as their own goals. In some cases, teen parents expressed goals, but they seemed to be ignored. Conflict also occurred in other aspects of practice. Although some TPSN staff appeared skillful in withholding opinions or sharing them tactfully, many other staff appeared to lecture teen parents in ways that might threaten the relationship.

Case records appeared to dwell on TPSN client failures and deficiencies more than on client successes. A negative tone pervaded many records, with little evidence of positive, strength-oriented techniques such as asking coping or exception questions (De Jong and Berg, 2007). Occasionally, TPSN clients appeared to be in need of advocacy and problem solving in dealing with issues in personal relationships. Little problem solving or obstacle analysis appeared to occur when difficulties arose. For example, if a teen parent was getting up late and missing class or being late for work, exploration of potential obstacles and solutions was not evident in the records. Finally, planned tasks were usually developed and carried out by TPSN staff members rather than teen parents.

Team Consultations

Patterns noted in the case records appeared in the team consultations as well. Discussions in team meetings revealed varying preferences about relationships between teen parents and staff. Many staff had formerly worked in the state department of child welfare and appeared to be accustomed to dealing with involuntary clients from a position of power. Some workers and teams appeared to prefer an assertive, confrontational style that focused on the teen parents' well-being but did not engage them as partners. For example, case records revealed a pattern of habitual lecturing, and this practice appeared to be associated with less frequent client contact and with teen parents not being home when the TPSN caseworker called. Such patterns seemed to lead to mounting unresolved conflict between TPSN staff and clients who were locked in a win-lose approach that required teen parents to capitulate to the TPSN staff member's beliefs about their well-being.

Some teams appeared to accept ongoing struggle with teen parents on multiple fronts as expectable occurrences in such work. Such conflicts also occurred about meeting times between TPSN staff and clients. TPSN staff members sometimes appeared to show up unannounced when they had other appointments in the neighborhood. Appointments were rarely scheduled from one session to the next. Too often, the purpose of such contacts appeared to be to demonstrate that a contact had occurred rather than to carry out action together on agreed-upon plans. Some workers and teams, however, were relatively supportive and nonjudgmental, and they made extra efforts to provide teen parents with the resources they needed and desired.

The emerging picture of this contact between teen parents and TPSN staff appeared to fit a pattern of involuntary contact. Practice was addressed to reaching goals that staff presumed to be in the best interest of the teen parents, and there was little emphasis on client-developed goals. Case records indicated that there was frequent conflict between workers and teen parents about goals and that teen parents rarely showed significant engagement with services. Hence the collaborative, client-goal-driven spirit of the task-centered approach appeared to be an uneasy fit with actual agency practice as revealed in the case records and team consultation.

Evaluation Study

A third way to use data to inform practice involves a systematic examination of randomly selected case records (Rooney, Rzepnicki & DeJong,

2007) to explore outcomes and their relationship to modes of client engagement. Researches selected a 10 percent random sample of TPSN clients from all seven participating agencies. The eighteen case files were of clients who had aged out of services, so they were complete from inception to termination. The sample included seventeen African-American females and one Hispanic male, aged thirteen through twenty-one. Average length of services was thirty-three months, five days, with a range of service duration from eleven to fifty-three months.

The researchers reviewed the literature, looking for measures of client engagement (Yatchmenoff, 2005; Finn and Rock, 1997). Littell, Alexander, and Reynolds's (2001) conception of engagement was selected as a starting point. These researchers considered engagement to include factors such as attendance, task completion, and treatment adherence, but also a more subjective assessment of the spirit of collaboration. Following their conception, the researchers developed a schema to measure activity level in case records and to assess perceived positive and negative worker-client relationships. It was expected that higher activity levels and more positive worker-client relationships would be related to the achievement of short-term goals such as school attendance and long-term goals such as high school and GED completion.

A coding scheme was developed on the basis of a study by Jessor, in which the level of activity and attitude toward formal education were scored on a scale from zero to four and compared to outcomes such as finishing school or dropping out (Jessor, Turbin, & Costa, 1998). In this coding scheme, a zero represented a total lack of involvement, a one or two represented moderate activity, and a three or four represented active participation and extracurricular activity.

This measure of participation was implemented with a matrix developed by Littell, Alexander, and Reynolds (2001). In this matrix, a high activity level and a negative working relationship is characterized as an active yet hostile relationship. On the other hand, high activity level and a positive working relationship is characterized as compliant. A third cell of the matrix describes a relationship that is positive yet reflects relative inactivity and is characterized as acquiescent. Finally a negative, inactive relationship is labeled as resistant. Utilizing this scheme, clients could score between zero and four for level of activity and between zero and four for quality of the relationship, so there were sixteen possible combinations of predictor variables. Each score for activity and quality of relationship represented an aggregate of all recorded worker-client contacts in a one-month period. It gave context to each individual contact and allowed for the vagaries of scheduling, such as "worker in neighborhood," "client not home," "client cancelled," and "worker cancelled."

The average score for all clients was 1.45 for activity and 1.51 for strength of relationship, with 61 percent of clients having scores higher than the mean for activity and 45 percent of clients having scores higher than the mean for strength of relationship. None of these scores were particularly high, but they suggested at least a continued emphasis on activity levels and on tasks valued by both the worker and the client, rather than on the value of the relationship.

There was also a slight bimodal nature to the data. Clients would start out with fairly low levels of activity and strength of relationship, build quickly until they reached or exceeded a score of two for each predictor variable, then generally drop and plateau slightly below the mean for a majority of the time. The activity level would noticeably increase months before termination then suddenly decrease just before termination. In addition, there was a general lack of variability between the scores in each pair. That is, activity levels and strength of relationship appeared to match, both being low or moderate or high.

At emancipation, two of the eighteen clients had finished high school, two clients had attended some college courses, and one client had attained her GED. Fifteen of the eighteen completed course work and other study but had not taken the GED examination. The hurdle of taking the examination appeared to be major for many of the adolescents. The cause of the difficulty in completing the examination was unclear in the records. All clients had been employed.

TPSN workers frequently noted in the case records that TPSN parents put the welfare and safety of their children first and consistently showed good to excellent judgment in parenting. As one of the original purposes of supportive services to TPSN clients was to help teen parents to raise their children safely, this objective often appeared to be realized in this sample of cases. Case records did not, however, reflect much praise or celebration of this fact. Case records appeared to be very much focused on tasks the adolescent parents needed to complete in order to become independent.

Clients and workers had relatively low levels of engagement as measured by application of the Littell index. Agreement on tasks and completion of tasks was not a common occurrence. Frequently workers requested that the teen parents complete tasks, and rarely did the teen parents do so.

Emergence of Appreciative Inquiry and Development of Training Videotapes

Encountering data suggesting that genuine collaboration between staff and clients was rare, the first author had several choices to consider in how to proceed in work with the agency. One alternative would be to present data to staff and supervisors related to the general lack of engagement and the deficit orientation reflected in case records and consultation. Ferguson describes a deficit orientation: "The culture of front line agencies too often becomes defined in deficit terms, whether through a focus on lack of resources, the pragmatics of managing risk or preventing the next mistake and reaching performance standards. The result is a deficit culture in social work, devoid of a tradition of celebration, pride or sense of achievement" (Ferguson, 2003, p. 1008). There appears to be a parallel process in which a focus on deficits is often reflected throughout the organization. That is, the emphasis is on eliminating problems rather than on discovering growth or successes. In this case there was a danger of repeating this parallel process of focusing on deficits. If the researchers focused on what staff and supervisors were not doing, it might elicit the same kind of negative response that staff encountered with teen parents.

In contemplating this problem, the first author began to explore appreciative inquiry for guidance in dealing with this deficit approach. In appreciative inquiry, an outside consultant does not play the role of problem solver, solution designer, or prescription giver. Rather, a process is initiated that is designed to include members of an organization in identifying what is working now and in exploring solutions to concerns that have been identified from within (Cooperrider & Srivastva, 1987; Cooperrider & Whitney, 1999). If part of the problem was a deficit orientation that was reflected in many areas of the organization, one part of the solution was to not participate in the deficit orientation but rather to model a more strength- and success-oriented approach.

Influenced by appreciative inquiry, the first author approached OIG staff and TPSN administrators about exploring in more detail those occurrences in which genuine collaboration appeared to occur. That is, in the face of evidence that positive engagement was rare, what might explain its occurrence when it did happen? Further, if engagement was to be fostered, examples from case managers who were skilled in engagement should be explored (Ferguson, 2003).

Engagement skills might best be employed around common obstacles to engagement. Examination of case records revealed five frequent conflicts. First, there were frequent conflicts between TPSN workers and young mothers about whether they should sleep with their infant children. Second, frequently staff had concerns about the young mothers' safety in relationships with paramours. A third issue was how to develop educational plans that focused on the clients' own goals rather than those that the case manager might impose upon them. A fourth issue related to how to carry out reviews of a case plan and to praise a client for progress. Finally, interpersonal conflicts often occurred between adolescent parents and their foster or kinship caretakers.

A way of addressing these frequent challenges to engagement was to develop training videotapes modeling the practice of TPSN staff who were skilled in such engagement. The first author nominated some TPSN staff on the basis of his assessment of promising practice in case records and observation in team consultations. In addition, supervisors were consulted about the prominence of issues to address in videos and asked to nominate other case managers to demonstrate promising practices.

Four videos were developed. A first video demonstrated a method of gathering ecomap information and developing a mutual plan for making safe sleeping arrangements with an infant. A second video was developed to demonstrate a review session toward reunification with a parent whose child had been removed (Center for Advanced Study in Child Welfare, 2007b). A third video demonstrated ways to negotiate between a teen parent and her foster parent about when the teen parent would return home from school to resume care of her child and differences between the teen and the foster parent related to child care (Center for Advanced Study in Child Welfare, 2007a). A final video presented a contracting session that demonstrated sensitivity to the teen parent's own goals and also a discussion of potential danger with a paramour and the development of a safety plan.

Those videos were edited and shared with supervisors, and plans were made for how they could be used to train staff in the following year. The videos were then previewed in meetings with TPSN staff. Although staff responses to the videos were generally favorable, specific plans were not made to follow up on the models or to link them to ongoing practice.

PHASE 3, 2008: FURTHER INFLUENCE OF APPRECIATIVE INQUIRY IN DEVELOPMENT OF VIDEOS AND IN PRELIMINARY TRAINING BASED ON VIDEOS

Because the evaluation study had revealed that completion of GED or high school was problematic for teen parents nearing emancipation, (Rooney et al., 2007), consultation with the OIG's office led to a more narrowly focused goal of preparing a training video around assisting teen parents in achieving educational goals. A script was developed that would depict case manager–client interaction across several sessions in both home and school settings. Because one obstacle identified in case records had been teen parents' failure to link with educational settings, the training video would model case manager support for attendance. Scenes were videotaped demonstrating these processes, as well as a problem-solving session based on the frequently occurring obstacle of a teen parent experiencing a crisis and stopping school attendance.

This was followed by a midsession review in which the teen parent revealed that although she had been attending school regularly, she was anxious about taking the GED exam. The TPSN case manager in the video accompanied her to visit the school site, where they worked together on solving the problem and talked with the educational staff about dealing with test anxiety. A major theme of the scenarios was the value of tangible, explicit support such as accompanying teen parents on educational visits (Center for Advanced Study in Child Welfare, 2008).

A second set of videos was developed that was also influenced by appreciative inquiry. Researchers made an effort to identify promising practices within the organization, with input from consumers and staff members (Cooperrider & Srivastva, 1987; Fry, Barrett, Seiling, & Whitney, 2002; Watkins & Mohr, 2001). Focus groups about promising practices were conducted and videotaped with TPSN staff and emancipated TPSN graduates who had completed educational goals. Glenda Dewberry Rooney led a focus group of emancipated TPSN parents, who reflected on their experiences and on what had helped them to complete their high school education (Center for Advanced Study in Child Welfare, 2010a). Second, Dewberry Rooney led a focus group of TPSN staff who were nominated by their supervisors because they were skilled in engaging TPSN clients (Center for Advanced Study in Child Welfare, 2010b). Those staff members shared their practice wisdom and beliefs about how to engage TPSN clients. A preliminary edited video version of the focus groups was shared with staff members. Staff found both the perspectives of emancipated teens and the insights of their nominated engagement experts useful.

In the fall of 2008, the Center for Advanced Studies in Child Welfare of the School of Social Work at the University of Minnesota provided a research assistant who was employed to assist in assessing and reviewing the three videos developed in May. Because four hours of role play had been taped, an extensive editing process was needed to condense them to thirty minutes of training video.

PHASE 4, 2009: FINAL DEVELOPMENT AND IMPLEMENTATION OF VIDEO ON REACHING EDUCATIONAL GOALS

The role play video was edited into two versions. One version was developed with Adobe Presenter so that a narrated PowerPoint and accompanying video links could be seen and heard at any facility with sufficient bandwidth. In a second version, videos were placed on a CD that could be viewed in conjunction with an in-person PowerPoint presentation. In May 2009, the video was shared with staff, and the case manager who appeared in the educational video role play was enlisted as a cotrainer to present the video.

The first day of training met with mixed success. The training site lacked sufficient bandwidth, so the Adobe Presenter presentation performed erratically. A backup DVD version was not sufficiently compressed and also worked sporadically. In addition, many of the workers attending the first day objected to the premise of the training, suggesting that they already accompanied teen parents to educational sites and that this rarely led to regular school attendance. Many felt that completing a GED or high school was not feasible for many teen parents whose reading levels were poor and whose motivation for completing their education was limited.

In addition, some staff members appeared ambivalent about the idea that of one of their peers was a copresenter with the first author. They suggested that the video seemed to have an underlying premise that if they were all Super Workers, their clients would achieve educational goals and live happily ever after. The training team assured them that they did not assume that all client educational challenges could be resolved by better TPSN worker performance. However, even skilled, experienced case managers might learn things that might help them engage better with some clients. The trainers shared their belief that most TPSN staff worked diligently and that many TPSN clients were difficult to engage around educational goals. Still, there might be clues in the training videos about additional ways to solidify the linkage with educational systems.

Fortunately, the second day of training worked much more smoothly. A DVD that had a better compressed version of the video operated better. The training team worked more fluently together and sent a clear message that the caseworker in the video was a cotrainer by positioning her at the front of the room alongside the first author. A stimulating discussion occurred about the message conveyed by extensive support of teen parents, such as accompanying them to educational settings as depicted in the video. Some had the opinion that such support could be a kind of coddling, enabling hand-holding that might inhibit independence. Those workers believed that teen parents would be ill-served by an expectation that workers could be relied on for such assistance when no one would be available in this fashion after their emancipation. Others felt that such tangible support at key times might be the necessary supportive step to facilitate the linkage with school.

Useful discussions ensued about the relationship between empowerment and nurturance. Extra, tangible support could be a key facilitator of progress at certain points, but this didn't mean that a case manager should take the teen parent to buy diapers. Special support also meant that case managers would have to clarify boundaries so the teen parent would know what she could rely on her case manager for and in what ways a case manager was not the same as a friend.

In this session staff members were much more positive about the cotraining team, saying that they had greater confidence in the training content because one of the trainers was experienced in the trenches with their clients. Similar training patterns occurred on the third and fourth days. The training team became more confident and fluent in working together, and the staff shared similar themes about appreciating the input from a seasoned TPSN worker.

Lessons Learned

Collaboration over a four-year period has presented both challenges and opportunities.

TRAINING

This collaboration revealed that a training program based on an empirically based intervention program, the task-centered approach, and work with involuntary clients could lead to promising results on a paper-and-pencil test of knowledge. That indication of impact does not, however, translate into treatment fidelity in practice. Indications of use of the approach were not consistently found in case records or in team consultations conducted after the training was completed.

The first author, TPSN administrators, and OIG staff shared the conclusion that training materials were more likely to be infused if they were based on an in-depth knowledge of the organizational environment. Consequently, efforts were made for the first author to get to know that context better through team consultations and review of agency records.

ENGAGING ADOLESCENT PARENTS

The initial premise of providing training based on the task-centered approach and supporting client-determined goals conflicted with a paternalistic emphasis on linking adolescent parents to services for their own good. Nonvoluntary clients in an organization that favors particular goals such as educational enhancement, parent training, and enhanced job skills can be relatively voluntary if the clients' goals fit or overlap with where the agency, acting as their parent, would like them to go. Looked at from the clients' perspective, it is also possible for the agency's priorities to be met if they are linked with teen parents' goals for themselves and their children. Posing these challenges as an either-or conflict between self-determination and best interest is less useful than exploring ways that these aims can be compatible.

Rather than forcing a false choice between purely self-determined goals and ones influenced by agency priorities, video models present both role plays demonstrating promising practice (Center for Advanced Study in Child Welfare, 2008) and practice wisdom from a focus group of workers skilled in engagement (Center for Advanced Study in Child Welfare, 2010b; McMillen, Morris, & Sherraden, 2004).

ORGANIZATIONAL CULTURE

The goal of engaging teen parents had been pursued in a deficit context in which the focus was often on what was not completed rather than on successes (Ferguson, 2003). Through a parallel process, this orientation was also often found in relationships with funding bodies, between managers and supervisors, and between supervisors and staff. Incentives often influenced clients' behavior in positive ways; similarly, case managers have received incentives for linking clients to services.

The influence of appreciative inquiry permitted the first author to seek models of promising practice rather than dwelling on and reinforcing deficits. Other ways to emphasize strengths would be to emphasize successes at each level: in contacts with funders, between managers and supervisors, and between supervisors and staff, as well as with staff and clients. In addition, if incentives are used to support staff members in making changes, then such incentives might be expanded to recognize linkage with the teen clients' self expressed goals.

SELF-DETERMINATION IN GOAL SETTING

The problem of whether teen parents could be self-determining was paralleled at the organizational level when the goals of training and the use of consultants was influenced by funding bodies and administrators, with lesser influence from line staff. Appreciative inquiry can support inclusion of staff in seeking solutions for problems and concerns. It does not, however, have a ready solution for circumstances in which there is a lack of goal consensus among administrators, agency staff, funders, and university staff. Continuing work is needed to find ways to use appreciative inquiry in social services in a way that appropriately engages line staff in change efforts.

Implications for Other Data-Informed Collaborations

Social work practitioners and researchers have long sought to collaborate with practitioners in agency settings. University collaborators should not assume that social work practitioners are free to implement evidence-based practices regardless of their organizational environment. This collaboration has shown how agency administrators, funders, and university collaborators can use data to assess practice and to influence decisions about programmatic directions. It has shown that such collaborations can feature both challenges and opportunities. Finally, appreciative inquiry is one framework for consultation that can be useful for bringing different parties to the table to explore and implement organizational initiatives.

References

Bickel R., Weaver, S., Williams T., & Lange L. (1997). Opportunity, community, and teen pregnancy in an Appalachian state. *The Journal of Educational Research, 90*(3), 175–181.

Caspi, J., & Reid, W. J. (2002). *Educational supervision in social work.* New York, NY: Columbia University Press.

Census Bureau. (2008). *American community survey, B20004: Median earnings in the past 12 months (in 2008 inflation-adjusted dollars) by sex by educational attainment for the population 25 years and over.* http://factfinder .census.gov.

Center for Advanced Study in Child Welfare. (2007a). *Problem solving with an adolescent mother and foster parent* (Video). St. Paul, MN: Center for Advanced Study in Child Welfare. http://mediamill.cla.umn.edu/mediamill/embed/ 24823.

Center for Advanced Study in Child Welfare. (2007b). *Working with teen parents toward reunification* (Video). St. Paul, MN: Center for Advanced Study in Child Welfare. https://mediamill.cla.umn.edu/mediamill/download.php? file = 79472.wmv.

Center for Advanced Study in Child Welfare. (2008). *Developing educational goals with teen parents* (Video). St. Paul, MN: Center for Advanced Study in Child Welfare. https://umconnect.umn.edu/tpe1.

Center for Advanced Study in Child Welfare. (2010a). *Healthy youth development for adolescent parents in foster care* (Video). St. Paul, MN: Center for Advanced Study in Child Welfare. https://umconnect.umn.edu/hdl/.

Center for Advanced Study in Child Welfare. (2010b). *Working with young parents in foster care: Lessons learned* (Video). St. Paul, MN: Center for Advanced Study in Child Welfare. https://umconnect.umn.edu/practl.

Circuit Court of Cook County, Illinois. (2009). Notice to plaintiff class members in *Hill v. Erickson.* http://www.state.il.us/DCFS/docs/REVISED%20Hill%20 Notice%20of%20Plaintiff%20Class%20Members%201-12-10.pdf.

Cooperrider, D. L., & Srivastva, S. (1987) Appreciative inquiry in organizational life. In W. Pasmore, & R. Woodman (Eds.), *Research in Organizational Change and Development,* Vol. 1 (pp. 129–169). Greenwich, CT: JAI Press.

Cooperrider, D. L., & Whitney, D. (1999). *Appreciative inquiry: Collaboration for change.* San Francisco, CA: Berrett Koehler.

DeJong, P., & Berg, I. K. (2007). *Interviewing for solutions.* Pacific Grove, CA: Wadsworth.

Epstein, L., & Brown, L. (2002). *Brief treatment and a new look at the task-centered approach* (4th ed.). New York, NY: Macmillan.

Ferguson, H. (2003). Outline of a critical best practice perspective on social work and social care. *British Journal of Social Work, 33,* 1005–1024.

Finn, J. D., & Rock, D. A. (1997). Academic success among students at risk for school failure. *Journal of Applied Psychology, 82,* 221–261.

Fortune, A. E., McCallion, P., & Briar-Lawson, K. (Eds.). (2010). *Social work practice research for the 21st century.* New York, NY: Columbia University Press.

Fry, R., Barrett, F., Seiling, J., and Whitney, D. (2002). *Appreciative inquiry and organizational transformation.* Westport, CT: Quorum.

Goldberg, E. M., Gibbons, J., & Sinclair, I. (1985). *Problems, tasks and outcomes: The evaluation of task-centered casework in three settings.* Winchester, MA: Allen & Unwin.

Jessor, R., Turbin, M., & Costa, F. (1998). Risk and protection in successful outcomes among disadvantaged adolescents. *Applied Developmental Science, 2*(4), 194–209.

Littell, J., Alexander, L., & Reynolds, W. (2001). Client participation: Central and underinvestigated elements of intervention. *Social Service Review, 75*(1), 1–28.

McMillen, J. C., Morris, L., & Sherraden, M. (2004). Ending social work's grudge match: Problems versus strengths. *Families in Society, 85*(3), 317–325.

Reid, W. J. (1992). *Task strategies: An empirical approach to clinical social work.* New York, NY: Columbia University Press.

Reid, W. J. (2000). *The task planner: An intervention resource for human service professionals.* New York, NY: Columbia University Press.

Reid, W. J., & Beard, C. (1980). An evaluation of in-service training in a public-welfare setting. *Administration in Social Work, 4*(1), 71–85.

Rooney, R. H. (1992). *Strategies for work with involuntary clients.* New York, NY: Columbia University Press.

Rooney, R. H. (Ed.). (2009). *Strategies for work with involuntary clients* (2nd ed.). New York, NY: Columbia University Press.

Rooney, R., Rzepnicki, T., & DeJong, M. (2007). Clients or suspects? Work with teen mothers in foster care. Paper presentation at Council on Social Work Education Annual Program Meetings. San Francisco.

Roosa, M. (1986). Adolescent mothers, school drop-outs and school based intervention programs. *Family Relations, 35*(2), 313–317.

Solomon R., & Liefeld, C. (1998). Effectiveness of a family support center approach to adolescent mothers: Repeat pregnancy and school drop-out rates. *Family Relations, 47*(2), 139–44.

Watkins, J. M., & Mohr, B. J. (2001). *Appreciative inquiry: Change at the speed of imagination.* New York, NY: Jossey-Bass.

Yatchmenoff, D. K. (2005). Measuring client perspective from the client's perspective in nonvoluntary child protective services. *Research on Social Work Practice, 15*(84), 84–96.

Contributors

Jennifer L. Bellamy, PhD, is assistant professor, School of Social Service Administration, University of Chicago.

Sharon B. Berlin, PhD, is Helen Ross Professor Emerita, School of Social Service Administration, University of Chicago.

Sarah E. Bledsoe, PhD, is assistant professor, School of Social Work, University of North Carolina at Chapel Hill.

William Borden, PhD, is senior lecturer, School of Social Service Administration, University of Chicago.

Harold E. Briggs, PhD, is professor, School of Social Work, Portland State University.

James J. Clark, PhD, LCSW, is associate professor and associate dean for research, College of Social Work, University of Kentucky.

Lisa Coconato, AM, JD, is lead investigator, Division of Child Death Investigations, Office of the Inspector General, Illinois Department of Children and Family Services.

Michael DeJong, MSSW, LCSW, is a doctoral student, School of Social Work, University of Minnesota, and proprietor/supervisor of De Jong Counseling Services, St. Joseph, Missouri.

Lin Fang, PhD, is assistant professor, Factor-Inwentash Faculty of Social Work, University of Toronto.

Anne E. Fortune, PhD, is professor and associate dean for academic affairs, School of Social Welfare, University at Albany.

Penny R. Johnson, PhD, is dean of students and lecturer (retired), School of Social Service Administration, University of Chicago.

Denise Q. Kane, PhD, is inspector general, Illinois Department of Children and Family Services.

Elisabeth Kinnel, BA, is a research assistant for the Evidence-Based Practice Project, Jewish Child and Family Services, Chicago.

Julia H. Littell, PhD, is professor, Graduate School of Social Work and Social Research, Bryn Mawr College.

Charlotte Mallon, AM, LCSW, is director of training for professional staff, Jewish Child and Family Services, Chicago.

Jennifer Manuel, PhD, LMSW, is assistant professor of clinical psychiatric social work, College of Physicians and Surgeons, Columbia University and Research Scientist, New York State Psychiatric Institute.

Jeanne C. Marsh, PhD, is George Herbert Jones Distinguished Service Professor, School of Social Service Administration, University of Chicago.

Stephen Edward McMillin, AM, MA, is a doctoral candidate, School of Social Service Administration, University of Chicago.

Diane Moncher, AM, is investigator, Division of Child Death Investigations, Office of the Inspector General, Illinois Department of Children and Family Services.

Stanley G. McCracken, PhD, LCSW, RDDP, is senior lecturer, School of Social Service Administration, University of Chicago.

Edward J. Mullen, DSW, is Wilma and Albert Musher Professor, School of Social Work, Columbia University.

Ronald H. Rooney, PhD, is professor, School of Social Work, University of Minnesota.

Tina L. Rzepnicki, PhD, is David and Mary Winton Green Professor and deputy dean for curriculum, School of Social Service Administration, University of Chicago.

Barbara Shulman, JD, is chief legal counsel, Office of the Inspector General, Illinois Department of Children and Family Services.

Fred Steffen is associate executive director (retired), Jewish Child and Family Services. Chicago.

Margaret Vimont, MSW, LCSW, is associate executive director and chief operating officer, Jewish Child and Family Services, Chicago.

Index